COOKING WITH Bon Appétit

Recipe Yearbook 1987

Editors' Choice of Recipes from 1986

THE KNAPP PRESS
Publishers
Los Angeles

Published by The Knapp Press
5900 Wilshire Boulevard, Los Angeles, California 90036

Library of Congress Cataloging-in-Publication Data

Recipe yearbook 1987.

(Cooking with Bon appétit)
Includes index.
1. Cookery, International. I. Series.
TX725.A1R423 1987 641.5′9 87-4125
ISBN 0-89535-182-X

On the cover: *Left to right, Southwest Salad with Cilantro Herbal Cream; Salmon Navajo with Orange Essence Butter Sauce; Peppered Lemon Saffron Pasta with Onions and Dill; Arizona Pecan Cake. Photographed by Rudi Legname.*

Printed and bound in the United States of America

10 9 8 7 6 5 4 3 2 1

Contents

Foreword

Welcome to the first annual collection of recipes from *Bon Appétit* magazine. While we don't have room to include all of the 1,428 recipes published in the magazine during 1986, this volume includes over 200 of the best, chosen by the editors to represent important food trends of the year.

What you'll find here is a surprising variety—new tastes and techniques as well as comfortably familiar foods. Perhaps the most prevalent "ethnic" influence this year has been Southwestern cooking, with its emphasis on grilled meats and fish and its distinctive flavorings of jalapeño and serrano chilies, cumin and cilantro. Southwest cuisine has become popular, and the expertise and innovation of our contributors have kept it vibrant, exciting, never trite—look for its influence in recipes throughout this book. The spicy cuisines of northern China and Indonesia, the Caribbean, and the full-bodied flavors of Italy and southern France have also had an impact on dining in 1986.

Something else you'll spot is a return to American "home cooking," a renaissance of such favorites as chili and pot roast, fruit pies and fritters and desserts with reassuring names like buckle and pandowdy. More and more dishes are featuring such all-American ingredients as cornmeal, maple syrup, sweet potatoes and hominy in interesting and even sophisticated ways.

In general, dishes have become lighter and easier to prepare, often depending on a pantry well-stocked with an intriguing array of oils and vinegars, imported mustards, dried mushrooms and pastas—combined with fresh produce and herbs from the supermarket. The availability of excellent-quality fruits and vegetables year-round now in most parts of the country, as well as the interest in healthier eating, have given a decidedly different look to the average meal, with colorful salads and leaner entrées and side dishes replacing the standard meat and potatoes of the past. (The paradox is, of course, that desserts—the richer the better—are more in demand than ever.)

In all, 1986 was a very good year for food—as well as a transitional one—and we hope you'll find our selection of recipes inspiring, entertaining and, most of all, delicious.

1 Appetizers

For starters, we offer a delectable array of recipes, from the traditional, such as Herbed Shrimp with Parsley Cheese (page 2) and Leek and Duck Terrine (page 9), to the new, with some unusual ingredients and delicious combinations: Chilled mussels highlighted by a spicy fresh corn relish and chili mayonnaise (page 3); sautéed sweetbreads combined with a blend of tomatoes, raisins and oil-cured olives in a flaky phyllo crust (page 6); oysters paired with bits of ham and served with a fresh watercress butter (page 8).

You may be surprised at the number of deep-fried foods in this chapter, but notice that they have a contemporary flair. A far cry from greasy food-stand fritters and fries, these appetizers are light, crisp and the perfect way to begin a meal. Try paper-thin strips of Parsnip Chips (page 3), crunchy Crab and Avocado Fritters (page 8) and Artichoke Fritters with Tarragon Mayonnaise (page 4).

Whether they're served singly as hors d'oeuvres, or as a meal in themselves—part of the up-and-coming dining trend known as "grazing"—these appetizers are a luscious sample of things to come.

Garden Vegetables with Creamy Beet Sauce

A colorful opener. For do-ahead preparation, blanch the vegetables two to three hours before serving.

16 servings

2 pounds medium beets, stems trimmed to 2 inches

7 tablespoons vegetable oil
7 tablespoons sour cream
3 to 4 tablespoons red wine vinegar
3 anchovies
1 small garlic clove
½ to 1 teaspoon salt
⅛ teaspoon freshly ground pepper

Baby green beans, trimmed
Baby carrots
Baby turnips
Baby beets, stems trimmed to 1 inch
Baby crookneck squash
Tiny new potatoes, strip peeled from center
Cauliflower florets
Broccoli florets
Peeled asparagus

Preheat oven to 400°F. Wrap 2 pounds beets in foil. Bake until tender when pierced with knife, 1 hour. Cool slightly. Peel and cut into quarters. Cool to room temperature.

Combine beets with oil, sour cream, 3 tablespoons vinegar, anchovies, garlic, ½ teaspoon salt and pepper in processor. Puree until smooth. Taste and add more vinegar and salt if desired. *(Can be prepared 1 day ahead and refrigerated. Bring to room temperature before serving.)*

Blanch vegetables separately in large pot of boiling salted water until just crisp-tender. Remove with slotted spoon and plunge into ice water. Drain thoroughly; pat dry. Peel baby beets.

Arrange vegetables on large platter. Serve with beet sauce.

Herbed Shrimp with Parsley Cheese

16 servings

8 cups water
1 garlic clove, minced
1 teaspoon salt
1 teaspoon cayenne pepper
½ teaspoon freshly ground pepper
½ teaspoon dried thyme, crumbled
½ teaspoon dried rosemary, crumbled
½ teaspoon paprika
⅛ teaspoon dried oregano, crumbled
2 pounds large shrimp with shells

Filling
1 cup packed fresh parsley
1 large garlic clove
½ cup cream cheese, room temperature
¼ cup (½ stick) butter, room temperature
1 tablespoon dry white wine
1 tablespoon fresh lemon juice
Salt and freshly ground pepper

Blanched green onion tops (optional)
Lemon wedges

Combine first 9 ingredients in heavy large saucepan and bring to boil. Add shrimp and boil until just cooked through, 3 to 4 minutes; do not overcook. Drain shrimp; rinse under cold water and drain again.

For filling: Combine parsley and garlic in food processor or blender and finely mince. Add cheese, butter, wine and lemon juice and mix well, stopping once to scrape down sides. Season with salt and pepper.

Peel shrimp, leaving tails on. Slit shrimp lengthwise along inner curve without cutting in half. Remove vein if visible. Transfer cheese mixture to pastry bag fitted with decorative tip. Pipe some of cheese mixture into each shrimp. Tie each with green onion top if desired. Cover and refrigerate. Remove from refrigerator 20 minutes before serving. Garnish with lemon.

Chilled Mussels with Fresh Corn Relish and Chili Mayonnaise

6 to 8 servings

Mussels

2 pounds mussels, scrubbed and debearded
1 cup dry white wine
2 bay leaves

Relish

3 bacon slices
1 small red bell pepper, finely diced
1 small white onion, finely diced
1 jalapeño chili, seeded, finely diced
2 garlic cloves, minced
2 ½ cups fresh corn kernels (about 3 ears)
3 tablespoons chopped fresh cilantro
3 tablespoons balsamic vinegar
Salt and freshly ground pepper

Mayonnaise

4 egg yolks
2 large Anaheim chilies, peeled, seeded and coarsely chopped
1 tablespoon fresh lemon juice
1 cup corn oil

Lemon slices
Cilantro sprigs

For mussels: Combine mussels, wine and bay leaves in large pot. Cover and steam over medium-high heat until mussels open, shaking pan occasionally, 3 to 4 minutes. Remove opened mussels. Steam remaining mussels 3 more minutes; discard any that do not open. Ladle liquid through strainer lined with several layers of dampened cheesecloth. Reserve liquid. Remove mussels from shells. Reserve half of each mussel shell. Cool mussels completely.

For relish: Fry bacon in heavy medium skillet over medium-high heat until very crisp. Remove bacon and drain on paper towels. Add bell pepper, onion, chili and garlic to skillet and cook until soft and lightly caramelized, stirring frequently, about 8 minutes. Stir in corn and cilantro. Crumble in bacon. Transfer to bowl. Stir in 2 tablespoons mussel liquid and vinegar. Season with salt and pepper. Cool completely.

For mayonnaise: Puree yolks, chilies and lemon juice in processor. With machine running, add oil through feed tube in slow stream. Transfer to another bowl. Season mayonnaise with salt and pepper.

To serve, arrange shell halves on platter. Place about 1 teaspoon relish in each. Top with mussels, then mayonnaise. Garnish with lemon slices and cilantro sprigs. Pass remaining relish separately.

Parsnip Chips

Serve these crunchy treats with cocktails.

6 servings

1½ pounds parsnips, peeled

2 quarts peanut oil

Salt

Cut parsnips lengthwise into 1/16-inch-thick slices, using mandoline or very sharp knife. *(Can be prepared 4 hours ahead. Place in large bowl and cover with cold water. Drain thoroughly and pat dry before continuing.)*

Heat oil in deep fryer or large saucepan to 325°F. Add parsnips in batches (do not crowd) and fry until limp, about 30 seconds. Transfer chips to paper towels, using slotted spoon.

Heat oil to 375°F. Add parsnips in batches (do not crowd) and fry until golden brown and crisp, about 2 minutes. Drain on paper towels. Sprinkle with salt and serve.

Artichoke Fritters with Tarragon Mayonnaise

Makes 48

6 medium artichokes
1 lemon, halved

1 lemon, quartered
1 tablespoon all purpose flour
1 tablespoon freshly ground white pepper
1 tablespoon salt
2 fresh thyme sprigs
1 bay leaf

Beer Batter
1 cup all purpose flour
2 eggs, separated
3 tablespoons olive oil
¼ teaspoon salt
¼ teaspoon cayenne pepper
1 cup flat beer, room temperature

Vegetable oil (for deep frying)

Lemon wedges
Tarragon Mayonnaise*

Break off stem of artichoke and rub exposed area with lemon half. Starting from base, bend each leaf back and snap off at natural break. Cut off tight cone of leaves above heart. Trim and shape heart carefully with knife until no dark green areas remain. Rub with lemon. Repeat with remaining artichokes. Spoon out chokes. Cut each artichoke heart into 8 wedges.

Fill large nonaluminum pan with water. Add juice and rind of quartered lemon, flour, pepper, salt, thyme and bay leaf, then artichokes. Bring to boil. Reduce heat and simmer until artichokes are just tender when pierced with knife, about 10 minutes. Drain thoroughly. Pat dry. *(Can be prepared 1 day ahead. Wrap tightly and refrigerate.)*

For batter: Combine flour, yolks, olive oil, salt and cayenne pepper in large bowl. Gradually whisk in beer. Refrigerate at least 1 hour.

Line baking sheet with paper towels. Preheat oven to lowest setting. Heat vegetable oil in deep fryer or deep skillet to 365°F to 370°F. Beat whites until stiff but not dry; fold into batter. Dip artichokes in batches in batter; drain off excess. Add to oil (do not crowd) and cook until golden brown, turning occasionally, about 7 minutes. Drain on prepared pan. Keep warm in oven. Repeat with remaining artichokes.

Sprinkle artichokes with salt if desired. Garnish with lemon and serve, passing mayonnaise separately.

*Tarragon Mayonnaise

Makes about 2 cups

1½ cups loosely packed fresh tarragon leaves
2 egg yolks, room temperature
2 tablespoons fresh lemon juice
Salt and freshly ground white pepper
1½ cups olive oil

Blend tarragon, yolks, lemon, salt and pepper in processor until thick. With machine running, slowly add oil through feed tube. *(Mayonnaise can be prepared 3 days ahead and refrigerated.)*

Baked Brie and Roasted Garlic

8 servings

4 large heads garlic (at least 2½ inches in diameter)
⅓ cup olive oil
1 teaspoon coarse salt
4 4-ounce wheels Brie
Toasted baguette slices

Preheat oven to 350°F. Remove all but one layer of skin from garlic; do not expose flesh. Arrange garlic tightly in small baking dish. Drizzle with oil. Sprinkle with salt. Cover with foil. Bake until garlic is very tender, 75 to 90 minutes.

Preheat broiler. Score large X in top of each wheel of cheese. Set each in small baking dish. Broil until browned and bubbly, 5 to 7 minutes. Serve immediately with garlic and toasted baguette slices.

Saga Blue Cheese and Ham Spirals

These hors d'oeuvres should be offered shortly after baking, but they can be formed one week ahead and frozen.

Makes about 40

Pastry

2 cups all purpose flour
½ teaspoon salt
1 cup (2 sticks) well-chilled unsalted butter, cut into ½-inch cubes
1 egg mixed with 1 tablespoon whipping cream

⅔ pound well-chilled Saga Blue cheese, rind removed
2 tablespoons plus 1½ teaspoons dry Sherry
⅓ pound paper-thin slices baked ham
2 egg whites beaten to blend (glaze)

For pastry: Combine flour and salt in large bowl. Cut in butter until coarse meal forms. Stir in egg and cream mixture. Gently knead dough on unfloured surface just until smooth ball forms. Flatten to rectangle. Cover and refrigerate until firm.

Roll dough out on lightly floured surface to 16x8-inch rectangle. Fold into thirds as for business letter. Give dough a quarter turn so it opens like a book. Repeat rolling and folding two more times. Wrap dough tightly in plastic and refrigerate at least 1 hour or overnight.

Using electric mixer, beat cheese until light. Mix in Sherry. Cut dough in half. Roll one piece out on lightly floured surface to 12x10-inch rectangle. Spread ½ of cheese mixture evenly over, leaving ½-inch border. Cover cheese with half of ham. Starting at one long side, roll dough up very tightly jelly roll fashion. Repeat with remaining dough, cheese and ham. Place rolls on baking sheet and freeze until firm, at least 45 minutes. *(Can be prepared to this point up to 1 week ahead. Wrap tightly. Soften slightly in refrigerator before continuing.)*

Position rack in center of oven and preheat to 400°F. Lightly grease baking sheets. Cut dough into ½-inch-thick slices. Arrange on prepared sheets. Brush with glaze. Bake until cheese is bubbly, 12 to 15 minutes. Turn baking sheets back to front and continue baking until spirals are light brown, 8 to 10 minutes. Transfer to platter. Let cool at least 5 minutes.

Cheese-filled Tortas with Tomatillo Sauce

Store-bought flour tortillas can also be used to prepare this zesty appetizer.

8 servings

Sauce

3 tablespoons vegetable oil
2 medium onions, minced
2 garlic cloves, minced
2 13-ounce cans tomatillos, drained

Tortas

12 Flour Tortillas*
½ cup (1 stick) butter, melted

½ pound Monterey Jack cheese, grated (2 cups)
2 to 3 tablespoons minced cilantro
2 fresh jalapeño chilies, seeded, deveined and thinly sliced
Freshly grated Parmesan cheese
Additional sliced jalapeño chilies (optional)

For sauce: Heat oil in heavy medium skillet over medium-low heat. Add onions and cook until soft, stirring occasionally, about 10 minutes. Add garlic and cook 1 minute. Add tomatillos and simmer until thickened, crushing with spoon, about 10 minutes.

For tortas: Preheat oven to 375°F. Arrange 4 tortillas on baking sheet. Brush lightly with butter. Bake until tortillas begin to crisp, about 8 minutes. For each torta, spread 1 tortilla lightly with ⅛ of tomatillo sauce. Cover with ⅛ of Monterey Jack cheese. Sprinkle with ⅛ of cilantro and chilies. Top with tortilla, pressing gently. Repeat layering, ending with tortilla. Brush tortas with butter. Sprinkle with Parmesan. Garnish with sliced chilies if desired. Bake until golden brown and cheese has melted, about 10 minutes. Cut each torta into 8 wedges. Serve immediately.

***Flour Tortillas**

Makes about 18

- **4 cups unbleached all purpose flour**
- **2 teaspoons salt**
- **⅓ cup solid vegetable shortening**
- **1½ cups (or more) warm water (105°F to 115°F)**

Combine flour and salt in large bowl. Cut in shortening until mixture resembles coarse meal. Gradually add water and stir until dough comes together (if dough does not come together, add up to 1 tablespoon more water 1 teaspoon at a time). Turn dough out onto lightly floured surface and knead 1 minute; do not overknead. Invert bowl over dough. Let stand 30 minutes.

Divide dough into 18 rounds. Roll rounds between hands until smooth; flatten into discs. Wrap in plastic and let stand 45 minutes to 1 hour.

Preheat griddle. Using a lightly floured dowel (do not use ball-bearing rolling pin), roll one disc out on lightly floured surface into 8-inch round, rolling from center of dough to edge and turning round often. Place round on fingers of one hand. Using fingers of other hand, pull and stretch tortilla into 10-inch round. Place on griddle. Count to 12 and turn over. Repeat counting to 12 and turning until tortilla has golden spots and has stopped bubbling, about 3 to 4 turns. Wrap tortilla in kitchen towel. Cool completely. Wrap in foil and place in plastic bag until ready to use. *(Can be prepared 1 week ahead and refrigerated or frozen.)* Repeat rolling, stretching and baking remaining discs.

Sweetbread, Raisin and Olive Croustades

An elegant and delicious appetizer. Begin the sweetbreads at least 24 hours before serving. If you do not have the correct ramekin to mold the croustades, use an empty tuna fish can.

Makes 6

- **⅔ pound sweetbreads**
- **3 ounces bacon, finely diced**
- **Freshly ground pepper**
- **2 tablespoons all purpose flour**
- **¼ cup olive oil**
- **7 medium garlic cloves, minced**
- **½ cup golden raisins**
- **⅓ cup oil-cured black Mediterranean olives, pitted and coarsely chopped**
- **¼ cup dry white wine**
- **2 tablespoons Sherry vinegar**
- **1 35-ounce can tomatoes, drained and crushed**
- **⅓ cup minced fresh parsley**
- **1 teaspoon minced fresh thyme or ½ teaspoon dried, crumbled**
- **½ teaspoon freshly grated nutmeg**
- **Salt**
- **12 phyllo pastry sheets, halved crosswise**
- **½ cup (1 stick) unsalted butter, melted**
- **2 cups Rich Brown Veal Stock (see recipe, page 51)**
- **½ cup minced fresh parsley**
- **6 oil-cured black Mediterranean olives, pitted and thinly sliced**

Soak sweetbreads in large bowl of cold water for about 2 hours.

Drain sweetbreads and transfer to medium saucepan. Cover with cold water. Cover and bring to boil. Reduce heat and simmer 2 minutes. Drain sweetbreads. Rinse and pat dry. Cut off membrane. Cut sweetbreads diagonally into 1½-inch-diameter slices, ⅛ to ¼ inch thick. Arrange in single layer on large plate. Cover with cutting board and 4-pound weight. Chill 24 hours, patting dry occasionally.

Blanch bacon in boiling water 2 minutes. Drain and pat dry.

Pat sweetbreads dry. Sprinkle with pepper, then dust lightly with flour. Heat oil in heavy large skillet over medium-high heat. Sauté sweetbreads in batches (do not crowd) until light brown, about 1 minute per side. Drain well on paper towels.

Reduce heat to low. Add bacon to skillet and stir 1 minute. Add garlic and cook 3 minutes, stirring occasionally. Mix in raisins and ⅓ cup olives. Increase heat to high and add wine and vinegar. Boil until liquid is almost completely evaporated, stirring occasionally, about 4 minutes. Transfer to bowl. Mix in tomatoes, ⅓ cup parsley, thyme and nutmeg. Season with salt and pepper. Cool completely. *(Can be prepared 1 day ahead. Wrap sweetbreads and tomato mixture separately and refrigerate.)*

Preheat oven to 425°F. Place 2 phyllo pastry sheet halves in 3¼-inch-diameter ramekin with 1¼-inch straight sides, allowing excess pastry to hang over sides (keep remaining pastry sheets covered with damp towel). Brush pastry in ramekin and 1 inch of overhang with butter. Add 2 more pastry sheets, at right angle to first 2, and brush with butter. Place ⅙ of sweetbreads in pastry. Stir tomato mixture and spoon ⅓ cup atop sweetbreads. Trim pastry, leaving 1 inch extending beyond rim of ramekin. Fold edges over filling. Brush with butter and invert onto grooved roasting pan. Remove ramekin. Cover croustade with damp towel. Repeat with remaining pastry and filling. Brush tops of pastries lightly with butter. Bake until crisp and golden brown, about 20 minutes. Cool 10 minutes.

Meanwhile, boil stock in heavy small saucepan until reduced to 1 cup. Add ½ cup parsley. Arrange croustades on heated plates. Fan sliced olive atop each. Surround with reduced stock.

Freshwater Bass with Lemon-Dill Sauce

For best flavor, prepare this one day before serving.

16 appetizer servings

1 3-pound freshwater bass, whitefish or other white fish, cleaned and halved lengthwise
2 tablespoons (¼ stick) butter, melted
Salt and freshly ground pepper

Lemon-Dill Sauce*

¼ cup raisins
2 tablespoons (¼ stick) butter
2 large yellow onions, thinly sliced
2 medium leeks (white part only), thinly sliced
1 tablespoon minced fresh thyme
1 tablespoon minced fresh oregano

Fresh dill or oregano sprigs

Preheat broiler. Generously grease broiler pan. Arrange fish skin side down on prepared pan. Brush with melted butter and sprinkle with salt and pepper. Broil 6 inches from heat until just opaque, about 9 minutes per 1-inch thickness. Cool.

Skin and bone fish. Flake into medium bowl. Blend in ¼ cup Lemon-Dill Sauce. Press mixture into 12x17½-inch glass baking dish.

Soak raisins in warm water 20 minutes.

Melt 2 tablespoons butter in heavy large skillet over low heat. Mix in onions, leeks, thyme and minced oregano. Cover and cook until very tender, stirring occasionally, about 25 minutes. Drain raisins and chop. Stir into onion mixture. Spread atop fish. Cover and refrigerate overnight.

Cut fish into 16 squares. Arrange each in center of plate. Garnish with dill. Let stand 20 minutes at room temperature. Serve with remaining sauce.

***Lemon-Dill Sauce**

Makes about 2 cups

4 egg yolks, room temperature
4 to 5 tablespoons fresh lemon juice
2 tablespoons Dijon mustard
¾ teaspoon salt
1 cup safflower oil
½ cup minced fresh dill

Combine yolks, lemon juice, mustard and salt in medium bowl. Slowly whisk in oil in thin stream. Mix in dill. Taste and adjust seasoning. *(Can be prepared 3 days ahead. Cover tightly and refrigerate. Let stand at room temperature 20 minutes before serving.)*

Oysters Country Gentleman

Making the watercress butter the night before allows the flavors to meld.

4 servings

3 tablespoons butter
2 tablespoons minced green onion
2 tablespoons minced celery
2 tablespoons minced fresh parsley
1 large garlic clove
1 cup chopped watercress leaves
5 tablespoons butter, cut into 5 pieces
2½ tablespoons dry breadcrumbs
2 tablespoons freshly grated Parmesan cheese
1 teaspoon freshly grated nutmeg
24 unshucked oysters
5 thin slices Smithfield or Black Forest ham, cut into 24 quarter-size pieces

Lemon wedges
Parsley sprigs

Melt 3 tablespoons butter in heavy small skillet over medium-low heat. Add green onion, celery, parsley and garlic and cook until green onion is tender, stirring occasionally, 3 to 4 minutes. Discard garlic. Add watercress and stir until wilted, about 1 minute. Transfer mixture to processor. Add 5 tablespoons butter, breadcrumbs, cheese and nutmeg and mix until smooth. Transfer to bowl. Cover watercress butter with plastic wrap; chill overnight.

Preheat oven to 425°F. Open oysters. Discard flat top shells. Loosen oysters in bottom shells; do not discard liquid. Arrange oysters in baking dish. Cover each with piece of ham. Top each with 1 tablespoon watercress butter. Bake until edges of oysters begin to curl, about 8 minutes.

To serve, arrange 6 oysters on each plate. Garnish with lemon and parsley.

Crab and Avocado Fritters

These spicy starters can be made one day ahead, then cooked before serving.

Makes about 4 dozen

2 pounds crabmeat
1 cup diced green onions
1 medium avocado, peeled and cut into ¼-inch pieces
2 eggs
½ cup hot chili salsa
Salt
¼ cup dry breadcrumbs

Corn oil (for deep frying)
All purpose flour
Thinly slivered green onion (optional)

Line baking sheet with parchment. Combine crab, 1 cup green onions and avocado in large bowl. Mix eggs, salsa and salt; add to crab. Mix in breadcrumbs. Form mixture into 1½-inch balls. Place on prepared sheet. Cover with plastic and refrigerate 3 hours. *(Can be prepared 1 day ahead and frozen. Do not thaw before cooking.)*

Preheat oven to lowest setting. Line another baking sheet with paper towels. Pour oil into large skillet to depth of 3 inches. Heat to 350°F. Dust fritters with flour. Carefully add to oil in batches (do not crowd) and cook until golden brown, about 2 minutes per side for refrigerated fritters and about 3 minutes per side for frozen. Drain on paper towels. Transfer to prepared sheet and keep warm in oven until all are cooked. Garnish with green onion slivers and serve immediately.

Lamb Pâté with Yogurt Herb Sauce

8 servings

Pâté

3 cups fresh white breadcrumbs
1 cup whipping cream
2 teaspoons salt
2 teaspoons minced fresh parsley
1 teaspoon poultry seasoning
1 teaspoon dried thyme, crumbled
1 teaspoon dried tarragon, crumbled
1 teaspoon freshly ground pepper
3 pounds lamb shoulder (not lean), ground through fine plate of meat grinder

Sauce

1 cup plain yogurt
½ teaspoon minced fresh parsley
½ teaspoon dried tarragon, crumbled
¼ teaspoon garlic powder
Salt and freshly ground pepper

Lettuce leaves

For pâté: Mix first 8 ingredients in large bowl. Let stand 15 minutes.

Preheat oven to 350°F. Grease 9x5-inch loaf pan. Add lamb to breadcrumb mixture and blend well. Pack into prepared pan. Cover tightly with foil. Bake until meat thermometer inserted in center registers 130°F, about 80 minutes.

Remove pâté from pan; drain off liquid. Wrap and refrigerate until ready to serve.

For sauce: Combine all ingredients.

To serve, line platter with lettuce. Cut pâté into ¼-inch slices. Arrange over lettuce. Pass yogurt sauce separately.

Leek and Duck Terrine

For best flavor, bake the terrine at least one day before serving.

8 to 10 servings

½ cup dried currants
½ cup Pineau des Charentes*

12 ounces trimmed and skinned duck meat, cut into ½-inch cubes
12 ounces pork fatback, cut into ½-inch cubes
8 ounces trimmed veal leg, cut into ½-inch cubes
8 ounces trimmed pork, cut into ½-inch cubes
½ cup shallots, minced
6 garlic cloves, crushed
4 eggs, beaten to blend
½ cup pine nuts, toasted
¼ cup fresh breadcrumbs
3½ tablespoons snipped fresh chives
2 tablespoons minced fresh basil
2 tablespoons minced fresh tarragon
2 tablespoons minced fresh parsley
2 teaspoons salt
1¼ teaspoons freshly ground white pepper
1 teaspoon Terrine Spice**

8 ¾-inch-diameter leeks, trimmed

Fresh herb sprigs
Toast

Soak currants in Pineau des Charentes until plumped, about 45 minutes.

Combine duck, fatback, veal, pork, shallots and garlic. Force through large disc of meat grinder into large bowl. Mix in eggs. Force through medium disc of meat grinder into another bowl. Fold in currants (do not drain), pine nuts, breadcrumbs, chives, minced herbs, salt, pepper and Terrine Spice. Pinch off small piece of mixture and fry until cooked through. Taste, then season uncooked portion with salt and pepper if necessary.

Cook leeks in large pot of boiling salted water until tender, about 6 minutes. Drain well. Pat dry. Cool.

Preheat oven to 375°F. Spoon ⅓ of meat mixture into 11x3½-inch terrine, smoothing surface. Top with 4 leeks, pressing into meat slightly. Repeat with another ⅓ of meat and remaining leeks. Cover with remaining meat, smoothing surface. (If all of meat mixture does not fit in terrine, smooth remainder into small baking dish and cook as for large terrine.) Cover with foil, shiny side down. Place terrine in large roasting pan. Add enough hot water to roasting pan to come halfway up sides of terrine. Bake terrine for 30 minutes.

Remove foil. Continue cooking terrine until skewer inserted in center comes out hot, about 40 minutes. Pour off any liquid in terrine. Place terrine on rack. Top with another pan filled with 1-pound weights. Cool completely. Remove top pan. Cover terrine and refrigerate overnight. *(Can be prepared 4 days ahead.)*

To unmold, run knife between meat and pan. Invert onto platter. Cut terrine into ⅜-inch-thick slices. Arrrange on platter. Let stand at room temperature 20 minutes. Garnish with herb sprigs. Serve with toast.

*A fortified wine from France's Cognac region. Available at liquor stores.

**Terrine Spice

Makes about 3 tablespoons

2 teaspoons ground allspice
1 teaspoon cinnamon
1 teaspoon freshly grated nutmeg
1 teaspoon ground coriander
1 teaspoon ground dried tarragon
½ teaspoon ground cloves
½ teaspoon ground dried marjoram

Combine all ingredients. Store in sealed jar in cool area.

2 ❦ *Soups and Breads*

Nothing satisfies like a bowl of good soup, and there are plenty of new and interesting ones here: rich Fennel and Shallot Soup (page 12); zippy Onion Soup El Paso (page 12), a twist on a French classic; a Cream of Tomato Soup (page 14) topped with roasted green chilies and a cilantro pesto (that is also good on pasta); and a thick soup made of white and sweet potatoes, served with tangy mint and curry butter (page 13). Some great soup favorites, classics that we have included from the last twelve months, are Ultimate Bean Soup (page 16), wholesome Brunswick Cod Chowder (page 18) and a flavorful Rich Beef Broth with Semolina Dumplings (page 16).

Bread lovers can indulge in hearty loaves that are wonderful with butter and jam as well as sliced for sandwiches. Try Farmhouse Potato Bread (page 19), Buttermilk Rye (page 19) and Whole Wheat Sourdough (page 20). Celebrate a leisurely breakfast or afternoon tea (both meals enjoyed new popularity in 1986) with a country pear and hazelnut loaf (page 23) or warm flaky biscuits (page 24) served with plenty of butter and jam.

Soups

Fennel and Shallot Soup

8 servings

- 2 tablespoons (¼ stick) butter
- 2 cups shallots, peeled

- 1 quart Poultry Stock (see page 83)
- 4 large fennel bulbs (about 4½ pounds), trimmed, cored and sliced
- ¼ cup fennel seeds

- 1 cup whipping cream
- ½ cup sour cream
- Salt and freshly ground white pepper
- ¼ cup minced fennel tops
- ¼ cup freshly grated Parmesan cheese (optional)

Melt butter in heavy large saucepan over low heat. Add shallots and cook until beginning to soften, stirring frequently, about 10 minutes. Add stock, fennel bulbs and fennel seeds. Simmer stock until fennel bulbs are very tender, stirring occasionally, about 2½ hours.

Puree soup in blender in batches. Strain. *(Can be prepared 2 days ahead and refrigerated.)* Return soup to saucepan and bring to simmer. Whisk in whipping cream and sour cream. Season with salt and pepper. Add fennel tops. Ladle soup into bowls. Garnish with cheese if desired.

Onion Soup El Paso

A delicious interpretation of the classic soup. The flavor depends on well-browned onions and a good stock.

8 servings

- 8 black peppercorns
- 3 bay leaves
- 1 teaspoon dried thyme
- 1 teaspoon dried marjoram
- ½ cup (1 stick) unsalted butter, clarified
- 2½ pounds yellow onions, thinly sliced
- 1 cup dry red wine
- 2 quarts rich veal or beef stock (preferably homemade)
- Salt and freshly ground white pepper

- 1 large red bell pepper
- 1 large green bell pepper
- 1 medium poblano chili

- 12 teaspoons applejack
- Parmesan Croutons*
- 8 ounces dry Monterey Jack cheese, thinly sliced
- Chili powder

Wrap first 4 ingredients in small square of cheesecloth. Heat butter in heavy large skillet over high heat. Add onions and cook until beginning to brown, turning frequently with spatula. Reduce heat to medium and cook until well browned, turning occasionally, about 20 minutes. Add wine and bring to boil, scraping up any browned bits. Reduce heat and simmer 10 minutes. Transfer mixture to large saucepan. Add stock and herb bag. Simmer soup 30 minutes. Season with salt and pepper. Discard herb bag. *(Can be prepared 1 day ahead and refrigerated.)*

Char bell peppers and poblano chili over gas flame or in broiler until blackened on all sides. Wrap in paper bag and let stand 10 minutes to steam. Peel and seed. Rinse if necessary; pat dry. Cut into ½-inch pieces.

Preheat oven to 500°F. Reheat soup. Measure 1½ teaspoons applejack into each ovenproof soup bowl. Fill to brim with soup. Cover each with croutons, then cheese. Top with peppers and chili. Bake until cheese is brown and bubbly, about 6 minutes. Sprinkle soup with chili powder and serve.

***Parmesan Croutons**

Makes 32

- **32 ¼-inch-thick slices French baguette**
- **¼ cup (½ stick) unsalted butter, melted**
- **¼ teaspoon minced garlic**
- **2 tablespoons grated Parmesan cheese**

Preheat oven to 350°F. Arrange bread in single layer on baking sheets. Mix butter and garlic; brush over bread. Sprinkle with grated Parmesan. Bake until croutons are dry, about 20 minutes.

Soup of Two Potatoes with Mint and Curry Butter

Makes about 7 cups

- **1 tablespoon unsalted butter**
- **2 medium leeks (white part only), chopped**
- **1 garlic clove, minced**
- **Pinch of cayenne pepper**
- **5 cups water**
- **1 pound boiling potatoes, peeled and coarsely chopped**
- **¾ pound sweet potatoes, peeled and coarsely chopped**
- **3½ teaspoons coarse salt**

Mint and Curry Butter*

Melt butter in heavy large pot over medium-high heat. Add leeks, garlic and cayenne and stir 1 minute. Add water, potatoes and 2 teaspoons salt. Bring to boil. Reduce heat, cover and simmer mixture until vegetables are tender, about 30 minutes.

Puree soup in batches in blender. *(Can be prepared 1 day ahead. Cool completely, cover and refrigerate.)* Return to pot. Add remaining salt. Simmer soup 5 minutes. Ladle into bowls. Top with Mint and Curry Butter and serve.

***Mint and Curry Butter**

Makes about ½ cup

- **1½ teaspoons unsalted butter**
- **¾ teaspoon curry powder**
- **⅛ teaspoon turmeric**
- **Pinch of minced garlic**

- **¼ cup (½ stick) unsalted butter, room temperature**
- **1 tablespoon minced fresh mint or ¼ teaspoon dried, crumbled**
- **2 teaspoons fresh lemon juice**

Melt 1½ teaspoons butter in heavy small skillet over medium heat. Add curry powder, turmeric and garlic and stir until butter and spices bubble, about 30 seconds. Cool mixture slightly.

Blend ¼ cup butter, mint and lemon juice until smooth. Stir in spice mixture. *(Can be prepared several days ahead and refrigerated. Bring butter to room temperature before using.)*

Cold Tomatillo Soup

6 servings

- **2 tablespoons vegetable oil**
- **2 small jalapeño chilies, seeded and finely diced**
- **1 small onion, finely diced**
- **2 pounds tomatillos, husked and quartered***
- **4 cups chicken stock (preferably homemade)**

Salt
- **2 tablespoons chopped cilantro leaves**

Heat oil in heavy large saucepan over medium-low heat. Add chilies and onion and cook until tender, stirring occasionally, about 10 minutes. Add tomatillos and stock and bring to boil. Reduce heat, cover and simmer until tomatillos are tender, about 10 minutes. Puree soup in blender or processor. Cool completely. Cover and chill.

Just before serving, season soup with salt. Ladle into bowls. Garnish with chopped cilantro.

*A vegetable that resembles a green tomato with a paper-thin husk. Available at Latin American markets.

Cream of Tomato Soup with Green Chilies and Cilantro Pesto

6 servings

- **2 tablespoons olive oil**
- **6 celery stalks (with leaves), chopped**
- **1 leek (white part only), chopped**
- **1 onion, chopped**
- **3 pounds ripe or canned tomatoes, coarsely chopped**
- **2 cups chicken stock (preferably homemade)**
- **½ bunch parsley, chopped**
- **½ cup fresh basil leaves, chopped**
- **3 bay leaves**
- **3 thyme sprigs or 1 teaspoon dried, crumbled**
- **3 marjoram sprigs or 1 teaspoon dried, crumbled**
- **6 tablespoons (¾ stick) butter**
- **6 tablespoons all purpose flour**
- **2 cups half and half**
- **4 poblano or Anaheim chilies, roasted, peeled, seeded and diced**
- **2 tomatoes, peeled, seeded and diced**
- **2 tablespoons Cilantro Pesto***
- **1 tablespoon sugar**
- **Salt and freshly ground white pepper**

Heat oil in heavy large saucepan over medium-low heat. Add celery, leek and onion and cook until translucent, stirring occasionally, about 15 minutes. Add next 7 ingredients and simmer until vegetables are very tender, about 45 minutes. Strain soup, pressing on solids to extract as much liquid as possible. *(Can be prepared 1 day ahead. Cool completely, cover and refrigerate. Reheat before continuing.)*

Melt butter in heavy large saucepan over medium-low heat. Add flour and whisk 10 minutes; do not let color. Whisk in soup and simmer until thickened and texture of whipping cream, 20 to 30 minutes. Stir in half and half and heat through. Add chilies, tomatoes, pesto and sugar. Season with salt and pepper. Ladle into bowls.

*Cilantro Pesto

This is also delicious with pasta or new potatoes.

Makes 1 cup

- **2 cups lightly packed cilantro leaves (about 3 large bunches)**
- **½ cup freshly grated Parmesan cheese**
- **⅓ cup hulled pumpkin seeds (pepitas)**
- **¼ cup olive oil**
- **5 teaspoons fresh lemon juice**
- **5 large garlic cloves, chopped**
- **½ teaspoon salt**

Mix all ingredients in processor until smooth, stopping to scrape down sides of bowl, about 2 minutes. Store in jar. *(Pesto can be prepared 2 weeks ahead and refrigerated.)*

Hungarian Creamy Chestnut Soup

A hearty, easy-to-make winter soup.

8 servings

1 pound prepared fresh* or vacuum-packed chestnuts (about 36)
¼ cup (½ stick) butter
½ pound lean pork, cut into ½-inch cubes, patted dry
1 cup chopped peeled parsnips
1 cup chopped peeled carrots
1 cup chopped celery with leaves
2 teaspoons Hungarian sweet paprika
5 cups chicken broth
1 cup whipping cream
3 egg yolks
Salt and freshly ground pepper
Hungarian sweet paprika

Chop chestnuts finely in processor. Set aside. Melt butter in heavy Dutch oven over medium heat. Add pork, parsnips, carrots and celery and cook until vegetables are tender, stirring occasionally, about 10 minutes. Mix in chestnuts and 2 teaspoons paprika, then broth. Simmer until pork is tender, stirring occasionally, about 20 minutes. *(Can be prepared 1 day ahead. Cover and refrigerate. Reheat before continuing.)* Beat cream and yolks in small bowl to blend. Slowly whisk 1 cup of soup into mixture; return to pan. Reduce heat and stir until soup thickens slightly, about 1 minute (do not boil). Season with salt and pepper. Ladle soup into bowls. Sprinkle with paprika.

***To Prepare Fresh Chestnuts**

Peel a thin strip of outer skin off side of chestnuts, using sharp knife. Place chestnuts in saucepan and cover with cold water. Cover and simmer until chestnuts are tender when pierced with knife, 25 to 30 minutes. Drain. Cover with cold water and let stand 15 minutes. Peel off remaining outer and inner brown skin, using sharp knife. You can do this up to one week before using. Chill in airtight jar.

Chicken, Hominy and Sweet Potato Chowder

6 servings

3 tablespoons unsalted butter
3 whole boneless chicken breasts (1½ pounds total), skinned, cut into 1-inch cubes
1 large slender sweet potato, peeled
1 medium onion, peeled and halved
4½ cups chicken stock or broth
2 small serrano chilies, stemmed
½ teaspoon ground coriander
¼ teaspoon ground cumin
1 15-ounce can golden hominy, drained
Salt
⅔ cup fresh cilantro leaves

Melt butter in heavy 5-quart saucepan over high heat. Add chicken and cook until no longer pink, stirring frequently, 3 to 4 minutes. Remove chicken cubes using slotted spoon and set aside.

Stand sweet potato in processor feed tube and slice, using thin slicer and firm pressure. Stand onion halves in feed tube and then slice using firm pressure.

Transfer contents of work bowl to saucepan. Add stock and bring to boil. Reduce heat, cover and simmer until sweet potato and onion are very soft, about 20 minutes. Strain cooking liquid into large bowl, pressing on solids to extract as much liquid as possible.

Puree potato mixture, chilies, coriander and cumin in processor until smooth, stopping once to scrape down sides of work bowl, about 1 minute. Add 1 cup cooking liquid and blend until very smooth, about 30 seconds. Reserve remaining liquid.

Return potato mixture to saucepan. Stir in chicken, hominy and salt. Cook over low heat until heated through. *(Can be prepared 3 days ahead, covered and refrigerated. Rewarm over low heat.)* Thin chowder to desired consistency with reserved cooking liquid. Mix in cilantro. Adjust seasoning. Serve hot.

Ultimate Bean Soup

Makes about 16 cups

1½ pounds dried navy beans

3 tablespoons butter
3 tablespoons olive oil
9 cups chopped leeks
6 garlic cloves, minced
12 medium carrots, chopped
12 medium celery stalks, chopped
9 cups water

6 cups rich chicken stock
6 cups whipping cream
9 tablespoons white wine vinegar
2 talespoons dried marjoram, crumbled
1 teaspoon freshly grated nutmeg
Salt and freshly ground pepper
Snipped chives or minced fresh parsley

Cover beans with cold water and soak overnight. Drain well.

Melt butter with oil in heavy large saucepan over medium-low heat. Add leeks and garlic and cook until tender, stirring occasionally, about 15 minutes. Stir in beans, carrots and celery. Add water and bring to boil. Reduce heat, cover partially and simmer until beans are tender, about 1¼ hours.

Puree bean mixture in blender until very smooth. Press through sieve into tureen. Stir in stock, cream, vinegar, marjoram and nutmeg. Season with salt and pepper. Refrigerate until well chilled. Top with chives or parsley.

Rich Beef Broth with Semolina Dumplings

To give the broth a rich hue, add the onion skin to the pot.

8 servings

4 pounds beef bones (not marrow bones)
8 quarts cold water
2 pounds beef brisket or boneless beef chuck, cut into ½-inch cubes
2 large beef marrow bones, cracked
½ pound beef liver, cut into 8 pieces
6 medium carrots, thinly sliced
4 medium leeks, trimmed and thinly sliced
2 large yellow onions (unpeeled), thinly sliced
1 cup coarsely chopped celery tops
1 bunch parsley (preferably Italian)
½ pound celery root, diced
4 medium garlic cloves
2 rosemary sprigs or 1 teaspoon dried, crumbled
2 sage sprigs or 2 teaspoons dried, crumbled
2 thyme sprigs or 2 teaspoons dried, crumbled
2 chervil sprigs or 2 teaspoons dried, crumbled
2 large bay leaves, crumbled
24 whole black peppercorns
½ teaspoon freshly grated nutmeg

Salt
Semolina Dumpling Dough*
⅔ cup snipped fresh chives

Preheat broiler. Spread 4 pounds beef bones on broiler pan. Broil 6 inches from heat until brown, about 5 minutes per side. Transfer to heavy large pot. Add all remaining ingredients except salt, dumpling dough and chives. Bring to boil, skimming surface. Adjust heat so liquid barely shimmers and cook 4 hours; do not boil. Strain broth through large colander, discarding solids. Refrigerate overnight.

Discard fat from surface of broth. Strain broth into pot through sieve lined with dampened towel. Simmer until reduced to 14 cups if necessary. Season with salt. Adjust heat so liquid boils gently. Roll dumpling dough into tablespoon-size balls. Drop into broth. Cover and simmer until dumplings are puffed and light, 18 to 20 minutes; do not lift lid during first 18 minutes. Ladle broth and dumplings into bowls. Top with chives and serve.

***Semolina Dumpling Dough**

Makes about 14

5 tablespoons unsalted butter
1 egg
¾ cup semolina flour or couscous*
1 tablespoon all purpose flour
½ teaspoon salt
¼ teaspoon freshly grated nutmeg

Cream butter and egg in processor until light. Add all remaining ingredients and process until dough forms ball, stopping once to scrape down sides, about 2 minutes. Transfer to bowl. Cover and refrigerate at least 2 hours. *(Can be prepared 1 day ahead.)*

*Available at Italian and Middle Eastern markets and some supermarkets.

Sole and Watercress Soup with Ginger

The watercress in this light soup is an appealing color contrast to the fish.

4 servings

6 ounces sole fillets
1 teaspoon vegetable oil
¾ teaspoon cornstarch
¼ teaspoon finely ground white pepper
Salt

5 cups chicken stock or 2 cups canned chicken broth and 3 cups water
2 thin slices fresh ginger
8 ounces watercress, stemmed
2 teaspoons soy sauce

4½ teaspoons vegetable oil
⅛ teaspoon Chinese cooking wine or dry white wine
¼ teaspoon oriental sesame oil

Holding knife almost parallel to work surface, cut fish across grain into ¹⁄₁₀x1-inch slices. Mix with 1 teaspoon vegetable oil, cornstarch, pepper and salt. Refrigerate mixture for 1 hour.

Bring stock and ginger to boil in medium saucepan. Add watercress and soy sauce. Season to taste with salt. Boil for 3 minutes. Reduce heat to low.

Heat 4½ teaspoons vegetable oil in wok or heavy large saucepan over high heat 1½ minutes. Add fish and stir 1 minute. Add wine, stock mixture and sesame oil. Cook 1½ minutes. Transfer soup to tureen, discarding ginger.

Oyster Cream Soup

The shucked oysters will yield enough "liquor" to strain and use in this soup.

8 servings

3 tablespoons unsalted butter
2 medium onions, chopped
1 bunch green onions (white part only), chopped
3 large garlic cloves, minced
2 medium tomatoes, peeled, seeded and chopped
1 teaspoon minced fresh basil leaves
1 teaspoon minced fresh thyme leaves
Salt and freshly ground white pepper
Cayenne pepper

4 cups whipping cream, boiled until reduced to 3 cups
½ cup strained oyster liquor
2 cups half and half
3 cups shucked oysters (about 24)
Basil leaves

Melt butter in heavy medium saucepan over medium-low heat. Add onions and garlic and cook until transparent, stirring occasionally, about 10 minutes. Add tomatoes. Increase heat to medium and cook until thickened, stirring occasionally, about 10 minutes. Stir in basil and thyme. Season with salt, pepper and cayenne. Cook until all moisture has evaporated. Cool completely. Cover. Chill overnight.

Puree onion mixture in processor. Transfer to heavy large saucepan. Add reduced cream and oyster liquor and bring to boil. Reduce heat. Add half and half and heat through. Adjust seasoning. Add oysters and poach until just opaque, about 2 minutes. Ladle into bowls. Garnish with basil leaves.

Brunswick Cod Chowder

6 to 8 servings

2 tablespoons (¼ stick) butter
½ cup chopped onion
1 garlic clove, minced
2 cups water
2 medium potatoes, peeled and diced
1 10-ounce package frozen baby lima beans (unthawed)
⅓ cup dry white wine
1 pound cod fillets, cut into 1-inch cubes
1 16-ounce can whole peeled tomatoes, drained and chopped
1 10¾-ounce can cream of celery soup
1 10-ounce package frozen corn (unthawed)
1 tablespoon chicken bouillon granules
1 teaspoon lemon pepper seasoning
1 teaspoon Worcestershire sauce
1 teaspoon fresh lemon juice
¼ teaspoon Old Bay seafood seasoning
1 cup half and half

Melt butter in Dutch oven over medium-high heat. Add onion and garlic and stir until soft, 1 to 2 minutes. Add water, potatoes, lima beans and wine. Bring to boil. Reduce heat to low, cover and simmer 15 minutes. Add next 9 ingredients. Cover and continue simmering 15 minutes. Stir in half and half. Cook until heated through, 2 to 3 minutes. Serve immediately.

Breads

Quick Egg Bread

Makes 16 rolls

3 to 3½ cups unbleached all purpose flour
2 tablespoons sugar
2 envelopes fast-rising dry yeast
1½ teaspoons salt
2 eggs
1 cup hot water (120°F to 130°F)
2 tablespoons vegetable oil
2 teaspoons sesame seeds

Grease 9-inch round cake pan. Combine 3 cups flour, sugar, yeast and salt in large bowl and mix well. Separate 1 egg; set white aside. Add yolk and remaining egg, hot water and oil to dry ingredients. Mix vigorously with wooden spoon until smooth. Turn dough out onto lightly floured surface. Knead until smooth and elastic, kneading in additional flour if necessary. Cover with mixing bowl and let rest 5 minutes.

Divide dough into 16 pieces. Arrange pieces in prepared pan. Beat reserved egg white until foamy. Brush over rolls and sprinkle with sesame seeds. Set wire rack in 9x13-inch baking dish. Add enough boiling water to come just below rack. Set pan on rack. Cover with towel and let rise in warm draft-free area until doubled in volume, about 25 minutes.

Preheat oven to 350°F. Bake until rolls are deep golden and sound hollow when tapped on bottom, about 20 minutes. Serve rolls warm.

Farmhouse Potato Bread

Moist, light loaves, perfect with the Plum and Apple Butter (see page 88). They are even better the day after they are baked.

Makes 2 loaves

½ pound Idaho potatoes, peeled and cut into 1-inch pieces

2 cups milk
8 tablespoons (1 stick) unsalted butter, room temperature
¼ cup sugar
1 tablespoon salt
1 envelope dry yeast
5 cups (about) unbleached all purpose flour

Place potatoes in small saucepan. Cover with cold salted water. Simmer until very tender, about 10 minutes. Drain. Force hot potatoes through sieve into large bowl.

Combine milk, 4 tablespoons butter, sugar and salt in heavy small saucepan. Bring to boil, stirring to dissolve sugar. Whisk into potatoes. Let cool to warm (105°F to 115°F). Sprinkle yeast over mixture, then stir in. Mix in 4 cups flour. Knead dough on generously floured surface until smooth and elastic, adding more flour if sticky, about 10 minutes. Grease large bowl with 2 tablespoons butter. Add dough, turning to coat entire surface. Cover bowl with towel. Let dough rise in warm draft-free area until doubled in volume, about 1½ hours.

Punch dough down. Knead until smooth, about 1 minute. Return to bowl. Cover and let rise until doubled in volume, about 1½ hours.

Butter two 6-cup loaf pans, using remaining 2 tablespoons butter. Punch dough down. Cut into 2 pieces. Shape each piece into loaf; transfer to prepared pans. Cover pans with towel. Let dough rise until level with tops of pans, about 45 minutes.

Position rack in lower third of oven and preheat to 400°F. Place bread in oven. Reduce temperature to 375°F. Bake until loaves are rich golden brown and sound hollow when tapped, about 30 minutes. Cool in pans 5 minutes. Transfer to racks and cool completely before serving.

Buttermilk Rye Bread

This bread makes delicious sandwiches. Use the food processor to quickly mix up a batch of dough.

Makes 1 loaf

1 envelope dry yeast
¼ cup warm water (105°F to 115°F)
2 tablespoons molasses

1½ cups (or more) bread flour
1½ cups rye flour
2 tablespoons safflower oil
1 teaspoon salt
1 teaspoon caraway seeds
1 teaspoon poppy seeds
¾ cup buttermilk, room temperature

Sprinkle yeast over warm water in small bowl; let dissolve. Add molasses and stir to blend. Let stand until foamy, about 5 minutes.

Combine 1½ cups bread flour, rye flour, oil, salt, caraway seeds, poppy seeds and yeast mixture in work bowl and mix. With machine running, pour buttermilk through feed tube and process until dough cleans sides of work bowl. If dough sticks to bowl, add more bread flour through feed tube 1 tablespoon at a time, incorporating each before adding next. If dough is dry and crumbly, add water through feed tube 1 teaspoon at a time, incorporating each before adding next. Process dough until uniformly smooth and elastic, about 2 minutes.

Transfer dough to oiled bowl, turning to coat entire surface. Cover bowl with oiled plastic wrap. Let dough rise in warm draft-free area until almost doubled in volume, about 1½ hours.

Grease 6-cup Pullman loaf pan* and underside of lid. Punch dough down on floured surface. Roll out into rectangle same length as pan. Roll up lengthwise, pinching ends to seal. Arrange seam side down in prepared pan, tucking ends under if necessary. Drape loosely with oiled plastic wrap. Let loaf rise in warm draft-free area until doubled in volume, about 45 minutes.

Position rack in center of oven and preheat to 375°F. Cover pan. Bake bread 45 minutes. Uncover pan and continue baking until top of loaf is golden brown, 5 to 10 minutes. Remove from pan. Cool completely on wire rack before slicing.

To slice for sandwiches, freeze bread until semifrozen. Trim crusts, leaving 2½x3½-inch core. Cut into ¼-inch-thick slices using serrated knife.

*A rectangular pan with right-angled corners and removable flat sliding lid. If unavailable, 8½x4½x2½-inch ovenproof glass loaf pan can be used. Let dough rise in pan as above. Oil bottom of baking sheet and set atop dough. Weight down with heavy ovenproof object. Bake at 350°F.

Whole Wheat Sourdough Bread

Makes 2 loaves

½ cup prepared sourdough starter*
2 tablespoons water
2 tablespoons all purpose flour

2 tablespoons sugar
1 envelope dry yeast
2 cups warm water (105°F to 115°F)
3 cups bread flour
2 teaspoons salt

¼ cup boiling water
¼ cup honey
1½ tablespoons butter

¼ cup rolled oats
¼ cup wheat germ
¼ cup unprocessed bran flakes
¼ cup wheat flakes**
2 tablespoons soy flour**
1½ teaspoons chia seeds**
3 to 4 cups whole wheat flour

Mix sourdough starter, 2 tablespoons water and all purpose flour. Let stand overnight or at room temperature.

Sprinkle sugar and yeast over ½ cup water in heavy-duty mixer bowl; let dissolve. Stir to blend. Let stand until foamy and proofed, about 10 minutes. Add sourdough starter mixture, remaining water, bread flour and salt and beat until smooth. Cover sponge and let stand in warm draft-free area until light and foamy, about 1 hour.

Whisk boiling water, honey and butter. Cool mixture completely.

Combine oats, wheat germ, bran, wheat flakes, soy flour and chia seeds. Beat oatmeal mixture and cooled honey mixture into sponge. Turn dough out onto floured surface. Knead 10 minutes, adding enough whole wheat flour to create slightly sticky dough. Butter large bowl. Add dough, turning to coat entire surface. Cover and let rise in warm draft-free area until doubled, about 1¼ hours.

Punch dough down. Cover and let rise in warm draft-free area until doubled in volume, about 1 hour.

Grease baking sheets. Punch dough down. Shape into 2 rounds. Set on prepared sheets. Slash tops. Cover and let rise in warm draft-free area until almost doubled, about 30 minutes.

Preheat oven to 350°F. Bake bread until golden brown, about 45 minutes. Cool bread completely.

*Available at natural foods stores and most supermarkets. Prepare starter according to package directions.

**Available at natural foods stores.

Baked Wheat Flour Bread with Cheese, Onion and Coriander Stuffing

A lovely bread to serve as an appetizer with cocktails, or as a light meal, accompanied by a yogurt salad.

Makes 12

4 cups bleached all purpose flour
1 tablespoon baking powder
2 teaspoons sugar
1 teaspoon salt
1¼ cups milk
¼ cup (½ stick) unsalted butter
1 egg
Vegetable oil

Stuffing
Simple Homemade Cheese*
⅓ cup thinly sliced onions, squeezed and drained
⅓ cup minced fresh cilantro
4 fresh hot green chilies (such as serrano), minced
4½ teaspoons fresh lemon juice
¼ teaspoon salt

All purpose flour

Melted clarified butter or vegetable oil (optional)

Combine flour, baking powder, sugar and salt in large bowl. Heat milk with butter in small saucepan until butter melts and milk is warm (115°F). Beat egg in another bowl; slowly beat in milk mixture. Add to dry ingredients and mix with hands until dough forms. Clean hands thoroughly and oil generously. Knead dough in bowl until smooth and satiny, adding oil to fingers and dough as necessary to prevent sticking, about 6 minutes. Cover dough and let rest 4 to 6 hours.

Divide dough into 12 pieces. Roll 1 piece into small round, oiling hands as necessary. Place on plate and cover with plastic. Repeat with remaining dough. Let rest 30 minutes. *(Can be prepared 4 days ahead and refrigerated.)*

For stuffing: Mix first 6 ingredients.

Stretch 1 dough round into 4-inch circle on work surface. Place 1 generous tablespoon filling in center. Gather sides of dough around filling, then roll dough into ball. Gently roll filled dough out on lightly floured surface to 5-inch round, dusting frequently with flour. Repeat rolling and filling with remaining dough and filling.

Preheat oven to 500°F. Arrange breads in single layer on baking sheets and bake until puffed and beginning to color, about 4 minutes for room temperature dough and 7 minutes for cold dough. *(Can be prepared 3 hours ahead. Cover tightly.)*

Preheat broiler. Just before serving, broil breads until tops are spotted brown, watching carefully. Brush with butter or vegetable oil if desired.

*Simple Homemade Cheese

Makes about ¾ cup

4 cups whole milk
2 tablespoons fresh lemon juice

Bring milk to simmer in heavy medium saucepan. Add lemon juice and stir gently until milk separates into curds and whey. Gently ladle into cheesecloth-lined strainer. Drain cheese 15 minutes. When cool enough to handle, squeeze to extract excess moisture. *(Can be prepared 2 days ahead. Wrap tightly and refrigerate.)*

Peppered Cheddar Cheese Loaf

Any leftover bread makes great croutons.

Makes 1 loaf

1 envelope dry yeast
1½ cups warm water (105°F to 115°F)

3 cups (or more) bread flour
1 cup grated sharp cheddar cheese
2 teaspoons coarsely ground pepper
1 teaspoon salt

¼ cup grated sharp cheddar cheese
Coarsely ground pepper

Sprinkle yeast over 1½ cups warm water in small bowl; stir to dissolve. Let mixture stand for 10 minutes.

Combine 3 cups flour, 1 cup cheddar, 2 teaspoons pepper and salt in large bowl; make well in center. (Can also be mixed in heavy-duty electric mixer.) Add yeast to well. Using wooden spoon, mix until dough forms ball and pulls away from sides of bowl, adding more flour if necessary. Knead dough on lightly floured surface until smooth and elastic, adding more flour if sticky, about 10 minutes. Grease large bowl. Add dough, turning to coat entire surface. Cover bowl with plastic. Let dough rise in warm draft-free area until doubled, about 2 hours.

Line baking sheet with parchment. Punch dough down. Knead on lightly floured surface until smooth, about 2 minutes. Knead into ball. Transfer to prepared sheet. Cut ¼-inch-deep cross in center of dough. Let dough rise in warm draft-free area until almost doubled in volume, about 45 minutes.

Preheat oven to 425°F. Sprinkle ¼ cup cheddar in cross atop loaf. Sprinkle pepper over cheese. Bake bread 20 minutes. Reduce temperature to 350°F. Continue baking until bread sounds hollow when tapped, about 25 minutes. Cool on rack.

Pumpkin Wheat Bread

Serve this with dinner and use it to make Pumpkin and Wild Mushroom Stuffing (see page 83); any leftovers make great toast for breakfast.

Makes 2 loaves

2½ cups all purpose flour
2 cups whole wheat flour
2 cups sugar
1 tablespoon baking powder
2 teaspoons baking soda
4 eggs, room temperature
2 cups canned solid pack pumpkin
2 teaspoons salt
1 cup (2 sticks) unsalted butter, room temperature

1 egg yolk beaten with ¼ cup whipping cream (glaze)

Position rack in lower third of oven and preheat to 350°F. Butter two 9x5-inch loaf pans. Sift flours, sugar, baking powder and baking soda into large bowl. Combine eggs, pumpkin and salt in another bowl. Add to dry ingredients and mix until smooth. Mix in butter 1 tablespoon at a time.

Divide batter between pans. Brush loaves with glaze. Bake until golden brown, about 45 minutes. Invert onto racks and cool before using. *(Can be prepared 2 days ahead. Wrap tightly.)*

Tandoor Baked Wheat Flour Bread with Mint

Although traditionally cooked in a tandoor *(Indian clay oven) in restaurants, these can also be baked in home ovens. They are very popular at Indian banquets, where they are offered with elegant braised dishes and grilled meats.*

4 cups all purpose flour
1 tablespoon baking powder
2 teaspoons sugar
1 teaspoon salt
1¼ cups milk
¼ cup (½ stick) unsalted butter
1 egg
Vegetable oil

Topping
6 tablespoons minced fresh mint or 3 tablespoons dried
1 tablespoon chat masala*
3 fresh hot green chilies (such as serrano), minced
2 small eggs
3 tablespoons water

12 tablespoons (1½ sticks) unsalted butter, melted

Makes 12

Combine flour, baking powder, sugar and salt in large bowl. Heat milk with butter until butter melts and milk is warm (115°F). Beat egg in another bowl. Slowly beat in milk mixture. Slowly add to dry ingredients, mixing with hand just until dough forms. Wipe hand clean and oil generously. Knead dough in bowl until smooth and satiny, oiling fingers and dough as necessary to prevent sticking, 5 to 6 minutes. Cover dough with plastic and let rest for 4 to 6 hours.

Divide dough into 12 pieces. Roll into smooth rounds between hands, oiling hands if necessary. Cover with plastic. Let rest 30 minutes. *(Can be prepared 4 days ahead and refrigerated.)*

For topping: Combine mint, chat masala and chilies in small bowl. Combine eggs and water in another bowl.

Stretch 1 piece of dough to 5x7-inch oval on work surface. Brush top with egg; sprinkle with mint mixture. Repeat with remaining dough. Arrange in single layer on baking sheets.

Position rack in center of oven and preheat to 550°F. Bake breads until they are beginning to color, about 4½ minutes. Drizzle each with 1 tablespoon butter. Serve breads immediately.

*Chat masala, a spicy salt blend, is available at Indian markets. Roasted ground cumin seeds can be substituted. Roast seeds in heavy small skillet over medium-high heat until several shades darker, shaking pan frequently. Cool. Grind to powder.

Pear and Hazelnut Country Bread

For best flavor and texture, serve this bread the same day it is baked, along with butter or cheese. It is also delicious sliced and toasted the next day for breakfast.

Makes 2 loaves

2 pounds Bartlett pears, peeled, cored and cut into 1-inch cubes
8 ounces dried pears, cut into ¼-inch pieces
1½ cups water

1 tablespoon dry yeast
1 teaspoon honey

¼ cup honey
2 tablespoons hazelnut oil or butter
1 egg, beaten to blend
1½ teaspoons salt
½ teaspoon ground ginger
1½ cups rye flour
4 cups (about) unbleached all purpose flour
1 cup hazelnuts, toasted and coarsely chopped

Hazelnut oil or vegetable oil

Rye flour

1 egg
2 tablespoons coarsely chopped hazelnuts

Combine Bartlett and dried pears and water in heavy nonaluminum saucepan. Bring to simmer. Cover partially and cook until fresh pears are just tender, about 8 minutes. Cool slightly. Drain well, reserving poaching liquid. Set aside 1⅓ cups pear mixture. Puree remainder in processor.

Pour ⅓ cup pear poaching liquid into small bowl and cool to 105°F to 115°F (reserve remaining liquid). Sprinkle yeast over; add 1 teaspoon honey and stir to dissolve. Cover and let stand until foamy, about 5 minutes.

Transfer yeast mixture to bowl of heavy-duty electric mixer (dough can also be mixed by hand). Mix in pear pieces and 1 cup pear puree. Combine ¼ cup honey, 2 tablespoons hazelnut oil, 1 egg, salt and ginger in small bowl; blend into yeast mixture. Add rye flour and beat until smooth. Add enough all purpose flour 1 cup at a time to form sticky dough that pulls away from sides of bowl. Knead until smooth and elastic, about 8 minutes. Knead in 1 cup hazelnuts.

Brush large bowl with hazelnut oil. Add dough, turning to coat entire surface. Cover bowl with plastic and kitchen towel. Let dough rise in warm draft-free area until doubled in volume, about 1½ hours.

Line baking sheet with parchment. Dust with rye flour. Punch dough down. Knead on floured surface until smooth, about 2 minutes. Cut dough in half. Knead each piece into round. Transfer to prepared sheet; flatten each to 7-inch diameter. Cover with kitchen towel and let rise in warm draft-free area until almost doubled in volume, about 50 minutes.

Position rack in lower third of oven and preheat to 350°F. Slash top of loaves ⅛ inch deep in crisscross pattern. Mix egg with 1 tablespoon pear poaching liquid. Brush over loaves. Sprinkle each with 1 tablespoon hazelnuts. Bake until loaves are deep golden brown and sound hollow when tapped, 45 to 55 minutes. Let loaves cool on racks before serving.

Flea St. Cafe Biscuits

Makes about 24

2 cups all purpose flour
2 cups whole wheat pastry flour
2 tablespoons baking powder
2 tablespoons sugar
1½ teaspoons salt
1 cup (2 sticks) well-chilled unsalted butter, cut into small pieces
4 eggs
⅔ cup buttermilk
2 egg whites, beaten to blend (glaze)
Sesame seeds

Preheat oven to 400°F. Lightly grease baking sheets. Combine flours, baking powder, sugar and salt in large bowl. Using pastry blender or 2 knives, cut in butter until mixture resembles coarse meal. Whisk eggs and buttermilk to blend in another bowl. Add to flour mixture. Using hands or fork, toss to moisten mixture completely.

Turn mixture out onto lightly floured surface. Knead briefly so dough comes together. Roll dough out into 12x15-inch rectangle. Bring both short ends of dough into center. Fold one half over other half. Roll dough out into 5x21-inch rectangle. Trim edges; cut in half lengthwise. Cut each strip into ten 2-inch squares. Gather scraps; re-roll and cut additional squares. Brush tops with glaze. Sprinkle with sesame seeds. Arrange on prepared sheets. Bake until golden brown, about 15 minutes. Serve biscuits hot with butter and jam.

3 ❦ *Salads*

More than any other item on the menu today, salads reflect how our attitudes about eating have changed. They're built on a healthy base of fresh greens and heightened with texture from grains and crunchy vegetables and the wholesome addition of bits of cooked meats or seafood. Salad dressings are different too—light and flavorful, enhanced with fresh herbs, spices and citrus juices.

In this chapter, we include a full array of salads, from family staples like one of new potatoes and peas with a tangy mint dressing (page 28), to intriguing newcomers like a refreshing combination of jicama and red bell peppers with a cilantro herbal cream (page 26), or tender strips of sweet potatoes tossed with yellow bell peppers, green onions and crisp snow peas, dressed with a honey-sweetened citrus vinaigrette (page 28).

Seafood, a salad staple, is here in force, with Mussel, Scallop and Corn Salsa Salad (page 30), tangy Calamari and Greens with Lemon Vinaigrette (page 31) and Shrimp and Celery Salad with Warm Dill Dressing (page 32).

Whether you serve them at the beginning or the end of a meal, or make one the focus of a light lunch or supper, you'll find these salads refreshing, colorful and very satisfying.

Garden Salad with "French" Dressing

This sweet and sour vinaigrette gradually evolved into the "French" dressing featured in supermarkets. Although there is nothing particularly French about it, it is delicious on crisp fresh summer vegetables. Best if never refrigerated, use it on the same day it is prepared.

10 servings

3 tablespoons sugar
1 tablespoon Hungarian sweet paprika
1½ teaspoons salt
⅓ cup red wine vinegar
2 tablespoons Dijon mustard
1 egg yolk, room temperature
Freshly ground pepper
2 cups vegetable oil

2 pounds green beans, trimmed

6 beefsteak tomatoes, cut into ½-inch-thick rounds
2 pounds cucumbers (peeled if waxed), cut diagonally into ½-inch-thick slices

Combine sugar, paprika and salt in medium bowl. Whisk in vinegar, mustard and yolk. Add generous amount of pepper. Whisk in oil in slow steady stream. Adjust seasoning.

Cook beans in large amount of boiling salted water until just crisp-tender, about 5 minutes. Drain. Cool beans in bowl of ice water. Drain well.

Just before serving, mound beans in center of large platter. Arrange tomatoes at one end; mound cucumbers at other end. Pass dressing separately.

Southwest Salad with Cilantro Herbal Cream

For maximum flavor, make the delectable salad dressing one day ahead.

6 servings

1½ cups mayonnaise, preferably homemade
1 cup buttermilk
2 tablespoons balsamic vinegar
1 tablespoon minced onion
2 teaspoons chopped fresh cilantro
2 teaspoons chopped fresh parsley
1 teaspoon chopped fresh basil leaves
1 medium garlic clove, chopped
¼ teaspoon freshly ground pepper

2 large heads Bibb lettuce, cut into 6 wedges and chilled
1 small jicama, peeled and cut julienne
1 large red bell pepper, cut julienne
6 sun-dried tomatoes, cut julienne

Mix first 9 ingredients in blender or processor until smooth. *(Can be made 1 day ahead and refrigerated.)*

Set lettuce wedge on each plate. Remove core. Spoon herbal cream over lettuce. Garnish with jicama, bell pepper and sun-dried tomatoes.

Watercress, Apple and Walnut Salad with Bleu Cheese Vinaigrette

6 servings

Vinaigrette
2 tablespoons minced shallots
2 tablespoons apple cider vinegar
2 tablespoons fresh lemon juice
¾ teaspoon coarsely cracked black peppercorns
½ teaspoon sugar
½ teaspoon salt
⅔ cup walnut oil
⅔ cup bleu cheese, crumbled

2 large bunches watercress, tough stems removed
1 small head romaine lettuce, cut crosswise into ½-inch ribbons
1 head Boston or Bibb lettuce, torn into large pieces
2 large Golden Delicious apples, quartered, cored and thinly sliced
⅔ cup walnut halves, toasted

For vinaigrette: Blend shallots, vinegar, lemon juice, peppercorns, sugar and salt. Whisk in oil in thin stream. Fold in bleu cheese. Let stand 30 minutes.

Mix watercress, lettuces, apples and walnuts in large bowl. Add vinaigrette and toss well. Serve immediately.

Salade Rouge

6 to 8 side-dish servings

1 small head red cabbage, cored and cut into wedges to fit feed tube
Ice water

1 cup safflower oil
½ cup raspberry vinegar
1 tablespoon honey
1½ teaspoons salt
1 teaspoon cinnamon
Freshly ground pepper

2 small beets, peeled
1 large unpeeled pear, halved and cored
1 cup walnuts, toasted

Arrange cabbage in feed tube and, using ultra thin slicer, slice using firm pressure. Transfer to large bowl. Add enough ice water to cover. Let soak 30 minutes. Drain well. Return cabbage to bowl.

Combine oil, vinegar, honey, salt, cinnamon and pepper in processor and blend 3 seconds. Leave dressing in work bowl.

Stand beets in feed tube and, using medium shredder, shred using firm pressure. Arrange pear in feed tube and shred using medium pressure. Add mixture to cabbage and toss well. *(Can be prepared 3 days ahead and chilled.)*

Just before serving, drain any liquid. Mix in walnuts. Adjust seasoning.

Spinach Salad with Bulgur

4 servings

1 cup boiling water
½ cup bulgur

1 bunch spinach, washed and patted dry
1 15½-ounce can garbanzo beans (chick-peas), drained
1 green bell pepper, cored and diced
⅓ cup chopped onion
1 hard-cooked egg, chopped
1 garlic clove, minced
¼ cup red wine vinegar
1 tablespoon Dijon mustard
6 tablespoons olive oil
Salt and freshly ground pepper

Combine boiling water and bulgur in small bowl. Soak 1 hour.

Drain bulgur. Transfer to large bowl. Add spinach, garbanzo beans, bell pepper, onion, egg and garlic. Whisk vinegar and mustard in small bowl. Add oil in slow stream and mix well. Season with salt and pepper. Pour over salad. Toss lightly.

Curly Endive, Apple and Gorgonzola Salad

6 servings

¾ cup whipping cream
3 tablespoons red wine vinegar
4 large Granny Smith apples, peeled, cored and thinly sliced
1 head curly endive (stems discarded), torn into bite-size pieces
½ cup crumbled Gorgonzola cheese
Salt and freshly ground pepper

Combine cream and vinegar in medium bowl. Mix in thinly sliced apples. *(Can be prepared 1 hour ahead.)*

Combine endive, cheese and apple mixture in large bowl. Toss to coat endive with dressing. Season with salt and pepper. Serve immediately.

New Potato Salad with Peas and Mint

10 servings

- **3 cups loosely packed fresh mint leaves**
- **3 eggs, room temperature**
- **5 tablespoons white wine vinegar**
- **3 tablespoons Dijon mustard**
- **1½ teaspoons salt**
- **¾ teaspoon freshly ground pepper**
- **2 cups vegetable oil**
- **4½ pounds new potatoes, cut into 1-inch pieces**
- **4½ cups shelled fresh peas (about 3½ pounds unshelled) or frozen peas, thawed and drained**
- **Salt and freshly ground pepper**
- **Mint sprigs**

Combine mint, eggs, vinegar, mustard, salt and pepper in processor. Blend 1 minute, stopping once to scrape down sides of work bowl. With machine running, slowly add oil through feed tube. Adjust seasonings. *(Can be prepared 1 day ahead. Cover tightly and refrigerate.)*

Place potatoes in large saucepan. Add cold salted water to cover. Simmer until potatoes are almost tender, about 7 minutes. If using fresh peas, add at this point and cook until just crisp-tender, about 4 minutes. Drain well. Rinse peas and potatoes under cold water until cool. Drain well. Transfer to large bowl (if using thawed frozen peas, add at this point). Mix in enough dressing to coat. Season with salt and generous amount of pepper. Garnish with mint sprigs and serve.

Sweet Potato Salad with Honey Citrus Dressing

6 servings

- **4 ounces snow peas, trimmed**
- **3 large slender sweet potatoes (2 pounds total), peeled**
- **1 ¼x½-inch piece fresh ginger, peeled**
- **½ cup fresh orange juice**
- **⅓ cup safflower oil**
- **4 to 5 tablespoons fresh lemon juice**
- **3 to 4 tablespoons honey**
- **1 egg**
- **¼ teaspoon salt**
- **Dash of hot pepper sauce**
- **2 medium yellow bell peppers**
- **4 medium green onions, trimmed and cut into 1-inch pieces**
- **Green leaf lettuce**

Cook snow peas in large saucepan of boiling salted water until just crisp-tender, about 1 minute. Remove using slotted spoon; drain. Rinse under cold water and drain again. Chill until ready to use. Return water to boil.

Stand sweet potatoes in feed tube and, using thick slicer blade, slice using firm pressure. Stack slices and arrange lengthwise in feed tube with slices perpendicular to slicing disc, packing tightly. Slice using medium pressure. Add sweet potatoes to boiling water and cook until just tender, about 2½ minutes. Drain well. Transfer potatoes to large bowl.

With machine running, drop ginger through feed tube and mince, using steel knife. Add orange juice, oil, 4 tablespoons lemon juice, 3 tablespoons honey, egg, salt, and pepper sauce and mix 5 seconds, stopping once to scrape down sides of work bowl. Pour dressing over warm potatoes and toss gently. Cover and refrigerate 3 hours.

Cut bell peppers into 4 pieces each, discarding cores and seeds.

Remove steel knife and insert thick slicer. Stand pepper pieces in feed tube, packing tightly. Slice using light pressure. Add to sweet potatoes. Add green onions and toss well. *(Can be prepared 2 days ahead and chilled.)*

Just before serving, mix snow peas into salad. Taste and adjust seasoning, adding remaining 1 tablespoon lemon juice and 1 tablespoon honey if desired. Arrange lettuce on large platter. Mound salad in center.

Oregon Blue Cheese Potato Salad

8 servings

¼ cup cider vinegar
2 tablespoons tarragon vinegar
2 teaspoons Dijon mustard
Salt and freshly ground pepper
⅔ cup olive oil
¼ cup minced shallots
2 tablespoons minced fresh parsley

4 pounds small red new potatoes (unpeeled)

Lettuce leaves
1 bunch watercress or parsley
½ cup crumbled Oregon Blue or other mild blue cheese
½ cup whipping cream
12 slices bacon, cooked until crisp, crumbled
3 tablespoons minced fresh chives or green onions

Mix vinegars, mustard, salt and pepper in small bowl. Whisk in oil in thin stream. Whisk in shallots and minced parsley. Set dressing aside.

Steam or boil potatoes until just tender. Cool slightly. Cut into ¼-inch slices. Place in large bowl. Gently mix ½ cup dressing into potatoes.

Line large platter with lettuce leaves. Top with alternating rows of potatoes and watercress. Whisk cheese and cream into remaining dressing. Spoon over potatoes. Top with bacon and chives. Serve warm or at room temperature.

Romaine Lettuce Leaves Stuffed with Warm Rice and Vegetable Salad

6 servings

1¾ cups water
1 cup short-grain brown rice
¼ teaspoon salt

3 tablespoons red wine vinegar
1 ¾x¾-inch piece fresh ginger, peeled and minced
1 garlic clove, minced
Salt and freshly ground pepper
⅓ cup olive oil

1 large red bell pepper, diced
7 radishes, diced
2 green onions, diced
½ cup minced fresh parsley
¼ cup fresh tarragon, minced or 2 teaspoons dried, crumbled
6 large romaine lettuce leaves
6 small romaine lettuce leaves

Preheat oven to 350°F. Combine water, rice and salt in medium ovenproof saucepan. Cover and bring to boil. Transfer saucepan to oven and bake 45 minutes. Let rice cool for about 10 minutes.

Blend vinegar, ginger, garlic and salt and pepper in large bowl. Whisk in oil in thin stream. Stir in rice. Let stand 10 minutes to blend flavors.

Mix bell pepper, radishes, onions, parsley and tarragon into rice. Season with salt and pepper. Divide rice among lettuce leaves and serve.

Mediterranean Couscous Salad

2 servings; can be doubled or tripled

1 cup plus 2 tablespoons chicken stock
¾ cup quick-cooking couscous

1 large tomato, seeded and chopped
3 ounces feta cheese, cut into ¼-inch dice
3 tablespoons minced arugula or ¼ cup minced watercress
3 tablespoons minced green onion
5 tablespoons olive oil
3 tablespoons fresh lemon juice
Salt and freshly ground pepper
Romaine lettuce leaves
Greek or Nicoise olives
Toasted pine nuts

Bring stock to boil in small saucepan. Mix in couscous. Cover and remove from heat. Let stand 5 minutes. Fluff with fork. Turn into bowl. Cool to room temperature.

Mix tomato, feta, arugula and green onion into couscous. Whisk together oil, lemon juice, salt and generous amount of pepper; mix into salad. Just before serving, line shallow bowl with lettuce. Spoon salad into bowl. Top with olives and pine nuts.

Summer Seafood Salade Composée with Tarragon Mayonnaise

Quick to prepare in the processor, the mayonnaise can be used to dress a variety of salads. The seasoning can also be stirred into 1¼ cups of purchased mayonnaise. If crab is not available, double the amount of shrimp.

2 servings; can be doubled or tripled

6 ounces green beans, trimmed
2 small yellow crookneck squash, ends trimmed
1 small head Boston lettuce
1 large beefsteak tomato, sliced into thick rounds
1 small cucumber, peeled, seeded and cut into ½-inch dice
¼ pound cooked bay shrimp
¼ pound cooked crabmeat
Tarragon Mayonnaise*

Blanch beans and squash in boiling salted water until beans are just crisp-tender and squash just yields to slight pressure, about 4 minutes. Rinse under cold water; drain thoroughly. Cut squash lengthwise into ⅓-inch-thick strips. Line platter with lettuce. Arrange tomato slices around edge of platter, leaving space between each slice. Combine beans and squash and arrange between tomato slices. Mix cucumber, shrimp, crabmeat and ¼ cup mayonnaise. Mound in center of platter. Serve salad, passing additional mayonnaise separately.

*Tarragon Mayonnaise

Makes about 1½ cups

1 egg, room temperature
2 tablespoons fresh lemon juice
1 tablespoon minced green onion or shallot
2 teaspoons coarse-grained Dijon mustard
½ cup plus 2 tablespoons vegetable oil
½ cup olive oil
1 tablespoon minced fresh tarragon or 1 teaspoon dried, crumbled
Salt and freshly ground pepper

Mix egg, lemon juice, green onion and mustard in processor. With machine running, add both oils through feed tube in slow stream. Mix in tarragon, salt and pepper. *(Can be prepared 5 days ahead, covered and refrigerated.)*

Mussel, Scallop and Corn Salsa Salad

Fall ingredients are imaginatively blended for this dish.

8 servings

½ medium red bell pepper
½ jalapeño chili
1 ear corn

½ cup water
½ cup dry white wine
4 thyme sprigs or 1 teaspoon dried, crumbled
1 small dried red chili
½ bunch parsley stems
24 mussels, scrubbed and debearded
¾ pound scallops

1 cup olive oil
¼ cup fresh lime juice
½ cup peeled, seeded and diced papaya
¼ cup diced green onions
1½ tablespoons minced fresh cilantro
1 tablespoon minced fresh mint
Hot pepper sauce
Salt

1½ heads red oak leaf lettuce, curly endive or Boston lettuce

Char red bell pepper and jalapeño over gas flame or in broiler until blackened on skin sides only. Wrap in paper bag and let stand 10 minutes to steam. Peel and seed. Rinse if necessary; pat dry. Cut bell pepper into ¼-inch dice. Mince jalapeño. Cut corn kernels from cob. Blanch kernels in boiling water until just tender, about 3 minutes. Drain thoroughly and set aside.

Bring ½ cup water, wine, thyme, dried chili and parsley to boil in large saucepan. Add mussels. Cover and cook 4 minutes. Remove opened mussels. Cover and cook remaining mussels 5 minutes longer. Remove mussels, discarding any that do not open. Add scallops to pan and simmer until just opaque, about 2 minutes. Drain.

Remove mussels from shells. Place in large bowl. Add scallops. Mix in oil and lime juice, then bell pepper, jalapeño, corn, papaya, green onions, cilantro and mint. Season with hot pepper sauce and salt. Refrigerate at least 2 hours, stirring occasionally. *(Can be prepared 6 hours ahead.)*

Let salad stand at room temperature 30 minutes. Line platter with lettuce leaves. Mix salad and spoon atop lettuce.

Calamari and Greens with Lemon Vinaigrette

6 servings

Calamari

1 pound squid (calamari), cleaned and sliced into ¼-inch rings
1 medium red onion, thinly sliced
1 medium red bell pepper, cut julienne
1 medium celery stalk, cut julienne
½ cup olive oil
3 tablespoons fresh lemon juice
2 tablespoons white wine vinegar
1 teaspoon grated lemon peel
½ teaspoon crushed dried pink peppercorns
Salt

Vinaigrette

4½ tablespoons fresh lemon juice
¼ cup balsamic vinegar
1½ teaspoons grated lemon peel
¾ teaspoon minced fresh lemon verbena leaves (optional)
¾ teaspoon minced fresh parsley
¾ teaspoon minced fresh basil
⅜ teaspoon cracked peppercorns
1 cup plus 2 tablespoons olive oil
Salt

1 head red leaf lettuce
1 head savoy cabbage
1 avocado, peeled and sliced
1 large tomato, cut into 6 wedges
6 radishes, sliced

For calamari: Blanch squid in boiling salted water 30 seconds. Refresh immediately in ice water. Drain well. Transfer to bowl. Add next 8 ingredients and toss well. Season with salt. Cover and refrigerate at least 3 hours.

For vinaigrette: Blend lemon juice, vinegar, peel, herbs and peppercorns in small bowl. Whisk in oil in thin stream. Season with salt. *(Can be prepared 1 day ahead.)*

To assemble: Line plates with lettuce and cabbage leaves. Mound calamari mixture in center. Garnish with avocado, tomato and radishes. Drizzle with vinaigrette. Serve immediately.

Shrimp and Celery Salad with Warm Dill Dressing

6 servings

4 quarts water
1 tablespoon salt
36 medium shrimp (about 1½ pounds), shelled and deveined
6 celery stalks, cut diagonally into 1-inch pieces

3 tablespoons white wine vinegar
2 tablespoons Dijon mustard
1 teaspoon sugar
Pinch of salt
⅓ cup whipping cream
¼ cup minced fresh dill
⅓ cup corn oil

1 head Bibb or Boston lettuce
1 medium red onion, sliced into thin rings
Freshly ground pepper

Bring water to boil in large pot. Stir in 1 tablespoon salt. Add shrimp and celery and cook 1 minute. Drain immediately. Cool to room temperature.

Blend vinegar, mustard, sugar and pinch of salt in heavy small nonaluminum saucepan. Whisk in cream. Set over medium heat and bring just to simmer, stirring constantly. Mix in dill. Remove from heat. Whisk in oil in thin stream. Cover.

Line salad plates with lettuce leaves. Divide shrimp and celery among plates. Garnish with onion. Rewhisk dressing. Spoon over salads. Sprinkle with pepper.

Chinese Chicken Salad with Spicy Dressing

6 to 8 main-course servings

4 green onions, trimmed
4 quarter-size slices fresh ginger
4 cups water
¼ cup rice wine or Scotch
2 1½-pound whole chicken breasts

Spicy Chili Oil Dressing
6 green onions
6 quarter-size slices fresh ginger
2 tablespoons oriental sesame oil
2 tablespoons safflower oil or corn oil
6 small dried red chilies, seeded and cut into ¼-inch pieces
6 tablespoons soy sauce
2 tablespoons plus 1½ teaspoons Chinese rice vinegar
2 tablespoons rice wine or Scotch
1 tablespoon sugar
2 large cucumbers, peeled, seeded and finely shredded
2 cups bean sprouts
16 green onions (green part only), cut into 1-inch pieces
3 medium carrots, peeled and finely shredded

Lightly crush green onions and ginger with flat side of cleaver. Combine with water and rice wine in heavy large saucepan. Simmer 15 minutes. Add chicken, increase heat to medium and bring to boil. Cover saucepan and remove from heat. Let stand until chicken is opaque, 20 to 30 minutes. Drain chicken and cool.

For dressing: Lightly crush 6 green onions and ginger with flat side of cleaver. Heat both oils in wok or heavy large skillet over high heat until smoking. Add red chilies, green onions and ginger. Cover and remove from heat. Cool to room temperature. Strain oil, discarding seasonings. Add soy sauce, vinegar, rice wine and sugar and stir until sugar dissolves.

Skin and bone chicken. Shred meat. Arrange in center of deep round bowl. Arrange cucumbers, bean sprouts, green onion pieces and carrots in concentric circles around chicken. Pour dressing over salad.

Italian Chicken Salad with Creamy Rosemary Dressing

6 main-dish servings

4 whole chicken breasts (2 pounds total), boned, split, skinned and cooked

8 small carrots, peeled and cut into feed-tube lengths
1 pound green beans, trimmed, cut into feed-tube widths
3 ounces Parmesan cheese (preferably imported), room temperature

Creamy Rosemary Dressing
1½ 2-ounce cans flat anchovies, drained, rinsed and patted dry
2 eggs
1 cup plus 2 tablespoons olive oil (preferably extra-virgin)
6 tablespoons fresh lemon juice
¼ cup whipping cream
1 tablespoon dried rosemary, crumbled
2 teaspoons rubbed sage
2 teaspoons sugar
Salt and freshly ground pepper

½ cup Niçoise olives

Cut 8 squares of plastic wrap. Place 1 chicken breast half on each square smooth side down. Fold in tapered end of chicken. Roll up tightly, using plastic as aid. Freeze until just firm but still easily pierced with tip of sharp knife.

Insert medium slicer in processor. Stand carrots in feed tube and slice using firm pressure. Cook carrots in medium pot of boiling salted water until just tender, about 2 minutes. Transfer to colander using slotted spoon. Rinse under cold water; drain well. Return water to boil. Add beans and cook until just tender, about 4 minutes. Drain in another colander. Rinse under cold water; drain well. Pat vegetables dry.

Unwrap chicken rolls. Insert ultra thick or thick slicing blade. Arrange length-wise in feed tube; slice using firm pressure.

Insert medium slicing blade. Arrange beans width-wise in feed tube and slice using light pressure. Leave in work bowl.

Shred cheese in processor using light pressure. Transfer mixture to bowl.

For dressing: Insert steel knife. Blend anchovies and eggs until smooth. Add oil, lemon juice, cream, rosemary, sage, sugar, salt and freshly ground pepper and blend mixture for 3 seconds.

Add some of dressing to chicken and toss to combine. Mix in carrots and olives. *(Can be prepared 3 days ahead, covered and refrigerated. Refrigerate remaining dressing.)* Adjust seasoning. Pass remaining dressing separately.

Cucumber and Cabbage Salad with Pork, Shrimp and Peanuts

6 to 8 servings

1 large cucumber, peeled, seeded and cut into feed-tube lengths
¾ teaspoon salt

1 5-ounce wedge green cabbage, cut to fit feed tube
3½ cups boiling water
4½ teaspoons (or more) distilled white vinegar

3 large carrots, peeled, cut into 2-inch pieces

3 large green onions, including green tops, cut into 2-inch pieces

1 4-ounce piece lean cooked pork, shredded

2 large garlic cloves
2 tablespoons fresh lime juice
4½ teaspoons vegetable oil
1 tablespoon fish sauce* (nuoc mam)
½ teaspoon sugar
¼ teaspoon dried red pepper flakes
½ cup unsalted dry-roasted peanuts
¼ cup dried shrimp,* rinsed under hot water, drained
½ cup fresh cilantro leaves

Using medium slicer, stand cucumber in feed tube and slice using light pressure. Transfer to colander and toss with ½ teaspoon salt. Let stand 30 minutes. Rinse under cold water. Squeeze dry. Transfer cucumber to large bowl.

Arrange cabbage cut side down in feed tube and slice using firm pressure. Transfer to medium bowl. Add 3½ cups boiling water and 3 teaspoons vinegar. Let soak 10 minutes. Drain; rinse under cold water. Squeeze dry. Add to cucumber.

Arrange carrots lengthwise in feed tube and slice using firm pressure. Stack slices and arrange lengthwise in feed tube with slices perpendicular to slicing disc. Slice using medium pressure. Add to cucumber.

Insert thin slicer. Arrange green onions lengthwise in feed tube and slice using light pressure. Add green onions and pork to cucumber. Wipe out work bowl with paper towel.

Insert steel knife. With machine running, drop garlic through feed tube and mince, stopping once to scrape down sides of work bowl. Add lime juice, oil, fish sauce, sugar, pepper flakes, remaining 1½ teaspoons vinegar and ¼ teaspoon salt and blend 10 seconds. Add to cucumber. Add peanuts to work bowl and coarsely chop using 3 to 4 on/off turns. Add to cucumber. Mix in shrimp and cilantro. *(Can be prepared 2 days ahead and chilled.)*

Just before serving, toss salad. Drain off any excess liquid. Adjust seasoning and add more vinegar if desired.

*Available at oriental markets.

4 ❦ Main Courses

This chapter is full of great ideas for delicious and satisfying entrées. There are hearty stews, succulent roasts, elegant seafood dishes—main courses for everyday or for a party.

Nothing is as comforting as home cooking, so try out our recipes for a wholesome stew of Beef Curry with Green Beans and Cilantro (page 49); a sophisticated Chicken Hash with Artichokes and Mushrooms (page 39); Roast Chicken with Cognac-spiked Hazelnut Cream Sauce (page 36) and a down-home Country Ham with Pickled Peach Glaze (page 55). Chili is about as American as you can get, with as many variations as there are cooks—we offer two possibilities from our excellent February '86 round-up: Texas Beef Chili (page 47) and Grilled and Toasted Pork and Onion Chili with Rhode Island Jonnycakes (page 57).

Grilling, probably the most popular cooking technique of the year, figures in many of our main-course recipes. But they go far beyond the typical backyard barbecue of ribs and burgers covered with a gooey sweet sauce. Hickory chips, mesquite or other fragrant woods were out in force in 1986 to help flavor simply grilled meats or fish. Their complementary vegetables and sauces were equally inventive. For example, there are Grilled Lamb Chops with Pecan Sauce and Roasted Garlic Custards (page 54), a Grilled Pork Loin with Spicy Black Beans and Tomatillo Salsa (page 56) and Hickory-barbecued Shrimp (page 61).

Seafood, light and quick to prepare, is still a main-dish favorite. In this chapter you'll see some exciting dishes using the familiar delectably, like Salmon Navajo with Orange Essence Butter Sauce (page 59) and Clams and Bluefish with Sweet Garlic Pasta (page 63), as well as some delicious new types such as Broiled Shark with Aïoli and Bell Peppers (page 60) and Monkfish with Saffron and Spinach (page 60).

We haven't overlooked the simple, last-minute recipes that are every busy cook's salvation. Quick and light but satisfying are the Fresh Corn, Brie and Jalapeño Frittata (page 64), Peppered Chicken Breasts with Balsamic Vinegar Sauce (page 38) and a basil- and garlic-scented Prosciutto, Provolone and Roasted Bell Pepper Sandwich (page 66).

Poultry

Roast Chicken with Hazelnut Cream Sauce

Serve with assorted roasted vegetables. If you can, use free-range chickens.

6 servings

⅔ cup toasted and husked hazelnuts
3 cups Rich Brown Poultry Stock*
3 3-pound chickens, halved
Vegetable oil
3 tablespoons Cognac
½ cup whipping cream
Salt and freshly ground pepper

Soak ½ cup hazelnuts in stock in heavy small saucepan overnight.

Set pan over medium-low heat and cook until hazelnuts are tender, stirring occasionally, about 1 hour.

Transfer hazelnut mixture to processor and puree. Return to saucepan.

Preheat oven to 450°F. Using small sharp knife, separate chicken breast from rib cage. Discard rib cage (or reserve for stock); leave breast, thighs, legs and wings intact. Heat thin layer of oil in roasting pan over medium-high heat. Arrange chicken in pan and brown well on all sides. Transfer to oven and roast until chicken is golden brown, 15 to 20 minutes. Keep warm.

Pour off fat from pan. Set over high heat. Stir in 2 tablespoons Cognac, scraping up browned bits. Add to stock mixture. Blend in remaining Cognac and cream and heat through. Season sauce with salt and pepper. Spoon onto plates. Top with chicken. Garnish with remaining hazelnuts.

*Rich Brown Poultry Stock

Makes 3 cups

First reduction
4 pounds chicken necks, wings and backs
2 celery stalks, diced
1 medium onion, diced
1 medium carrot, diced
1 medium leek, diced
1 cup dry red wine
10 whole black peppercorns
1 bouquet garni (4 parsley sprigs, 4 thyme sprigs, 1 bay leaf)
10 cups unsalted chicken stock (preferably homemade)

Second reduction
1 tablespoon butter
3 tablespoons minced shallots
½ cup dry red wine
2 thyme sprigs
Stock from first reduction

For first reduction: Preheat oven to 425°F. Arrange chicken parts in large roasting pan and roast until browned, turning occasionally, about 1 hour. Add vegetables and roast until browned, turning occasionally, about 30 minutes. Transfer to stockpot. Pour off fat from pan. Set pan over high heat. Stir in wine, scraping up browned bits, and bring to boil. Add to stockpot. Add peppercorns and bouquet garni to pot. Pour in stock and bring to boil, skimming foam from surface. Reduce heat and simmer gently until liquid is reduced to 5 cups. Strain stock; degrease if necessary.

For second reduction: Melt butter in heavy small skillet over medium-low heat. Add shallots and stir until soft, about 3 minutes. Add wine and thyme and boil until reduced to 1 tablespoon. Add to first reduction and simmer until reduced to 3 cups.

Tandoori-style Chicken

4 servings

5 garlic cloves
1 1-inch cube peeled ginger
1 medium onion, cut into 8 wedges
1 cup plain lowfat yogurt
3 tablespoons fresh lemon juice
1 tablespoon olive oil
2 teaspoons ground coriander
1 teaspoon cumin
1 teaspoon turmeric
½ teaspoon freshly ground pepper
½ teaspoon salt (optional)
¼ teaspoon cardamom
¼ teaspoon freshly grated nutmeg
¼ teaspoon ground cloves
¼ teaspoon cinnamon
¼ teaspoon cayenne pepper
8 chicken pieces, skinned

Chopped green onion
Lemon wedges

Mince garlic in processor. Add ginger and mince. Add onion and mince. Add next 13 ingredients and puree. Transfer to bowl. Cut deep slashes in chicken pieces. Add to marinade, turning to coat well. Cover. Refrigerate overnight.

Preheat broiler. Generously butter broiler pan and large shallow ovenproof glass baking dish. Arrange chicken on pan and broil about 3 inches from heat source 5 minutes per side. Reduce oven temperature to 325°F. Transfer chicken to prepared dish. Bake until juices run clear when pierced with tip of sharp knife, basting frequently with marinade, 20 to 25 minutes. Garnish chicken with chopped green onion and lemon wedges.

"Catfish-fried" Chicken

The same crunchy cornmeal coating that covers fried catfish (an Iowan specialty) does wonders for old-fashioned fried chicken. This will be enough for ten if you are also having another entrée; if not, double the recipe. This chicken is best served warm, not hot.

10 servings

2 3-pound chickens, cut into pieces
2 cups buttermilk

1½ cups all purpose flour
1½ cups yellow cornmeal (preferably stone-ground)
2 teaspoons dried thyme, crumbled
2 teaspoons paprika
2 teaspoons salt
Freshly ground pepper

2 pounds (about) solid vegetable shortening (for deep frying)

Pat chicken dry. Place in large bowl; add buttermilk. Let stand 2 hours, turning occasionally.

Mix flour, cornmeal, 2 teaspoons thyme, 2 teaspoons paprika, 2 teaspoons salt and generous amount of pepper in shallow bowl. Shake buttermilk off chicken. Sprinkle chicken with additional salt, pepper, thyme and paprika. Roll in flour mixture 1 piece at a time, coating thoroughly; shake off excess. Arrange chicken in single layer on baking sheets. Let stand for 30 minutes to firm coating.

Add enough shortening to two heavy large skillets to come ½ inch up sides. Melt over low heat. Increase heat to high and cook until almost smoking. Add chicken skin side down in batches (do not crowd). Reduce heat to medium, cover and cook 12 minutes. Turn chicken and cook uncovered until rich dark brown and just springy to touch, about 12 minutes. Transfer chicken to paper towels and drain well. Serve warm.

Peppered Chicken Breasts with Balsamic Vinegar Sauce

2 servings; can be doubled or tripled

1 large chicken breast, boned and halved
Salt
Freshly ground white and black pepper
2 tablespoons (¼ stick) unsalted butter
1 teaspoon unsalted butter
1 large shallot, minced
3 tablespoons balsamic vinegar
1¾ cups low-sodium chicken broth
1 to 2 tablespoons unsalted butter
2 teaspoons minced fresh marjoram or ¾ teaspoon dried, crumbled

Preheat oven to 200°F. Pat chicken dry. Sprinkle with salt and peppers. Melt 2 tablespoons butter in heavy medium skillet over high heat. Add chicken, skin side down, and cook until skin is crisp. Reduce heat to medium-low and continue cooking until chicken is just springy to touch, turning occasionally, about 12 minutes. Transfer to heated platter. Tent with foil and keep warm in oven.

Pour off fat from skillet. Add 1 teaspoon butter and shallot to skillet. Cook over medium-low heat until shallot is translucent, scraping up any browned bits, about 3 minutes. Increase heat to high. Add vinegar and boil until reduced to glaze, stirring constantly, about 3 minutes. Add broth and boil until reduced to ¼ cup, stirring occasionally. Season with white and black pepper. Remove sauce from heat and whisk in 1 to 2 tablespoons butter and marjoram. Adjust seasoning. Whisk in any juices from chicken. Spoon sauce over chicken and serve immediately.

Spicy Chicken with Lemongrass

6 servings

4 whole chicken breasts (3¾ pounds total), boned, split and skinned

4 fresh lemongrass stalks*

4 egg yolks
½ cup oyster sauce*
3 tablespoons fish sauce* (nuoc mam)
4 teaspoons honey
4 teaspoons hoisin sauce*

3 teaspoons ground red pepper paste* (sambal oeleck)

6 large green onions, including green tops, cut into feed-tube lengths
1 small head iceberg lettuce, cored, cut into wedges to fit feed tube
2 tablespoons peanut oil
2 medium tomatoes, cored and sliced
Cilantro sprigs

Beginning at narrow end of each chicken breast, roll up tightly. Wrap each roll in plastic. Freeze chicken on baking sheet until just firm but still easily pierced with tip of sharp knife. *(Can be prepared 1 month ahead and frozen. Thaw in refrigerator just until easily pierced with sharp knife.)*

Discard tough outer leaves of lemongrass. Cut into ½-inch pieces.

With machine running, drop lemongrass through processor feed tube and mince. Add yolks, oyster sauce, fish sauce, honey, hoisin sauce and red pepper paste and blend 3 seconds. Leave marinade in work bowl.

Unwrap chicken rolls. Discard plastic.

Insert thick slicer. Stand chicken rolls in feed tube and slice using firm pressure. Transfer chicken mixture to large plastic bag. Refrigerate 2 to 12 hours, turning bag occasionally.

Stand green onions in feed tube and slice using light pressure. Remove from work bowl. Stand lettuce in feed tube and slice using light pressure. Remove from work bowl. Heat oil in heavy 12-inch skillet over high heat. Add chicken and marinade and stir-fry until chicken is just opaque, 2 to 3 minutes; do not overcook. Remove from heat. Mix in green onions.

Divide lettuce among plates. Mound some of chicken mixture in center of each. Arrange tomato slices around chicken. Garnish with cilantro sprigs.

*Available at oriental markets.

Chicken Hash with Artichokes and Mushrooms

Large chunks of chicken, artichokes and wild mushrooms make for a sophisticated version of an old favorite.

8 servings

1 pound baby artichokes (maximum 2-inch diameter)

1½ quarts rich chicken stock (preferably homemade)
3¼ pounds boned chicken breasts

½ cup corn oil
2 cups ½-inch cubes peeled baking potatoes

¼ cup (½ stick) unsalted butter
2 cups diced onion

2 cups ¾-inch pieces stemmed morel or button mushrooms
1½ cups Crème Fraîche*
6 tablespoons cream Sherry
¾ teaspoon salt
¼ teaspoon pepper

½ cup minced fresh parsley
8 parsley sprigs
Crème Fraîche

Cook artichokes in large pot of boiling water until tender, about 10 minutes. Drain. Rinse under cold water. Drain well. Discard tough outer leaves and trim off any dark green skin. Quarter each artichoke. Remove any choke, using spoon. *(Can be prepared 1 day ahead. Wrap tightly and refrigerate.)*

Bring stock to simmer in large saucepan. Add chicken. Adjust heat so liquid barely shimmers. Cook until chicken is opaque on outside and just pink inside, 4 to 10 minutes, depending on size. Transfer chicken to plate, using slotted spoon. Cool completely. Simmer stock until reduced to 1 cup, about 40 minutes. Discard chicken skin. Cut meat into ¾-inch pieces.

Heat oil in heavy large skillet over medium-high heat. Add potatoes and cook until light brown, stirring frequently, about 5 minutes. Transfer potatoes to paper towels, using slotted spoon. Reserve oil in skillet.

Melt butter in another heavy large skillet over high heat. Add onion and mushrooms. Cook until light brown, stirring frequently, about 8 minutes. Transfer mushrooms and onion to bowl. Add artichokes and reduced stock to skillet. Simmer until liquid coats artichokes, about 5 minutes. Add 1½ cups Crème Fraîche, Sherry, salt and pepper. Simmer 5 minutes. Add mushrooms and simmer until sauce thickens slightly, stirring occasionally, about 8 minutes. Add chicken and stir until heated.

Meanwhile, reheat oil in skillet over medium-high heat. Add potatoes and stir until crisp and tender, about 4 minutes. Drain on paper towels. Add potatoes and minced parsley to chicken mixture. Simmer until sauce coats hash, 1 to 2 minutes. Spoon onto plates. Garnish with parsley sprigs and dollop of Crème Fraîche.

*Crème Fraîche

Makes 2 cups

1 cup whipping cream
1 cup sour cream

Scald whipping cream in heavy small saucepan. Remove from heat and whisk in sour cream. Transfer mixture to glass jar. Set in pan of warm water. Maintain temperature at 110°F for 12 hours. Refrigerate overnight. *(Can be prepared 5 days ahead.)*

Chicken Chiricahua

To make the corn bread for the stuffing, use your favorite corn bread recipe and add two roasted, peeled, seeded and diced Anaheim chilies.

6 servings

6 6-ounce chicken breast halves, boned and pounded lightly to even thickness
Salt and freshly ground pepper
2 cups Corn Bread Stuffing*
3 tablespoons melted butter
½ cup sour cream
¼ cup pomegranate seeds or diced red bell pepper
¼ cup chopped green onions
¼ cup chopped black olives
¼ cup canned drained white hominy

2 cups Mole Sauce**

Preheat oven to 375°F. Grease baking sheet. Arrange chicken breasts skin side down on work surface. Sprinkle with salt and pepper. Shape stuffing into 6 rounds. Set one on each piece of chicken. Roll up to enclose stuffing completely. Set seam side down on prepared sheet. Brush with melted butter. Season with salt and pepper. Bake until chicken is opaque and firm to touch, 30 to 35 minutes.

Set chicken on plates. Ladle about 3 tablespoons sauce over each. Whip sour cream until smooth. Spoon into pastry bag fitted with small plain tip. Pipe cream in S shape atop sauce. Sprinkle chicken with pomegranate seeds, onions, olives and hominy and serve.

*Corn Bread Stuffing

Makes about 2 cups

¼ cup chicken fat or butter
½ cup chopped onions
½ cup chopped celery
2 cups day-old green chili corn bread, crumbled
1 egg
Pinch *each* of dried basil, marjoram and sage, crumbled
Pinch of ground cumin
Salt and freshly ground pepper
Chicken broth

Melt fat in heavy medium skillet over medium-low heat. Add onions and celery and cook until translucent, stirring occasionally, about 10 minutes. Stir in corn bread, egg, herbs and cumin. Season with salt and pepper. (If stuffing is too dry, stir in enough chicken broth to bind.) Transfer to bowl. Cool completely. Cover and refrigerate. *(Can be prepared 1 day ahead.)*

**Mole Sauce

The remaining sauce can be refrigerated or frozen; serve with grilled meats, poultry or sausages.

Makes 1 quart

3 tablespoons lard or solid vegetable shortening
¼ cup chopped onion
1 tablespoon pure chili powder
½ teaspoon ground cumin
1 medium garlic clove, minced
⅓ cup all purpose flour
3 cups (or more) chicken broth, heated
¾ cup red chili paste***
Salt and freshly ground pepper

Melt lard in heavy medium saucepan over medium-low heat. Add onion, chili powder, cumin and garlic and cook until onion is translucent, stirring occasionally, about 10 minutes. Add flour and stir 3 minutes. Whisk in 3 cups broth and bring to boil. Whisk in chili paste. Season with salt and pepper. Reduce heat and simmer until sauce is thick and smooth, adding more chicken broth to thin if necessary, about 20 minutes. *(Can be prepared 1 day ahead. Cool, cover and chill.)*

***Available at Latin American markets. If unavailable, soak 8 large dried pasilla chilies in hot water until softened, about 40 minutes. Drain well. Puree in processor.

Maple-glazed Turkey with Apple and Ginger Butter Sauce

A splendidly glazed turkey with a sweet, zesty sauce. Use the turkey giblets to make the Poultry Stock (see page 83).

8 servings

1 16-pound turkey
1 tablespoon salt
1 tablespoon pepper
1 tablespoon minced fresh rosemary
¼ cup (½ stick) unsalted butter, room temperature
1 cup pure maple syrup
¼ cup applejack or Calvados

Sauce
2 tablespoons (¼ stick) unsalted butter
1¼ pounds Granny Smith apples, peeled, cored and thinly sliced
2 cups Poultry Stock (see page 83)
½ cup applejack or Calvados
Ginger Butter*
Snipped fresh chives

Sliced apples
Fresh herb sprigs

Position rack in lower third of oven and preheat to 475°F. Pat turkey dry. Sprinkle inside with salt, pepper and rosemary. Truss turkey to hold shape. Rub butter into skin. Arrange breast side up on rack in roasting pan. Cook 45 minutes. Reduce temperature to 375°F. Combine syrup and applejack and baste turkey. Continue cooking until thermometer inserted in thickest part of thigh registers 170°F, about 80 minutes, basting frequently. Transfer turkey to heated platter. Tent with foil.

For sauce: Melt 2 tablespoons butter in heavy nonaluminum skillet over high heat. Add 1¼ pounds apples and stir 3 minutes. Add stock and boil until reduced by ¾, stirring frequently, about 14 minutes. Add applejack and boil until sauce thickens and coats spoon, about 3 minutes. *(Can be prepared 6 hours ahead. Reheat before continuing.)* Reduce heat to low. Whisk in Ginger Butter 1 tablespoon at a time, lifting pan from heat briefly if beads of melted butter appear. Transfer sauce to bowl and whisk 1 minute. Sprinkle with snipped fresh chives.

Garnish turkey with sliced apples and herb sprigs. Pass sauce separately.

*Ginger Butter

Makes about 1 cup

¾ cup water
½ cup sugar
½ cup finely diced fresh ginger
¾ cup (1½ sticks) unsalted butter, room temperature

Combine water, sugar and ginger in small saucepan and cook over low heat, swirling pan occasionally, until sugar dissolves. Increase heat and simmer until ginger is tender and liquid is reduced to thick syrup, about 25 minutes. Puree mixture in processor until smooth, stopping occasionally to scrape down sides of work bowl. Press puree through strainer. Beat butter in small bowl until light. Mix in ginger puree. Refrigerate until firm. *(Can be prepared 3 days ahead.)*

Breast of Turkey in Savoy Cabbage with Red Pepper Concassé

The turkey roll is served in slices to show off the colorful spiral of stuffing.

4 to 6 servings

1 ounce dried porcini mushrooms
1 medium onion (preferably Maui), thinly sliced
1 4-pound savoy cabbage

1 1¼-pound boned turkey breast, fat and skin discarded

¾ cup cooked kasha (cracked buckwheat)

3 ounces thinly sliced Black Forest or Westphalian ham
2 teaspoons minced jalapeño chili
1 large red bell pepper, peeled and cut into ¼-inch-thick strips

Red Pepper Concassé*

Soak mushrooms in warm water to cover 2 hours. Blanch onion in boiling water 1 minute. Drain. Remove 10 large outer leaves from cabbage (reserve remainder for another use). Blanch in boiling water until just pliable, about 2 minutes. Drain. Rinse with cold water; drain. Pat completely dry. Cut off raised part of veins.

Drain mushrooms. Rinse to remove sand. Squeeze out liquid. Slice, discarding any hard parts. Butterfly turkey. Pound between sheets of waxed paper to thickness of ¼ inch, using meat pounder or flat side of cleaver.

Overlap 8 cabbage leaves on work surface, forming 15x22-inch rectangle. Set turkey atop cabbage. Spread kasha over turkey. Top with ham, onions, mushrooms and chili. Arrange bell pepper strips on one short end. Fold in long sides of cabbage leaves. Roll cabbage and turkey up tightly, starting at end with bell pepper and patching with remaining cabbage leaves if necessary. Wrap in double layer of plastic wrap to hold shape. Twist ends and secure with wire twists.

Bring water to boil in steamer. Place turkey roll on rack. Cover and steam until just springy to touch, about 40 minutes. Cool 5 minutes. Remove plastic. Cut roll into ¾-inch-thick slices. Arrange 3 on each plate. Garnish with concassé and serve.

***Red Pepper Concassé**

Peel the peppers with a vegetable peeler.

Makes about 1 cup

2 tablespoons olive oil
1½ teaspoons minced garlic
2 cups diced peeled red bell peppers
1 dried red chili, crumbled
2 tablespoons water

Heat oil in heavy large skillet over low heat. Add garlic and cook until tender, stirring occasionally, about 3 minutes. Mix in peppers and chili. Add water. Cook until all liquid evaporates, stirring occasionally, about 35 minutes. *(Can be prepared 1 day ahead and refrigerated.)* Serve warm.

Twice-fried Game Hens

The double cooking yields succulent hens with wonderfully crisp skin. Cherry tomatoes simply sautéed with dill are an attractive accompaniment.

6 servings

6 12- to 16-ounce Cornish game hens
6 tablespoons soy sauce
¼ cup dry Sherry
6 quarter-size slices fresh ginger, minced

Vegetable oil (for deep frying)

Coarse kosher salt
Lemon wedges

Pat hens dry and arrange in glass baking dish. Mix soy sauce, Sherry and ginger; brush over hens, inside and out. Let stand in cool place 2 hours.

Heat oil in deep fryer or large saucepan to 375°F. Pat game hens dry. Add one to oil and cook until golden brown and leg is tender, 5 to 7 minutes. Transfer to paper towel, using frying basket or Chinese deep-fry strainer. Repeat with remaining hens, allowing oil to return to 375°F before cooking each. *(Can be prepared 3 hours ahead. Let stand at room temperature.)*

Preheat oven to lowest setting. Line baking sheet with paper towels. Heat oil in deep fryer to 400°F. Add 1 hen and cook until dark brown and crisp, 4 to 5 minutes. Drain on paper towels. Place on prepared sheet and keep warm. Repeat with remaining hens, allowing oil to return to 400°F before cooking each. Just before serving, sprinkle hens with coarse salt and garnish with lemon wedges.

Cornish Game Hens with Rancho Mole Sauce

The rich sauce refrigerates and freezes beautifully. In fact, it gets better as the flavors age and mellow. It really perks up grilled meats, poultry and sausages.

8 servings

8 Cornish game hens
2 lemons, halved
Salt and freshly ground pepper
½ cup (1 stick) butter, melted
4 cups Rancho Mole Sauce*
2 teaspoons honey

Sesame seeds, toasted

Preheat oven to 400°F. Pat hens dry. Squeeze lemon juice into cavities. Rub cavities with salt and pepper. Arrange hens in large roasting pan. Brush hens with 6 tablespoons melted butter. Roast 20 minutes, basting often.

Mix remaining butter with ¼ cup sauce and honey. Brush hens with mixture; roast 10 minutes. Brush hens again with mixture; roast 5 minutes.

Transfer hens to platter. Gently heat remaining sauce. Stir in ¼ cup pan juices. Drizzle ¾ cup sauce over hens. Sprinkle with sesame seeds. Serve immediately. Pass remaining sauce.

*Rancho Mole Sauce

Makes about 10 cups

8 dried pasilla chilies**
6 dried pasilla negro chilies**
2 dried New Mexico or mulato chilies**

½ cup unblanched almonds
¼ cup sesame seeds
¼ cup pine nuts
1 slice French bread, torn
1 corn tortilla

3 tablespoons raw pepitas (pumpkin seeds)
4 unpeeled garlic cloves
4 whole cloves
1 2-inch cinnamon stick

1 quart turkey or chicken stock
1 pound tomatoes, roasted, peeled and seeded
¼ cup raisins, soaked in hot water until ready to use

3 tablespoons vegetable oil
3 tablespoons all purpose flour
1 to 2 3.3-ounce rounds Mexican chocolate**

Stem, seed and devein chilies. Break up into pieces. Rinse under cold water. Place in large metal bowl. Cover with boiling water. Cover tightly with foil. Let chilies steep 1 to 2 hours.

Preheat oven to 350°F. Arrange almonds, sesame seeds, pine nuts, bread and tortilla on baking sheets. Toast until golden brown, about 10 minutes.

Place pepitas in heavy small skillet over medium heat and toast well, about 2 minutes (watch carefully, pepitas may pop out of skillet). Remove from skillet. Add garlic to skillet and toast well, tossing mixture occasionally, about 4 minutes.

Grind almonds to powder in spice mill or coffee grinder; transfer to bowl. Grind sesame seeds to powder; transfer to bowl. Grind pine nuts, pepitas, cloves and cinnamon to powder; transfer to bowl. (Do not use processor for grinding; mixture will be gummy.)

Transfer ⅓ of chilies and ½ cup soaking liquid to blender and puree until smooth. Pour into large bowl. Repeat. Transfer remaining ⅓ of chilies, bread, tortilla and ground-nut mixture to blender. Add some of stock to moisten and puree until smooth. Pour some of mixture into bowl. Add undrained raisins, garlic and tomatoes to blender and puree until smooth. Pour mixture into bowl. Stir well.

Heat oil in heavy large saucepan over medium-low heat. Whisk in flour and stir until golden, about 5 minutes. Add chili mixture. Stir in remaining stock ½ cup at a time and simmer 45 minutes to thicken and blend flavors.

Add 1 round of chocolate and simmer 15 minutes. Taste and add more chocolate if richer flavor is desired. Cool sauce completely. Cover and refrigerate until ready to serve. *(Can be prepared 1 week ahead and refrigerated.)*

**Available in Latin American markets.

Honey-glazed Squabs

Cabernet Sauvignon or Burgundy complements these flavors nicely.

4 servings

4 ¾- to 1-pound squabs or Cornish game hens
1 tablespoon Chinese Seasoned Salt*
1 tablespoon dried thyme, crumbled
3 tablespoons honey
1 tablespoon Chinese rice wine or dry Sherry
1 tablespoon dark soy sauce

Cornmeal, Green Onion and Ginger Waffles (see page 83)

Cut each squab down both sides of backbone; discard backbone. Spread squab out on work surface skin side up. Press heel of hand down on breastbone until bone snaps. Mix salt and thyme in small bowl. Rub inside of each squab with mixture. Arrange squabs skin side up in roasting pan. Blend honey, wine and soy sauce. Brush generously over each squab. Let stand at room temperature 1 hour.

Position rack in center of oven and preheat to 450°F. Roast squabs 15 minutes. Reduce oven temperature to 350°F. Continue roasting until skin is crisp and meat is tender, 10 to 15 minutes; do not overcook. Let cool 10 minutes. Cut out breastbones from each squab. Degrease pan juices. Set each squab atop waffle. Spoon pan juices over. Serve immediately.

*Chinese Seasoned Salt

Makes about ⅓ cup

¼ cup (generous) Szechwan peppercorns**
2 tablespoons coarse kosher salt

Heat peppercorns and salt in heavy small skillet over high heat. Reduce heat to medium and stir until peppercorns are aromatic and lightly browned, about 2 minutes. Cool.

Coarsely grind mixture in blender or processor. Store in jar.

**Available at oriental markets.

Duck with Plum Sauce

6 servings

3 cups Rich Brown Poultry Stock (see page 36)
1½ pounds Italian prune plums, halved and pitted

3 medium ducks, trimmed
3 large garlic cloves, halved
Peanut oil
1 tablespoon Cognac
12 Italian prune plums, halved and pitted

¼ cup (½ stick) well-chilled unsalted butter, cut into 4 pieces
Salt and freshly ground pepper
1½ tablespoons minced fresh dill

Bring stock to simmer over very low heat in heavy small nonaluminum saucepan. Add 1½ pounds plums and poach until soft and liquid has reduced by half, skimming surface occasionally, about 1 hour.

Meanwhile, preheat oven to 450°F. Pat duck dry. Rub inside and outside with garlic. Heat thin layer of oil in heavy large roasting pan over medium-high heat. Add ducks and brown well on all sides. Transfer to oven and roast until juices run light pink when thigh is pierced, about 25 minutes.

Using slotted spoon, transfer plums to processor; puree. Return to saucepan.

Transfer duck to cutting surface; keep warm. Pour off fat from pan. Set pan over high heat. Stir in Cognac, scraping up browned bits. Add to sauce and bring to simmer. Add 12 plums and poach 5 minutes. Remove using slotted spoon. Allow plums to cool slightly, then peel.

Cut duck into pieces. Cut duck off bone into thin serving slices. Bring sauce to simmer. Whisk in butter 1 piece at a time. Season with salt and pepper. Spoon onto plates. Arrange duck in sauce. Garnish with poached plums and dill. Serve immediately.

Duck and White Bean Ragout

6 servings

1 pound Great Northern beans, sorted

2 5-pound ducks, giblets (not livers) reserved

1 cup water

1 pound slab bacon, cut into ¼-inch dice

2 large leeks, white part only, finely chopped
2 medium onions, finely chopped
1 large carrot, finely chopped
10 large garlic cloves, chopped
6 Italian parsley sprigs
1½ tablespoons dried thyme, crumbled
2 bay leaves

3 cups chicken stock
2 cups dry white wine

1 pound carrots, peeled and cut diagonally into 1-inch pieces
1 cup canned crushed tomatoes

2 teaspoons salt
Freshly ground pepper

1 cup chopped Italian parsley

Soak Great Northern beans in enough cold water to cover overnight.

Cut wings off ducks and reserve. Skin ducks, reserving breast skin. Cut into 1-inch squares. Bone ducks; cut meat into approximately 1-inch chunks.

Combine skin and water in heavy small skillet and bring to boil. Reduce heat and simmer until water has evaporated and skin is crisp, about 50 minutes. Remove cracklings using slotted spoon and drain on paper towels.

Cook bacon in 4- to 5-quart pot over medium heat until crisp and brown, stirring frequently, 20 to 30 minutes. Remove using slotted spoon and drain on paper towels. Pour off all but ¼ cup rendered bacon fat.

Add duck (in batches if necessary) to same pot over high heat and brown well on all sides, stirring frequently, about 10 minutes. Remove using slotted spoon. Add giblets and wings and brown well on all sides, stirring frequently, about 15 minutes. Remove using slotted spoon. Reduce heat to medium-low. Stir in leeks, onions, chopped carrot, 5 garlic cloves, parsley sprigs, thyme and bay leaves. Cover and cook until golden brown, stirring occasionally, about 20 minutes.

Stir stock and wine into pot, scraping up browned bits, and bring to boil. Reduce heat, cover and simmer 30 minutes, skimming surface.

Strain stock mixture into bowl, pressing on solids to extract as much liquid as possible. Wipe pot; return mixture. Stir in beans, sliced carrots and tomatoes and bring to boil. Reduce heat, cover partially and simmer ½ hour.

Stir in duck meat, salt and pepper and simmer until beans are very tender, stirring occasionally, about 1 hour.

Transfer 1 cup cooked beans and 1 cup cooking liquid to processor. Add remaining garlic and chopped parsley and puree. Stir back into pot. Cover and let stand 1 minute. Adjust seasoning. Ladle into bowls. Garnish with cracklings and bacon and serve immediately.

Braised Goose with Peppercorns, Fresh Thyme and Madeira Sauce

Goose cooked in fat becomes tender and succulent—and is surprisingly not greasy. The carcass can be used to make a stock for the sauce.

12 servings

- **2 11-pound geese**
- **6 fresh thyme sprigs, chopped**
- **Salt and freshly ground white pepper**
- **6 cups goose fat***
- **10 medium garlic cloves**
- **1 tablespoon black peppercorns**
- **Madeira Sauce****

Cut legs with thighs attached from goose. Cut down length of breastbone on goose. Holding blade of knife against bones, scrape breast meat from carcass with small cuts, gently pulling flesh from carcass with fingers. Place goose pieces on baking pan. Repeat with second goose. Season both sides of meat with thyme, salt and white pepper. Let stand 45 minutes.

Melt fat in heavy large pot over low heat. Add garlic and peppercorns, then goose legs skin side down. Adjust heat so fat barely shimmers. Cook 1 hour. Add breasts, skin side down, pressing to submerge. Continue cooking until goose is tender when pierced with fork, about 3 hours. *(Can be prepared 3 months ahead. Refrigerate completely covered with cooking fat. To rewarm, scrape most of fat from meat. Place meat in baking pan. Cover and heat in 350°F oven about 20 minutes.)* Remove goose from fat. Discard skin. Serve goose; pass Madeira Sauce separately.

Geese can also be cooked in oven. Arrange legs skin side up in roasting pan just large enough to accommodate. Add garlic and peppercorns; cover with fat. Bake in 300°F oven 1 hour. Add breasts skin side up and cook until tender, about 3 hours.

*If unavailable, 5 pounds pork fatback can be substituted. Discard skin from fatback. Cut fatback into 1-inch pieces. Add to pan of boiling water and return to boil. Drain well. Puree in processor in batches until smooth. Melt in heavy large saucepan over low heat. Strain rendered fat.

**Madeira Sauce

Makes about 1½ cups

- **1 tablespoon butter**
- **6 tablespoons sliced shallots**
- **6 tablespoons sliced mushrooms**
- **2 cups Madeira**
- **1½ quarts brown goose, duck or chicken stock**
- **3 tablespoons well-chilled butter, cut into small pieces**

Melt 1 tablespoon butter in heavy medium saucepan over medium heat. Add shallots and mushrooms and cook until brown, stirring occasionally, about 3 minutes. Add Madeira. Increase heat and boil until reduced by half, about 4 minutes. Add stock. Reduce heat and simmer until reduced to 1½ cups liquid, skimming frequently, about 30 minutes. Remove sauce from heat and whisk in cold butter a little at a time. Strain into sauceboat.

Texas Beef Chili

6 to 8 servings

Meat
- 2 pounds well-marbled beef chuck or shin, cut into ½-inch cubes
- 3 tablespoons olive oil
- 2 tablespoons medium-hot chili powder, preferably Grandma's

- 3 to 5 tablespoons olive oil
- 1 pound Spanish chorizo, sliced ¼-inch thick (optional)
- 3 medium onions, chopped
- 8 garlic cloves, minced
- 3 tablespoons medium-hot chili powder, preferably Grandma's
- 1 tablespoon dried oregano, crumbled
- 2 teaspoons ground cumin
- 2 teaspoons salt
- 1 teaspoon freshly ground pepper
- 2 2-pound cans Italian plum tomatoes, drained and coarsely chopped (preferably in processor)
- 2 12-ounce bottles beer
- 1 6-ounce can tomato paste

Beans
- 1 pound dried pinto beans, soaked in cold water to cover overnight and drained
- 3 tablespoons olive oil
- 2 large onions, chopped
- 4 to 6 garlic cloves, minced
- 1 tablespoon dried oregano, crumbled
- Salt and freshly ground pepper

Salsa
- 3 ripe tomatoes, peeled, cored, seeded and cut into ½-inch dice
- 1 cup fresh lemon or lime juice or combination
- 1 small red onion, minced
- 2 to 3 tablespoons chopped fresh cilantro
- 2 garlic cloves, minced
- 2 to 4 fresh or canned jalapeño chilies, seeded, deveined and minced
- Salt and freshly ground pepper

- 2 tablespoons red wine vinegar or Sherry vinegar
- Sour cream
- Avocado slices
- Lime wedges
- Corn tortillas

For meat: Toss meat with 3 tablespoons oil and 2 tablespoons chili powder in non-aluminum pan; rub powder into meat. Cover and chill overnight.

Heat 3 tablespoons oil in heavy large skillet over medium-high heat. Brown beef in batches (do not crowd) on all sides, about 5 minutes. Transfer to heavy large pot, using slotted spoon. Add chorizo to skillet and brown well. Transfer to pot, using slotted spoon. Reduce heat to medium-low. Add more oil to skillet if necessary. Add onions and cook until translucent, stirring occasionally, about 10 minutes. Add garlic, chili powder, oregano, cumin, salt and pepper and stir 3 minutes. Transfer to pot. Stir tomatoes, beer and tomato paste into pot. Bring to boil. Reduce heat, cover and simmer until meat is very tender, stirring occasionally, about 3 hours. (Uncover during last hour if necessary to thicken liquid into sauce.)

Meanwhile, prepare beans: Combine beans with enough water to cover by 2 inches in large saucepan and slowly bring to boil, skimming foam.

Heat oil in heavy large skillet over medium-low heat. Add onions and garlic and cook until translucent, stirring occasionally, about 10 minutes. Add oregano and cook 1 minute. Stir onion mixture into beans. Cover saucepan partially and simmer beans until tender but not mushy, adding more water as necessary to keep beans covered, about 1½ hours. Season generously with salt and pepper. *(Can be prepared 5 days ahead. Refrigerate chili and beans separately.)*

For salsa: Combine first 8 ingredients in nonaluminum bowl.

To serve: Degrease chili. Adjust seasoning. Stir in vinegar. Reheat chili and beans if necessary. Ladle chili into bowls. Garnish with sour cream, avocados and lime. Pass beans, salsa and corn tortillas separately.

Hash of Brisket and Winter Vegetables with Ale-spiked Cheddar Sauce

6 servings

1 2¾-pound beef brisket
1 onion
1 bay leaf
4 whole cloves
4 whole black peppercorns

¾ pound small boiling potatoes
¾ pound rutabagas, peeled and halved
¾ pound carrots, peeled

6 ounces thick-sliced smoked bacon, cut into ½-inch dice
1 large onion, cut into ½-inch dice
2 garlic cloves, minced
½ cup (1 stick) unsalted butter
2 teaspoons salt
1 teaspoon firmly packed light brown sugar
1 teaspoon dried thyme, crumbled
1 teaspoon dried savory, crumbled
1 teaspoon dried marjoram, crumbled
Freshly grated nutmeg
1 tablespoon all purpose flour
⅓ cup English ale

Freshly ground pepper
½ cup whipping cream

Minced fresh parsley
Ale-spiked Cheddar Sauce*
Toasted country bread

Combine brisket, onion, bay leaf, cloves and peppercorns in heavy large pot. Add enough water to cover and bring to boil. Reduce heat and simmer until brisket is tender, about 2½ hours. Let cool completely in liquid. Drain, reserving liquid. Dice brisket and set aside.

Bring reserved liquid to simmer in heavy large saucepan. Cook potatoes, rutabagas and carrots separately in simmering liquid until just tender. Drain, reserving ⅓ cup liquid. Cool vegetables. Peel potatoes and cut into ½-inch dice. Cut rutabagas into ½-inch dice. Halve carrots lengthwise and cut crosswise into ½-inch slices.

Fry bacon in heavy large skillet over medium-high heat until just beginning to crisp. Add onion and stir until just beginning to color, about 5 minutes. Add garlic and stir 2 minutes. Add cooked vegetables and ¼ cup butter and toss until vegetables begin to color, about 10 minutes. Sprinkle with salt, sugar, thyme, savory and marjoram. Season with nutmeg. Sprinkle with flour and cook 3 minutes. Stir in reserved ⅓ cup liquid and ale and cook until mixture is thick, stirring frequently, about 5 minutes.

Position rack in center of oven and preheat to 400°F. Generously grease 13x10x2-inch oval gratin dish. Melt remaining ¼ cup butter in heavy large skillet over medium heat. Add diced brisket and cook until golden brown, stirring frequently, about 7 minutes. Stir beef into vegetable mixture. Season with pepper. Blend in cream. Spoon into prepared dish. *(Can be prepared 1 day ahead. Cool completely, cover and refrigerate. Bring to room temperature before baking.)* Bake 15 minutes. Reduce temperature to 375°F. Continue baking until top is crusty, about 30 minutes. Sprinkle with parsley. Serve immediately with sauce and bread.

*Ale-spiked Cheddar Sauce

Makes 2½ cups

1 pound sharp cheddar cheese, very coarsely grated
1 cup English ale
2 tablespoons (¼ stick) unsalted butter
1 tablespoon prepared horseradish
1 tablespoon Dijon mustard
Several drops hot pepper sauce

Combine cheese, ale, butter, horseradish and mustard in double boiler over gently simmering water; stir until smooth. Season with hot pepper sauce.

Five-Treasure Toss

The beef is easier to slice if cooked one day ahead and refrigerated.

6 servings

3 green onions
3 quarter-size slices fresh ginger
1 whole star anise
2 cups water
½ cup rice wine or Scotch
⅓ cup soy sauce
3 tablespoons sugar

2 tablespoons safflower oil or corn oil
2½ pounds beef chuck, trimmed and cut into 1½-inch squares

Garlic and Ginger Dressing
2 tablespoons soy sauce
4½ teaspoons rice wine or Scotch
4½ teaspoons Chinese rice vinegar
4½ teaspoons sugar
2 teaspoons minced garlic
2 teaspoons minced fresh ginger
¼ teaspoon freshly ground pepper

3 tablespoons oriental sesame oil
2 medium red bell peppers, cored and cut into matchstick julienne
2 medium yellow bell peppers (optional), cored and cut into matchstick julienne
½ pound snow peas, trimmed, strings removed, halved lengthwise
2 cups 1-inch pieces green onions (green part only)
1 cup enoki mushrooms, trimmed
Minced green onions (green part only)

Lightly crush green onions, ginger and star anise with flat side of cleaver. Combine with water, rice wine, soy sauce and sugar in heavy large saucepan. Bring to boil. Reduce heat and simmer for 20 minutes.

Heat wok or heavy large skillet over high heat. Add safflower oil and heat until very hot. Add meat and cook until golden brown on all sides, about 10 minutes. Transfer to simmering liquid, using slotted spoon. Cover partially and simmer until meat is tender and sauce is reduced to thick glaze, stirring occasionally, about 1 hour. Transfer meat to medium bowl, using slotted spoon. Strain cooking liquid into another medium bowl. Cool meat to room temperature. *(Can be prepared 1 day ahead. Refrigerate meat and cooking liquid separately. Rewarm liquid before continuing.)* Slice meat thinly across grain. Mix into cooking liquid.

For dressing: Combine first 7 ingredients in small bowl and mix to blend.

Heat wok or heavy large skillet over high heat. Add sesame oil and heat until very hot. Add bell peppers, snow peas, green onion pieces and mushrooms. Stir-fry until vegetables begin to soften, about 1½ minutes. Stir in dressing. Transfer mixture to platter. Make well in center of vegetable mixture. Spoon beef into well. Garnish with minced green onions. Serve warm or at room temperature, mixing gently.

Beef Curry with Green Beans and Cilantro

4 servings

3 tablespoons vegetable oil
2 pounds boneless beef chuck, trimmed, patted dry and cut into 1¼- to 1½-inch pieces
1 large onion, chopped
1 tablespoon plus 1 teaspoon all purpose flour

2¼ pounds tomatoes, peeled, seeded and chopped
1¾ to 2¼ cups water
3 tablespoons minced fresh cilantro
2 large garlic cloves, minced
1 tablespoon curry powder
1 tablespoon minced fresh ginger
Salt and freshly ground pepper

¾ pound green beans, trimmed and halved crosswise

Position rack in lower third of oven and preheat to 450°F. Heat oil in heavy 4- to 5-quart flameproof casserole over medium-high heat. Add ⅓ of beef and brown on all sides, making sure piecess do not touch, 6 to 7 minutes. Transfer beef to plate using slotted spoon. Repeat with remaining beef. Add onion to pan, reduce heat to low and cook until translucent, stirring often, about 7 minutes. Return beef to pan; reserve any juices on plate. Sprinkle beef with flour. Toss gently until well coated. Transfer to oven and bake uncovered, stirring once, 5 minutes. Remove from oven.

Reduce oven temperature to 325°F. Pour reserved juices from plate over beef. Add tomatoes and enough water to barely cover. Add 2 tablespoons cilantro, garlic, curry powder, ginger, salt and pepper. Bring mixture to boil on top of stove, scraping down any browned bits from sides and bottom of pan. Transfer to oven, cover and bake, stirring occasionally, 1¼ hours. Add more water if mixture appears dry or sauce is too thick. Continue baking until beef is tender when pierced with tip of knife, about 15 to 30 minutes.

Meanwhile, bring medium saucepan of salted water to boil. Add green beans and boil until almost tender, about 3 minutes. Drain; rinse green beans under cold water and drain again.

Transfer stew to top of stove and uncover. Add beans and simmer until tender, about 7 minutes. Sauce should be thick enough to lightly coat back of spoon. If sauce is too thick, stir in additional water. If sauce is too thin, carefully remove beef and vegetables using slotted spoon and boil sauce, stirring often, until slightly thickened. Return beef and vegetables to sauce. *(Can be prepared 3 days ahead, covered and refrigerated or 1 month ahead and frozen.)* Stir in remaining cilantro. Adjust seasoning. Serve stew hot.

Grilled Flank Steak with Shiitake Mushrooms

A wonderful main course for a barbecue. Marinate the steaks 24 hours for best flavor, and use either fresh or dried shiitake mushrooms.

6 servings

2 1¼- to 1½-pound flank steaks, fat trimmed
½ cup soy sauce
½ cup oriental sesame oil
3 tablespoons red wine vinegar
Freshly ground pepper
2 medium garlic cloves, crushed

Mushroom Sauce
1 pound fresh shiitake mushrooms* (discard stems)
3 tablespoons unsalted butter
3 tablespoons vegetable oil
2 cups (or more) unsalted beef stock
4 teaspoons Dijon mustard
4 teaspoons coarse-grained mustard
½ cup whipping cream
Salt and freshly ground pepper

1 tablespoon unsalted butter
1 tablespoon vegetable oil

Place steaks in nonaluminum pan. Whisk soy sauce, sesame oil, vinegar and generous amount of pepper in medium bowl. Mix in garlic. Pour over steaks, turning to coat all sides. Cover pan tightly and refrigerate 24 hours, turning steaks occasionally.

For sauce: Reserve six 2-inch-diameter mushrooms for garnish. Cut remaining into ½-inch-wide strips. Melt 3 tablespoons butter with 3 tablespoons oil in heavy large skillet over medium-high heat. Add mushroom slices and stir 3 minutes. Mix in 1 cup stock and both mustards. Increase heat to high and boil until reduced by half, about 5 minutes. Add 1 cup stock ¼ cup at a time, boiling until sauce is reduced by half after each addition. Stir in cream. Boil until sauce coats spoon, about 3 minutes. Season with salt and pepper. *(Can be prepared 1 day ahead. Chill sauce and reserved mushrooms separately.)*

Prepare barbecue grill (high heat). (Steaks can also be cooked in broiler.) Remove steaks from marinade and arrange on grill rack. Cook about 4 minutes per side for medium-rare. Transfer to platter and let rest 5 minutes.

Reheat sauce over low heat, stirring occasionally. Melt 1 tablespoon butter with 1 tablespoon oil in heavy small skillet over high heat. Add reserved mushroom caps and cook until heated through, about 2 minutes per side. Drain mushroom caps on paper towels. Cut steaks across grain diagonally into ⅜-inch-thick slices. Arrange in circular pattern on heated platter. Thin sauce with stock if desired. Ladle half of sauce in center of platter. Arrange mushroom caps in 2 clusters on platter edge. Serve immediately, passing remaining sauce separately.

*If unavailable, 4 ounces dried shiitake mushrooms can be substituted. Soak in hot water to cover 30 minutes. Drain. Squeeze out excess moisture. Discard hard cores.

Veal Scallops with Pimiento-Caper Sauce

4 to 6 servings

All purpose flour
Spanish paprika
Salt and freshly ground pepper
12 1½-ounce veal scallops

Sauce
2 cups Rich Brown Veal Stock*
½ medium green bell pepper, coarsely chopped
¼ cup amontillado Sherry
¼ cup diced pimientos
4 teaspoons drained capers
8 tablespoons (1 stick) well-chilled unsalted butter, cut into 8 pieces

¼ cup (½ stick) butter
¼ cup olive oil

Combine flour, paprika, salt and pepper on large plate. Using flat mallet or rolling pin, pound veal between sheets of waxed paper to thickness of ⅛ to ¼ inch. Cover tightly with waxed paper.

For sauce: Boil stock, green pepper and Sherry in heavy medium saucepan until reduced to ⅔ cup.

Strain stock and return to pan. Add pimientos and capers. Whisk in 2 tablespoons chilled butter. Set pan over low heat and whisk in remaining 6 tablespoons chilled butter 1 piece at a time, removing pan from heat briefly if drops of melted butter appear. (If sauce breaks down at any time, remove from heat and whisk in 2 tablespoons cold butter.) Remove pimiento-caper sauce from heat and keep warm.

Melt ¼ cup butter with oil in large heavy skillet over medium-high heat. Dredge veal in seasoned flour, shaking to remove excess, and add to skillet in batches (do not crowd). Cook until light brown, about 1 minute on each side. Drain on paper towels. Dip veal in sauce and place 2 to 3 scallops on each plate. Nap with remaining sauce and serve immediately.

*Rich Brown Veal Stock

Makes about 2 quarts

12 pounds veal bones
3 large onions, sliced
3 cups coarsely chopped celery
3 cups coarsely chopped carrot
3 medium garlic cloves, mashed
½ cup brandy
4 cups chopped tomato
2 cups fresh parsley
12 peppercorns
3 bay leaves

Preheat oven to 400°F. Arrange bones in single layer in roasting pan. Bake until dark brown, turning every 30 minutes, about 1½ hours. Spread next 4 ingredients atop veal bones. Reduce heat to 350°F and cook 1 hour.

Transfer contents of roasting pan to large pot. Add brandy to roasting pan and bring to boil, scraping up any browned bits. Add to pot with all remaining ingredients. Add water to cover. Bring to boil, skimming surface occasionally. Reduce heat and simmer 16 hours, skimming surface occasionally. Strain stock and degrease. Boil until reduced to 8 cups if necessary. *(Can be prepared ahead and refrigerated 3 days or frozen for up to 3 months.)*

The Tombstone T-Bone

Add julienne of jalapeño chilies to the colorful sauce to create a spicy version of this succulent veal dish.

8 servings

2 mild green chilies, such as poblano or Anaheim
1 large red bell pepper

1 ounce Carne Seca* or beef jerky
1 cup rich beef stock (preferably homemade)

Mesquite wood or mesquite charcoal

1 tablespoon butter
½ large onion, thinly sliced
¼ cup canned, drained golden hominy
14 tablespoons rich beef stock (preferably homemade)
½ cup whipping cream
2 teaspoons cornstarch dissolved in 2 tablespoons beef stock

8 1-inch-thick veal T-bone steaks
Vegetable oil
Salt and freshly ground pepper

Char chilies and bell pepper over gas flame or in broiler until blackened on all sides. Wrap in paper bag and let stand 10 minutes. Peel and seed. Rinse and pat dry. Cut into julienne strips.

Pound Carne Seca with mallet to shred. Pull apart into fine shreds. Soak in 1 cup stock until softened, about 30 minutes. Drain, reserving liquid.

Prepare barbecue grill with hot fire, using mesquite wood or charcoal.

Melt butter in heavy large skillet over medium-low heat. Add onion, then chilies, bell pepper, Carne Seca and hominy and cook until onion is tender, stirring occasionally, about 8 minutes. Add Carne Seca soaking liquid, 14 tablespoons beef stock and cream. Boil until mixture is reduced to 2¼ cups, stirring occasionally, about 10 minutes. Add cornstarch mixture and stir until sauce thickens, about 2 minutes. Cover and keep warm.

Brush steaks with oil, sprinkle with salt and pepper. Place steaks on grill rack and cook to desired degree of doneness, about 3 minutes per side for medium-rare. Transfer steaks to platter. Nap tails with sauce and serve.

*Carne Seca

Makes about 2 ounces

4 ounces well-trimmed lean beef top round, cut into paper-thin slices
Salt and freshly ground pepper

Preheat oven to 200°F. Sprinkle meat lightly with salt and pepper. Arrange in single layer on metal cooling racks. Bake on racks until dry, 2 to 4 hours. *(Carne Seca can be prepared 3 months ahead. Store in airtight container.)*

Orange Veal Piccata

2 servings; can be doubled or tripled

All purpose flour
Salt and freshly ground pepper
2 tablespoons (¼ stick) butter
1 teaspoon vegetable oil
½ pound ⅛-inch-thick veal scallops
½ cup strained fresh orange juice
½ teaspoon minced fresh sage or generous pinch of dried, crumbled
1 tablespoon butter
Minced fresh sage or parsley

Place flour on large plate. Season with salt and pepper. Melt 2 tablespoons butter with oil in heavy large skillet over high heat. Dredge veal in flour, shaking off excess. Add to pan (in batches if necessary; do not crowd) and cook 30 seconds on each side. Transfer to plate; keep warm.

Discard pan drippings. Add ¼ cup orange juice to skillet and boil until reduced to glaze, scraping up browned bits, about 1 minute. Add remaining orange juice and ½ teaspoon sage. Season with salt and pepper. Boil until mixture thickens and just coats spoon, about 1 minute. Remove from heat and swirl in 1 tablespoon butter. Pour in any juices accumulated from veal. Transfer veal to heated plates. Spoon sauce over. Sprinkle with sage.

Veal Shanks with Oranges, Prunes and Red Wine

4 servings

4 2-inch-thick veal shank pieces, preferably from meaty part of hind shanks (about 3 pounds total), tied around center
Salt and freshly ground pepper
¼ cup all purpose flour
2 tablespoons (¼ stick) unsalted butter
2 tablespoons vegetable oil or olive oil

1 medium onion, minced
1 medium carrot, finely chopped
1 medium celery stalk, finely chopped
1 large navel orange
3 thyme sprigs or ¾ teaspoon dried, crumbled
2 parsley sprigs
1 bay leaf
½ cup dry red wine
3 medium garlic cloves, minced
1½ cups brown veal stock or rich chicken stock

16 small pitted prunes
4 ounces small white onions, peeled

1 tablespoon minced fresh parsley

Preheat oven to 350°F. Pat veal dry. Sprinkle both sides with salt and pepper. Dredge in flour, patting off excess. Melt butter with oil in heavy large skillet with high sides or Dutch oven over medium-high heat. Add veal and brown on all sides. Transfer to plate.

Reduce heat to low. Add onion, carrot and celery to skillet. Stir until vegetables are tender, scraping up any browned bits, about 5 minutes. Cut 2½x3-inch strip peel from orange, using vegetable peeler. Reserve orange. Tie peel, thyme, parsley sprigs and bay leaf in cheesecloth. Add to skillet. Mix in wine and garlic. Boil until most of liquid evaporates, stirring constantly. Return veal bone side up to skillet. Add stock. Bring mixture to boil. Cover, transfer to oven and bake until veal is very tender when pierced with tip of sharp knife, about 1½ hours.

Meanwhile, cover prunes with hot water and let stand until softened, about 1½ hours. Cook white onions in small pan of boiling water 1 minute. Drain. Rinse under cold water; drain well. Cut off half of remaining peel from orange (orange part only) and cut into fine julienne. Reserve orange. Place 1 tablespoon firmly packed peel into small saucepan of cold water. Boil 3 minutes. Drain. Rinse peel; drain well. Cut remaining peel and all white pith from orange. Cut between membranes of orange with small sharp knife to release segments; reserve segments.

Discard herb bag from veal. Transfer veal to platter. Tent with foil to keep warm. Strain cooking liquid, pressing firmly on vegetables to extract as much liquid as possible. Discard vegetables. Return cooking liquid to pan. Drain prunes. Add prunes and onions to cooking liquid. Bring to boil. Reduce heat and simmer until onions are just tender, about 10 minutes. Remove prunes and onions from skillet using slotted spoon and arrange around veal. Cover and keep warm. Boil sauce until reduced to ¾ cup, stirring frequently, about 7 minutes. Stir in orange peel julienne. Reduce heat and simmer 1 minute. Adjust seasoning. Spoon sauce over veal. Sprinkle with parsley. Garnish with orange segments.

Grilled Lamb Chops with Pecan Sauce and Roasted Garlic Custard

6 servings

Custard

1 tablespoon olive oil
6 large garlic cloves, peeled
2 cups whipping cream

4 egg yolks, room temperature
1 egg, room temperature
Salt and freshly ground white pepper

Sauce

½ cup finely chopped toasted pecans
3 tablespoons unsalted butter, softened
2 tablespoons finely choppped onion
1 tablespoon finely chopped celery
¾ cup (about) rich veal, lamb or chicken stock
½ cup dry red wine
3 tablespoons red wine vinegar
1 shallot, minced
⅓ cup whipping cream
½ cup (1 stick) well-chilled butter, cut into tablespoons
3 drops of hot pepper sauce
Salt and freshly ground pepper

1 cup aromatic wood chips (apple, alder or hickory), soaked in water to cover 15 minutes and drained
12 2-ounce lamb chops, trimmed
Vegetable oil
6 pecan halves
Grilled vegetables (such as yellow squash, bell peppers and snow peas)

For custard: Preheat oven to 400°F. Heat olive oil in heavy medium ovenproof skillet over medium heat. Add garlic and toss 1 minute. Transfer skillet to oven and roast until garlic is soft, about 12 minutes. Set skillet over high heat. Add cream and bring to boil. Transfer garlic and cream to blender and puree. Pour into bowl.

Reduce oven temperature to 350°F. Grease six ¾-cup ramekins. Beat yolks and egg to blend in small bowl. Whisk into garlic cream. Season with salt and pepper. Divide mixture among ramekins. Arrange in roasting pan. Pour enough boiling water into pan to come halfway up sides of ramekins. Bake until custard is just set, about 25 minutes. Turn oven off. Let custards stand in oven with door ajar until serving time.

For sauce: Mix pecans, 3 tablespoons butter, onion and celery in processor 1 minute, stopping to scrape down sides of bowl. Add enough stock to mix to paste, about ¼ cup.

Boil remaining ½ cup stock, wine, vinegar and shallot in heavy medium saucepan until liquid is reduced to 2 tablespoons. Add cream and boil until slightly thickened. Remove from heat and whisk in 2 tablespoons butter. Set pan over low heat and whisk in remaining butter 1 tablespoon at a time, removing pan from heat briefly if drops of melted butter appear. Whisk in pecan mixture. Add hot pepper sauce. Season with salt and pepper. Keep sauce warm in water bath.

Prepare barbecue (very high heat). Sprinkle aromatic chips over coals. Grease grill rack. Rub chops with oil. Sprinkle with salt and pepper. Arrange chops on rack and grill 3 minutes per side for medium rare. Spoon sauce onto one side of each plate. Arrange 2 chops atop sauce. Invert custard onto each plate. Top each with pecan. Garnish plates with grilled vegetables. Serve immediately.

Potato-topped Lamb with Eggplant and Tomatoes

6 to 8 servings

18 ounces baking potatoes, peeled

2 tablespoons olive oil
1 medium onion, minced
1 teaspoon minced garlic
¾ teaspoon ground cinnamon
½ teaspoon ground coriander
½ teaspoon ground cumin
Pinch of dried red pepper flakes
1 pound ground lamb
1 1-pound can whole tomatoes with juice, coarsely chopped
¾ cup dry red wine
1 pound eggplant, peeled and cubed
1 teaspoon salt
½ cup chopped parsley
1 tablespoon fresh lemon juice
Freshly ground pepper

¼ pound Monterey Jack cheese, grated (1 cup)
1 ounce Parmesan cheese, grated (¼ cup)
3 tablespoons milk
1 egg
⅛ teaspoon freshly grated nutmeg

Cook potatoes in boiling salted water until very tender. Drain. Puree through food mill or sieve into bowl (you should have about 1½ cups packed puree). *Do not use food processor.*

Butter 9x12-inch oval gratin or baking dish. Heat oil in heavy large skillet over high heat. Add onion, garlic, cinnamon, coriander, cumin and red pepper flakes and stir 1 minute. Add lamb and brown well, stirring frequently and pouring off fat as necessary. Stir in tomatoes and wine and bring to boil. Reduce heat to medium-low. Add eggplant and ¾ teaspoon salt. Cook until eggplant is tender, stirring occasionally and skimming fat from surface, about 30 minutes. Increase heat to medium and cook until almost all liquid is absorbed. Remove from heat. Stir in parsley, lemon juice, ¼ teaspoon salt and pepper. Pour into prepared dish.

Preheat oven to 350°F. Blend potato puree, cheeses, milk, egg and nutmeg until smooth. Season with salt and pepper. Pipe or spread potato topping over lamb mixture. *(Can be prepared 1 day ahead. Cool completely, cover and refrigerate.)* Cover and bake 15 minutes. Uncover and bake until topping is browned, about 30 minutes.

Country Ham with Pickled Peach Glaze

Perfect for a buffet. Make the glaze at least two days before cooking the ham.

10 servings

1 16- to 18-pound fully cooked, bone-in ham
2 cups chicken broth
Pickled Peach Glaze*

Cut away rind and all but ¼-inch-thick layer of fat from upper surface of ham. Score ¼-inch-deep diamond pattern in upper surface. Set ham in shallow baking pan just large enough to accommodate. Bring ham to room temperature before baking.

Preheat oven to 325°F. Set ham in oven; add broth to pan. Bake ham 2 hours, basting every 15 minutes. Spoon off pan drippings. Spread glaze over top of ham. Bake until glaze is light brown, about 45 minutes. Let ham rest 20 minutes before serving.

***Pickled Peach Glaze**

Makes 1½ cups

- **1 cup sugar**
- **¾ cup cider vinegar**
- **¾ cup golden raisins**
- **12 whole cloves**
- **1 2-inch cinnamon stick**
- **2 pounds peaches, peeled, pitted and coarsely chopped or one 20-ounce bag frozen unsweetened sliced peaches, thawed and chopped**

Combine sugar, vinegar and raisins in heavy nonaluminum saucepan. Wrap cloves and cinnamon in cheesecloth and add to pan. Cook over low heat, swirling pan occasionally, until sugar dissolves. Increase heat, cover and simmer 10 minutes. Add peaches and simmer uncovered until mixture is reduced to 1½ cups, skimming surface and stirring occasionally, 30 to 40 minutes. Cool glaze to room temperature. Cover and refrigerate for at least 2 days. Bring glaze to room temperature and discard spice bag before using.

Grilled Pork Loin with Spicy Black Beans and Tomatillo Salsa

All the elements of this dish come together for a terrific main course. The pork is also good with just the onions.

6 servings

Pickled Onions

- **½ cup olive oil**
- **2 pounds white onions, cut into ⅛-inch-thick wedges**
- **1½ cups sugar**
- **1 cup red wine vinegar**
- **¼ cup catsup**
- **2 tablespoons sea salt**
- **2 teaspoons dried red pepper flakes**
- **Freshly ground white pepper**

Salsa

- **½ jalapeño chili**
- **¾ pound tomatillos, peeled**
- **½ cup minced green onions**
- **¼ cup minced fresh parsley**
- **2 tablespoons olive oil**
- **2 tablespoons fresh lime juice**
- **3 medium garlic cloves, minced**
- **1 teaspoon grated lime peel**
- **¼ teaspoon salt**
- **¼ teaspoon freshly ground white pepper**

Pork

- **1 4-pound pork loin, boned and cut into ¾-inch-thick slices**
- **1 cup mesquite chips, soaked in water to cover 30 minutes and drained**

- **Spicy Black Beans***
- **Jalapeño chilies (optional), halved, seeded and grilled**

For onions: Heat oil in heavy large saucepan over low heat. Mix in onions. Cover and cook until tender, stirring occasionally, about 15 minutes. Add all remaining ingredients and simmer 3 minutes. Serve warm or at room temperature. *(Can be prepared 5 days ahead and refrigerated.)*

For salsa: Char chili over gas flame or in broiler until blackened on all sides. Wrap in paper bag and let stand 10 minutes to steam. Peel and seed. Rinse if necessary and pat dry. Blanch tomatillos in boiling salted water 3 minutes. Rinse under cold water; pat dry. Transfer to processor or blender. Add chili and all remaining ingredients. Puree until smooth. *(Can be prepared 1 day ahead and refrigerated.)*

For pork: Prepare barbecue grill (high heat). Place pork slice between sheets of waxed paper. Pound to thickness of ½ inch using mallet or flat side of cleaver. Repeat with remaining pork. Sprinkle pork with salt and pepper. Grease grill rack. Sprinkle coals with mesquite chips. Arrange pork on grill rack and cook until springy to touch, about 2½ minutes per side.

Grilled and Toasted Pork and Onion Chili

Jerry Friedman

Maple-glazed Turkey with Apple and Ginger Butter Sauce; Pumpkin and Wild Mushroom Stuffing; Pumpkin Wheat Bread; Brussels Sprouts and Chestnuts; steamed carrots; Cranberry Puree

Irwin Horowitz

Irwin Horowitz

From left: Fresh Blueberry Yogurt Tart; Rougemont Apple Cake; Calvabec and Apple Cheesecake

Jerry Friedman

Clockwise from top left: "Catfish-fried" Chicken; Country Ham with Pickled Peach Glaze; Garden Salad with "French" Dressing; New Potato Salad with Peas and Mint; Farmhouse Potato Bread accompanied with Plum and Apple Butter

Orzo- and Feta-stuffed Tomatoes; Pita Pockets with Parsley and Chick-Pea Salad; Ultimate Bean Soup

Brian Leatart

Arrange pork in center of plates. Spoon some of salsa over. Mound onions on one side of pork and black beans on other. Garnish with grilled jalapeño chilies and serve immediately.

***Spicy Black Beans**

6 servings

1 pound dried black beans

¼ pound bacon, chopped
5 medium garlic cloves, minced
2 medium celery stalks, minced
1 large carrot, peeled and diced
1 medium onion, diced
1 jalapeño chili, seeded and minced

1 bay leaf
1 tablespoon chili powder
1 teaspoon ground cumin
1 teaspoon cayenne pepper
¾ teaspoon freshly ground white pepper
8 cups chicken or beef broth
Salt

Soak beans in water to cover 24 hours. Drain. Transfer to large saucepan. Cover with generous amount of cold water. Boil 20 minutes. Drain. Rinse beans and drain again.

Cook bacon in heavy large saucepan over medium heat until golden brown and crisp, stirring frequently, about 5 minutes. Mix in garlic, celery, carrot, onion, jalapeño chili and bay leaf. Cook until vegetables are tender, stirring occasionally, about 10 minutes. Add chili powder, cumin, cayenne and pepper. Stir until aromatic, about 1 minute. Add beans and broth. Simmer until beans are tender and liquid is absorbed, stirring occasionally, about 1½ hours. Season with salt.

Grilled and Toasted Pork and Onion Chili

The accompanying jonnycakes lend a New England twist to this chili.

6 to 8 servings

30 medium garlic cloves, peeled and trimmed

4 pounds 2-inch-thick loin pork chops
Salt and freshly ground pepper
Vegetable oil
2 large yellow onions, cut into ¾-inch-thick slices

½ cup vegetable oil
¼ cup unbleached all purpose flour

¼ cup Hungarian sweet paprika
2 tablespoons chili powder
1 tablespoon (heaping) minced garlic
1 tablespoon filé powder
1 jalapeño chili, seeded, deveined and finely chopped
5 cups chicken stock
1 cup canned crushed tomatoes in puree
2 dried ancho or pasilla chilies, trimmed and chopped

Thin Rhode Island Jonnycakes*
Cooked Rice

Blanch garlic cloves in boiling water until tender, 7 to 10 minutes. Drain.

Prepare very hot fire in barbecue grill. Position grill rack 4 inches above fire. Season pork with salt and pepper; brush lightly with oil. Grill until crisp on outside but very rare inside, about 5 minutes per side. Cool on platter. Brush onions with oil. Grill until charred, about 8 minutes per side. Cool on platter. Remove bones from pork and reserve. Cut pork and onions into ½-inch dice. Set aside.

Heat ½ cup oil in heavy large Dutch oven over medium-high heat until very hot. Whisk in flour. Immediately reduce heat to medium. Whisk until roux is deep brown, about 15 minutes. Cool roux completely.

Combine paprika, chili powder, minced garlic, filé powder and jalapeño in small bowl. Bring stock, tomatoes and ancho chilies to simmer in saucepan. Place roux over low heat; whisk in spices. Cook 8 minutes, stirring frequently. Whisk in simmering stock 1 cup at a time. Add grilled onions and reserved pork bones. Increase heat and bring mixture to boil. Reduce heat and simmer 1 hour, skimming and stirring occasionally. Add blanched garlic and simmer until sauce thickens and coats spoon, stirring occasionally, about 30 minutes. Add pork and simmer until cooked through, about 10 minutes. Discard pork bones. Season chili with salt. Refrigerate overnight to blend flavors.

Reheat chili over medium-low heat. Serve hot with jonnycakes and rice.

***Thin Rhode Island Jonnycakes**

Makes about 25

2½ cups stone-ground cornmeal
½ teaspoon salt
¾ cup cold water
1½ cups milk

Vegetable oil

Combine cornmeal and salt in large bowl. Gradually add water, stirring until smooth. Mix in milk. Let batter stand for 30 minutes.

Generously grease griddle or heavy large skillet over medium heat. Add batter by 1½ tablespoons in batches (do not crowd) and cook until cakes are golden brown, about 2 minutes on each side. Drain on paper towels. Serve jonnycakes immediately.

Seafood

Baked Salmon with Lime, Jalapeño, Chive and Sour Cream Sauce

2 servings; can be doubled or tripled

1 ¾- to 1-pound salmon fillet
1 tablespoon fresh lime juice
1½ teaspoons butter, melted
Salt and freshly ground pepper

Sauce
1½ teaspoons butter
2 jalapeño chilies, seeded and cut julienne
⅓ cup sour cream
¾ teaspoon fresh lime juice
Salt and freshly ground white pepper

Snipped fresh chives
Lime wedges

Preheat oven to 500°F. Butter baking dish. Place salmon in dish skin side down. Mix lime juice and butter. Brush over salmon. Sprinkle with salt and pepper. Let stand 15 minutes. Bake until fish is almost opaque, about 9 minutes per inch of thickness.

Meanwhile, prepare sauce: Melt butter in heavy small saucepan over medium-low heat. Add chilies and cook until tender, stirring occasionally, about 3 minutes. Add sour cream and stir until heated through; do not boil. Mix in lime juice. Add salt and white pepper.

Transfer fish to platter. Spoon sauce over. Sprinkle generously with chives. Garnish with lime wedges.

Salmon Navajo with Orange Essence Butter Sauce

6 servings

3 navel oranges
2 tablespoons grenadine

3 cups water
1¾ cups dry white wine
½ medium onion, sliced
½ medium carrot, sliced
½ medium celery stalk, sliced
2 parsley sprigs
1 bay leaf
1 teaspoon Sonoran Seasoning*

¾ cup fresh orange juice
2 large shallots, chopped

6 6- to 7-ounce salmon fillets, skinned and boned

¼ cup whipping cream
1 cup (2 sticks) well-chilled unsalted butter, cut into 16 pieces
1 tablespoon fresh lemon juice
Salt and freshly ground white pepper

1 large avocado, cut into 18 slices

Grate orange peel (colored part only). Mix peel and grenadine in small bowl. Remove white pith from oranges. Cut between membranes to separate sections. Set orange sections aside.

Combine water, 1 cup wine, onion, carrot, celery, parsley, bay leaf and seasoning in medium saucepan and simmer 20 minutes. Strain and set aside; this is court bouillon. *(Can be prepared 2 days ahead. Cool, cover and refrigerate.)*

Combine remaining ¾ cup wine, orange juice and shallots in heavy medium saucepan and boil until reduced by ⅓, about 20 minutes.

Arrange salmon in deep skillet. Add enough court bouillon just to cover. Bring to simmer. Poach fish until opaque, adjusting heat so poaching liquid barely shakes, about 10 to 15 minutes.

Add cream to shallot reduction and bring to boil. Remove from heat. Whisk in 2 tablespoons butter. Return to low heat and whisk in remaining butter 1 piece at a time, removing pan from heat if drops of melted butter appear. Season sauce with lemon juice, salt and freshly ground white pepper.

Transfer salmon to plates using slotted spatula. Arrange 3 orange sections and 3 avocado slices atop each fillet. Spoon sauce over. Sprinkle with peel.

*Sonoran Seasoning

This distinctive spice blend is good on grilled seafood, meats and poultry.

Makes about 1 cup

1 tablespoon pure chili powder
6 tablespoons plus 1½ teaspoons salt
4½ teaspoons black peppercorns
4 teaspoons cumin seeds
4 teaspoons granulated garlic
1 tablespoon chamomile*
1 tablespoon granulated onion
1½ teaspoons paprika
¾ teaspoon white peppercorns
1 star anise point*
¼ teaspoon (scant) dried orange bits*
¼ teaspoon (scant) dried orange blossoms*
Pinch of cinnamon

Preheat oven to 250°F. Spread chili powder on small baking pan. Bake until beginning to darken, 5 to 7 minutes. Combine with all remaining ingredients in blender. Grind finely, about 1 minute. Store in jar.

*Available at specialty shops and natural foods stores. If orange bits and dried orange blossoms are unavailable, substitute ¼ teaspoon orange spice tea.

Broiled Shark with Aïoli and Bell Peppers

4 servings

1 medium green bell pepper
1 medium red bell pepper

1½ pounds 1-inch-thick shark fillet, cut into 4 pieces, rinsed and patted dry

Salt and freshly ground pepper
4 teaspoons olive oil

½ cup Basic Aïoli or jalapeño aïoli (see page 87), room temperature

Preheat broiler. Broil peppers about 2 inches from heat source until skins are charred and blistered, turning often, about 15 minutes. Transfer to plastic bag; let stand 10 minutes. Peel peppers. Halve and core. Rinse if necessary; pat dry. Slice halves lengthwise into ⅜-inch-wide strips.

Position broiler rack 4 inches from heat source. Season shark with salt and pepper. Brush with oil. Broil 3 minutes. Turn fish over and broil until knife inserted in center comes out hot to touch and fish is just opaque, about 3 minutes.

Reserve 8 red and 4 green pepper strips for garnish. Arrange remaining pepper strips over fish in single layer. Spoon aïoli over pepper strips and gently spread to edge of fish. Broil just until aïoli browns, watching carefully, about 30 seconds. Garnish fish with reserved pepper strips and serve.

Monkfish with Saffron and Spinach

4 servings

1 1-pound monkfish fillet
½ teaspoon salt

Saffron Sauce
1 tablespoon butter
1 garlic clove, minced
5 anchovies
2½ cups whipping cream
¼ teaspoon saffron threads, crushed

Sifted all purpose flour
6 tablespoons clarified butter

12 ounces spinach, stemmed
Freshly ground pepper
½ pound tomatoes, peeled, seeded and coarsely chopped
1 teaspoon Sherry vinegar

Holding sharp knife almost parallel to work surface, cut monkfish into 12 thin, broad slices. Sprinkle salt on both sides. Arrange on large pan. Refrigerate for 1½ hours.

For sauce: Melt 1 tablespoon butter in heavy medium saucepan over medium-high heat. Add garlic and anchovies and stir 2 minutes. Add cream and saffron. Bring to boil. Adjust heat so liquid barely shimmers and cook until sauce is reduced to 1½ cups, stirring occasionally, about 1½ hours.

Pat fish dry. Score edges of each slice with ¼-inch cuts. Dust with flour. Heat clarified butter in heavy large skillet over high heat. Cook fish in batches (do not crowd) until just opaque, about 1 minute on each side.

Meanwhile, sprinkle spinach with salt and pepper. Steam until just wilted. Bring tomatoes and vinegar to boil in heavy small saucepan.

Bring sauce to boil. Strain through fine sieve. Spoon onto plates. Arrange 3 spinach nests on each plate. Arrange 1 fish slice atop each nest. Garnish each with ¼ teaspoon tomato mixture. Serve immediately.

Red Snapper Hot Pot

To finish this dish, use a traditional Chinese clay or metal pot or casserole. Uncover it at the table to reveal the bubbling, savory stew.

3 to 4 servings

- **1 pound fresh red snapper or rock cod fillets, skinned, boned and cut into 1½-inch squares**
- **1 tablespoon cornstarch**
- **½ egg white**
- **½ teaspoon salt**
- **¼ teaspoon finely ground white pepper**

- **1¼ teaspoon fermented black beans***
- **1½ teaspoons water**
- **3 tablespoons water**
- **4 teaspoons oyster sauce***
- **1 teaspoon dark soy sauce**
- **1 teaspoon cornstarch**
- **¾ teaspoon sugar**
- **½ teaspoon oriental sesame oil**
- **½ large onion, thinly sliced**
- **1 tablespoon minced garlic**
- **1 teaspoon finely chopped fresh ginger**
- **1 teaspoon coarsely chopped seeded hot chili**

- **2 cups vegetable oil (for deep frying)**
- **8 ounces Chinese long beans,* trimmed and cut into 1-inch pieces or 8 ounces green beans, trimmed, cut into 1-inch pieces and halved lengthwise**
- **⅛ teaspoon salt**
- **2 medium firm tomatoes, stemmed and cut into 8 wedges each**

Pat fish dry. Mix with 1 tablespoon cornstarch, egg white, ½ teaspoon salt and white pepper in medium bowl. Refrigerate for 1½ hours.

Soak black beans in lukewarm water to cover 30 minutes. Drain. Rinse and drain well. Puree in mortar with pestle. Mix in 1½ teaspoons water. Mix 3 tablespoons water, oyster sauce, soy sauce, 1 teaspoon cornstarch, sugar and sesame oil in small bowl. Combine onion, garlic, ginger and hot chili in another small bowl.

Heat vegetable oil in wok or heavy 2-quart saucepan over high heat until smoking. Add fish in batches (do not crowd) and cook 30 seconds on each side. Drain on paper towels. Drain oil. Wipe wok clean and return 4½ teaspoons oil. Heat over high heat 1 minute. Add green beans and ⅛ teaspoon salt. Stir until crisp-tender, 2 to 3 minutes. Add onion mixture and stir 15 seconds. Add black beans and stir 1 minute. Add fish and stir 10 seconds. Add oyster sauce mixture and tomatoes. Stir gently 1 minute. Transfer to 2-quart Chinese pot or 7- to 8-cup casserole. Cover and cook over high heat 8 minutes, stirring occasionally and reducing heat if fish begins to stick.

*Available at oriental markets.

Hickory-barbecued Shrimp

An easy-to-prepare entrée for summer parties. Guests shell their own shrimp and dip them in a garlic sauce.

6 servings

- **1 cup (2 sticks) butter**
- **3 bunches green onions (white part and 2 inches of green part), chopped**
- **12 medium garlic cloves, chopped**
- **1¾ cups dry white wine**
- **2 tablespoons plus 1 teaspoon fresh lemon juice**
- **Freshly ground pepper**
- **36 large shrimp in shell, legs removed**
- **1 cup minced fresh parsley**
- **8 2-inch hickory chunks, soaked in water 15 minutes and drained**

- **Hot pepper sauce**
- **Salt**

- **Lemon and lime wedges**
- **2 tablespoons minced fresh parsley**
- **2 tablespoons minced green onions**
- **2 tablespoons snipped fresh chives**

Melt butter in heavy Dutch oven over medium-low heat. Add 3 bunches green onions and garlic and stir 3 minutes. Add wine and simmer 15 minutes. Remove from heat and stir in lemon juice and generous amount of pepper. Cool. Cut shrimp down back and remove vein; do not peel. Add shrimp and 1 cup parsley to butter mixture. Refrigerate 6 hours or overnight, turning occasionally.

Prepare barbecue grill. When coals are gray, add hickory chunks and let heat until wood smokes, about 15 minutes.

Meanwhile, remove shrimp from marinade. Heat marinade in heavy medium saucepan. Strain and return to pan. Cook over medium-high heat until reduced by half, about 5 to 10 minutes. Add hot pepper sauce and salt to taste. Cover sauce and keep warm.

Place shrimp on grill rack and cook until just opaque, turning once, about 5 minutes. Mound shrimp on platter. Garnish with lemon and lime wedges. Pour sauce into ramekins or serving bowls; sprinkle with minced parsley, green onions and chives. Serve shrimp and dipping sauce immediately.

Jade Prawns

Oriental beer or a fruity rosé would be a delightful beverage choice here. Cooking the prawns in the shell retains their flavor and moisture.

4 servings

2 tablespoons olive oil
1½ pounds uncooked prawns, trimmed, rinsed and patted dry
3 tablespoons minced fresh basil
3 tablespoons minced green onion
2 tablespoons minced cilantro
1½ tablespoons minced fresh Italian parsley
1½ tablespoons minced garlic
1 tablespoon whole bean sauce*
Salt and freshly ground pepper

Heat oil in wok or heavy large skillet over medium-high heat. Add prawns and stir-fry until shells turn pink. Add next 6 ingredients and stir-fry 3 minutes. Season with salt and pepper. Serve prawns immediately.

*Also frequently called brown bean sauce. Available at oriental markets.

Scallop Packets with Sun-dried Tomatoes

Accompany with rice or pasta—spinach fettuccine is especially attractive—for soaking up the delicious tarragon- and dill-scented sauce.

4 servings

2 tablespoons fresh dill
2 tablespoons fresh tarragon leaves
2 medium shallots (1 ounce total)
¼ cup (½ stick) well-chilled unsalted butter, cut into 4 pieces

½ cup whipping cream
6 sun-dried tomatoes,* cut into ⅛-inch-thick julienne
1 teaspoon fresh lime juice
⅛ teaspoon salt
Freshly ground pepper

1½ pounds sea scallops, halved horizontally
4 fresh tarragon or dill sprigs

Place 2 tablespoons dill and 2 tablespoons tarragon in processor work bowl. With machine running, drop shallots through feed tube and mince. With machine running, drop butter pieces through feed tube and blend until smooth, stopping to scrape down sides of work bowl, 1 to 2 minutes.

Transfer butter mixture to heavy small nonaluminum saucepan. Cook over low heat until shallots are soft, about 5 minutes. Stir in cream, tomatoes, lime juice, salt and pepper. Increase heat and simmer until reduced to ⅔ cup, stirring frequently, about 5 minutes. Taste and adjust seasoning.

Position rack in center of oven and preheat to 500°F. Cut four 15-inch squares of heavy-duty foil. Spoon 1 tablespoon sauce in 4-inch circle in center of each. Arrange scallops in circle atop sauce, overlapping slightly. Season lightly with salt and pepper. Spoon 1 tablespoon sauce over. Top each with tarragon or dill sprig. Bring 2 opposite sides of foil up and double-fold to form packet. Double-fold ends to seal tightly. *(Can be prepared 1 day ahead and refrigerated.)* Arrange packets on baking sheet. Bake until scallops are just opaque, about 8 minutes. Place 1 packet on each plate and serve.

*If using sun-dried tomatoes packed in oil, drain well; pat dry with paper towels.

Clams and Bluefish with Sweet Garlic Pasta

Mussels and sea bass work just as well in this entrée.

4 servings

3 tablespoons olive oil
2 bay leaves
1 medium onion, finely diced
2 teaspoons minced garlic
½ cup fish stock or clam juice
¼ cup dry white wine
½ cup minced fresh parsley
2 teaspoons snipped fresh chives
2 teaspoons minced fresh basil
24 littleneck clams, scrubbed
4 5-ounce bluefish fillets, trimmed
Salt and freshly ground pepper

Sweet Garlic Pasta*

½ cup (1 stick) unsalted butter, cut into 8 pieces

Heat oil in heavy large saucepan over medium heat. Add bay leaves and stir until browned. Remove leaves. Add onion and garlic and cook until lightly browned, stirring frequently, about 5 minutes. Add stock and wine and bring to boil. Reduce heat to simmer. Stir in herbs. Add clams. Cover and simmer until clams open. Remove clams from saucepan; reserve liquid.

Preheat broiler. Pat bluefish dry. Season with salt and pepper. Broil as close to heat source as possible until fish is browned, 3 to 4 minutes per side.

Meanwhile, cook pasta in large amount of boiling salted water until just tender but still firm to bite. Drain.

To serve, mound pasta on platter. Top with bluefish. Surround pasta and bluefish with clams. Reheat clam cooking liquid over low heat. Whisk in butter 1 piece at a time. Spoon sauce over pasta.

*Sweet Garlic Pasta

Makes 2 pounds

1 whole head garlic
Olive oil
6 eggs
1 teaspoon salt

4 cups semolina flour

Preheat oven to 300°F. Sprinkle garlic with oil. Wrap loosely in foil. Bake until tender, about 1 hour. Cool to room temperature. Squeeze pulp from skin. Puree garlic pulp in processor.

Mound flour on work surface. Make well in center. Add garlic puree, eggs and salt to well and blend with fork. Gradually draw flour from inner edge of well into center until all flour is incorporated. Knead dough into smooth ball. Wrap in plastic and let stand at room temperature 30 minutes.

Cut dough in half. Flatten 1 piece of dough (keep remainder covered), then fold in thirds. Turn pasta machine to widest setting and run dough through several times until smooth and velvety, folding before each run and dusting with flour if sticky. Adjust machine to next narrower setting. Run dough through machine without folding. Repeat narrowing rollers after each run until pasta is 1/16 inch thick, dusting with flour as necessary. Hang dough sheet on drying rack or place on kitchen towels. Repeat with remaining dough. Set aside until sheets look leathery and edges begin to curl, 10 to 30 minutes, depending on dampness of dough. *Pasta must be cut at this point or dough will be too brittle.*

Run sheets through fettuccine blades of pasta machine (or cut by hand) into ¼-inch-wide strips. Arrange pasta on kitchen towel, overlapping as little as possible, until ready to cook.

Portuguese Mussel Stew

Offer crusty bread with this one-dish meal to soak up the savory broth.

6 servings

- **6 ounces smoked hard sausage such as summer sausage or Polish cabanassi**
- **1 medium red bell pepper, cored and seeded**
- **1 medium green bell pepper, cored and seeded**
- **1 medium yellow bell pepper, cored and seeded**
- **1 medium yellow onion**
- **1 small zucchini**
- **1 small yellow crookneck squash**
- **3 cups fish stock or clam juice**
- **¾ cup white Port**
- **5 pounds New Zealand Green Lip mussels or standard mussels, scrubbed and debearded**
- **1 large tomato, peeled, seeded and cut into ½-inch cubes**
- **½ cup julienne of pitted Kalamata olives**
- **Salt and freshly ground pepper**
- **2 tablespoons minced fresh parsley**

Cut sausage, peppers, onion, zucchini and crookneck squash into 2x⅛-inch julienne. Set mixture aside.

Bring stock and Port to boil in large pot. Add mussels, julienne of sausage and vegetables, tomato and olives. Cover and boil just until mussels open, about 10 minutes. Discard any mussels that do not open. Season stew with salt and pepper. Sprinkle with parsley and serve immediately.

Eggs, Cheese and Sandwiches

Fresh Corn, Brie and Jalapeño Frittata

Place cheese in the freezer briefly to facilitate peeling and cutting. Recipe can be doubled; use a 12-inch skillet.

2 servings

- **1 tablespoon butter**
- **½ cup minced onion**
- **¾ cup fresh corn kernels (cut from 1 large ear of corn) or frozen, thawed**
- **2 jalapeño chilies, seeded and finely chopped**
- **5 eggs**
- **6 ounces Brie cheese, peeled and finely diced**
- **Salt and freshly ground pepper**
- **2 tablespoons (¼ stick) butter**
- **6 fresh basil leaves, shredded**

Melt 1 tablespoon butter in heavy small skillet over medium-low heat. Add onion and stir 3 minutes. Add corn and jalapeños and cook until corn is tender, stirring occasionally, about 5 minutes. Cool slightly.

Beat eggs lightly in medium bowl to blend. Stir in corn mixture, cheese, salt and pepper. Melt 2 tablespoons butter in heavy 9-inch ovenproof skillet over medium heat. Add egg mixture. Pierce holes in eggs and lift up edges with spatula, tipping pan to allow uncooked egg to flow under until edge forms, about 1 minute; do not stir. Reduce heat to low. Cover skillet and continue cooking until eggs are almost set, about 5 minutes.

Meanwhile, preheat broiler. Uncover skillet and broil frittata until eggs are set and top is golden brown, watching carefully. Garnish with basil.

Pork Sandwiches with Wilted Red Cabbage and Horseradish Butter

Makes 12 open-face sandwiches

1 pound cooked pork tenderloin, trimmed

Red Cabbage
½ small head red cabbage (8 ounces), cored, cut into wedges to fit feed tube
½ small tart apple (3 ounces), unpeeled, cored and halved
1 1-ounce piece red onion
4½ teaspoons red wine vinegar
1½ teaspoons firmly packed light brown sugar
⅛ teaspoon salt
⅛ teaspoon cinnamon
Freshly ground pepper

Horseradish Butter
2 tablespoons prepared horseradish, well drained
2 teaspoons Dijon mustard
¼ cup (½ stick) well-chillled unsalted butter, cut into 4 pieces

12 slices Buttermilk Rye Bread (see page 19)

Line baking sheet with waxed paper. Cut pork into 3-inch pieces. Set pork on prepared sheet. Freeze until just firm but still easily pierced with tip of sharp knife. *(Can be prepared 1 month ahead. Wrap tightly and return to freezer. Let thaw in refrigerator just until easily pierced with sharp knife.)*

For cabbage: Insert ultra thick slicer blade in processor. Stand cabbage in feed tube and slice using firm pressure. Add to medium pot of boiling salted water and cook until tender, about 4 minutes. Drain well. Transfer to large bowl. Carefully remove slicer blade and insert fine shredder.

Shred apple and onion using firm pressure. Add to cabbage. Immediately mix in vinegar, sugar, salt, cinnamon and pepper. Adjust seasoning. *(Can be prepared 3 days ahead, covered and refrigerated. Bring to room temperature before using.)*

Slice pork in processor using firm pressure. Remove from work bowl.

For horseradish butter: Insert steel knife. Place horseradish and mustard in work bowl. With machine running, drop butter pieces through feed tube and blend until smooth, stopping as necessary to scrape down sides of bowl.

Spread 1½ teaspoons horseradish butter on each bread slice. Cover with 2 generous teaspoons cabbage mixture, spreading evenly. Top with 3 to 4 pork slices, overlapping slightly. Spoon about 2 teaspoons cabbage mixture in center of each. *(Can be prepared 6 hours ahead, covered and refrigerated. Bring sandwiches to room temperature before serving.)*

Danish Blue Cheese, Salami and Radish Sandwiches

Makes 12 open-face sandwiches

4 large radishes, trimmed, bottoms cut flat
1 cup parsley leaves
2 ounces Danish blue cheese
2 ounces cream cheese, room temperature
1 medium green onion including green top, cut into 1-inch pieces
6 tablespoons (¾ stick) unsalted butter, room temperature
12 slices Buttermilk Rye Bread (see page 19)
6 ounces hard salami
12 small parsley sprigs

Insert ultra thin slicer blade in processor. Slice radishes using firm pressure. Remove from bowl. Carefully remove blade and insert steel knife.

Mince parsley leaves in processor. Transfer to large square of waxed paper. Process both cheeses and green onion until smooth, stopping as necessary to scrape down sides of bowl.

Spread 1½ teaspoons butter evenly on top and sides of each bread slice. Dip sides in parsley. Spread about 2 teaspoons cheese mixture on top of each sandwich. Cut salami into 18 paper-thin slices, then cut each slice into quarters. Place 6 salami quarters down center of each sandwich, overlapping and alternating geometrically. Arrange 6 radish slices in rosette atop salami. Place parsley sprig in center. *(Can be prepared 6 days ahead, covered and refrigerated. Bring sandwiches to room temperature before serving.)*

Prosciutto, Provolone and Roasted Red Bell Pepper Sandwich

6 to 8 servings

2 medium red bell peppers

½ cup loosely packed fresh basil leaves
1 ounce Parmesan cheese, preferably imported
1 medium garlic clove
¼ teaspoon salt
3 tablespoons olive oil, preferably extra-virgin
3 tablespoons safflower oil
1 tablespoon red wine vinegar

1 16-inch loaf Italian or French bread
8 ounces thinly sliced prosciutto
5 ounces thinly sliced provolone cheese

Char bell peppers over gas flame or in broiler until blackened on all sides. Transfer to paper bag and let stand 10 minutes to steam. Peel; rinse under cold water and pat dry. Cut bell peppers lengthwise into 4 pieces each, discarding cores and seeds.

Combine basil, Parmesan, garlic and salt in work bowl and mince finely with steel knife. Add both oils and vinegar and blend 5 seconds. Remove from bowl.

Halve bread lengthwise. Hollow out bread, leaving 1-inch shell. Brush inside with basil oil. Layer prosciutto and provolone in bottom half. Arrange bell pepper pieces over. Cover with top half of bread and press together lightly. *(Can be prepared 2 hours ahead, wrapped tightly and refrigerated. Bring to room temperature before serving.)*

Cut loaf diagonally into 1½-inch slices. Arrange on platter cut side up. Serve sandwich immediately.

Pita Pockets with Parsley and Chick-Pea Salad

24 servings

8 cups chopped fresh parsley (about 4 bunches)
4 15½-ounce cans chick-peas (garbanzo beans), drained
2 large green bell peppers, chopped
2 large tomatoes, peeled, seeded and diced
4 green onions, chopped
½ cup fresh lemon juice
2 garlic cloves, minced
Salt and freshly ground pepper
1 cup olive oil
24 mini pita breads or 12 standard pita breads, halved

Combine parsley, chick-peas, bell peppers, tomatoes and onions in large bowl. Blend lemon juice, garlic and salt and pepper in another bowl. Whisk in olive oil in thin stream. Toss with vegetable mixture. *(Can be prepared 1 day ahead and refrigerated.)* Divide mixture among pita breads.

5 Vegetables and Side Dishes

What do you serve to go with a trendy, new-wave grill? Or to complement a traditional roast? In this chapter of tempting dishes you'll find plenty of variety and flavorful ideas.

Vegetables are getting more interesting every year. They're quick, incredibly versatile and at the top of the healthy-foods list. To go with a roast, make our caraway-scented Brussels Sprouts and Chestnuts (page 71) or a quickly prepared potato pancake speckled with rosemary (page 75). For a change, try Baked Spaghetti Squash with Two Cheeses (page 76), heady with garlic, parsley and goat cheese. Some of these vegetables, like the Chard, Zucchini, Onion and Turnip Torte in Whole Wheat Crust (page 72), are hearty enough to make a meal in themselves.

Pasta is also being showcased. Inexpensive, easy to prepare and good with practically everything, it offers the bonus of being a good source of essential complex carbohydrates. The health aspects aside, who could resist such specialties as Linguine with Spinach, Cucumbers and Scallops (page 80) or delicate Crabmeat Ravioli with Herb Oil (page 80)?

Black beans, wild rice, cracked wheat and cornmeal add texture and an all-American appeal to dinnertime, too. Some of the best examples from last year include Wild Rice with Shiitake Mushrooms (page 82), Cracked Wheat and Winter Squash Pilaf (page 82) and the unusual Cornmeal, Green Onion and Ginger Waffles (page 83).

Vegetables

Three-Vegetable Puree

6 servings

2 cups chopped peeled pumpkin
1 24-ounce head cauliflower, separated into florets
1 11-ounce bunch broccoli, florets separated, stems peeled and cut into 1-inch pieces
¾ cup whipping cream
6 tablespoons (¾ stick) butter, melted
3 eggs
Freshly grated nutmeg
Salt and freshly ground pepper

Fresh watercress or parsley sprigs

Steam pumpkin until tender, about 15 minutes. Drain well. Steam cauliflower until tender, about 10 minutes. Drain well. Steam broccoli until tender, about 5 minutes. Drain well. Puree each vegetable separately in blender or processor with ¼ cup cream, 2 tablespoons butter and 1 egg. Season each puree with nutmeg, salt and pepper.

Preheat oven to 325°F. Butter six ¾-cup ramekins. Using spoon or small spatula, layer purees in ramekins, using ¼ cup puree for each layer and spreading evenly. Place ramekins in roasting pan. Add enough hot water to pan to come halfway up sides of ramekins. Cover ramekins with waxed paper. Bake until set, 30 to 45 minutes, adjusting oven temperature so water remains just below simmer. Remove ramekins from water bath. Run small knife around edge of each and invert purees onto plates. Garnish with watercress or parsley. Serve immediately.

Basic Vegetable Timbales

These delicate vegetable custards are easy to prepare and make elegant side dishes. For best results, puree the vegetables in the processor or in small batches in the blender with a few tablespoons of cream from the recipe. The puree can be made a day ahead and refrigerated.

4 to 5 servings

2 cups vegetable puree (see Variations)

⅔ cup whipping cream, room temperature

3 eggs, beaten to blend
1 teaspoon salt
¼ teaspoon freshly ground white pepper
¼ teaspoon freshly grated nutmeg

1 cup Dill Cream Sauce, Garlic Butter Sauce or Quick Cumin Hollandaise Sauce (optional) **(see page 86)**

Generously butter four 5-ounce ramekins or five 4- to 4½-ounce timbale molds. Generously butter piece of foil large enough to cover molds. Prepare vegetable puree (see Variations below).

Stir 2 cups vegetable puree in heavy medium saucepan over low heat until excess liquid is evaporated, about 5 minutes. Stir cream into puree. Increase heat and bring puree to boil. Reduce heat to medium and cook, stirring frequently, until cream is absorbed and puree is reduced to 2 cups, about 5 minutes. Transfer puree to medium bowl and cool 7 minutes.

Preheat oven to 375°F. Gradually whisk eggs into puree. Blend in 1 teaspoon salt, pepper and nutmeg. Spoon mixture into ramekins or molds. Tap ramekins on counter to pack mixture and avoid air pockets. Carefully smooth tops with small knife.

Set ramekins in roasting pan; transfer to oven. Add enough boiling water to pan to come halfway up sides of ramekins. Cover with prepared foil. Bake until timbales are firm to touch and tester inserted in centers comes out clean, adding more water to pan if necessary, 35 to 55 minutes, depending on vegetable used. *(Do not allow water to boil; add several tablespoons cold water to pan if necessary.)* Cool timbales in ramekins on rack 5 minutes. Carefully run thin knife around edge of 1 ramekin. Set plate over ramekin and invert. Tap bottom of ramekin and gently remove. Repeat with remaining ramekins. If serving with sauce, spoon 2 to 3 tablespoons around base of each timbale. Pass remaining sauce separately.

Variations

For asparagus timbales: Peel 3 pounds asparagus spears and cut into 2-inch pieces. Add to medium saucepan of boiling salted water and boil until very tender when pierced with tip of sharp knife, 3 to 5 minutes. Drain thoroughly. Return asparagus to dry saucepan and cook over very low heat, stirring and mashing with wooden spoon until excess liquid evaporates, about 7 minutes. Drain thoroughly in strainer, pressing to remove excess liquid. Puree in processor until very smooth.

For broccoli timbales: Cut florets from 2 pounds broccoli. Discard 2 inches of each stalk. Peel remaining stalks and cut into ½-inch slices. Add florets and sliced stalks to large saucepan of boiling salted water and boil until very tender when pierced with tip of sharp knife, about 8 minutes. Drain broccoli; rinse under cold water and drain thoroughly. Puree broccoli in processor until very smooth.

For carrot timbales: Peel 1½ pounds carrots. Cut into ½-inch slices. Transfer to medium saucepan. Add enough water to cover. Stir in pinch of salt. Bring to boil. Reduce heat to medium, cover and cook until carrots are very tender when pierced with tip of sharp knife, about 20 minutes. Drain thoroughly. Puree carrots in processor until very smooth.

For cauliflower timbales: Cut 2 pounds cauliflower into medium florets. Add to large saucepan of boiling salted water and boil until very tender when pierced with tip of sharp knife, about 8 minutes. Drain; rinse under cold water and drain thoroughly. Puree cauliflower in processor until very smooth.

For spinach timbales: Stem 4 pounds spinach. Add to very large saucepan of boiling salted water and boil until very tender, pushing leaves down into water often, about 3 minutes. Drain; rinse under cold water and drain thoroughly. Squeeze by handfuls until dry. Puree in processor until very smooth.

For winter squash timbales: Cut 2 pounds squash into 2x2x1-inch pieces. Add to large saucepan of boiling salted water and boil until very tender when pierced with tip of sharp knife, about 10 minutes. Drain; rinse under cold water. Cut off and discard skin. Return squash to dry saucepan and cook over very low heat until excess liquid evaporates, stirring and mashing with spoon, about 5 minutes. Drain thoroughly in strainer 15 minutes. Puree in processor until very smooth.

California-style Stuffed Peppers

4 servings

4 green bell peppers, tops cut off, cored and seeded

1 large carrot, peeled and grated
1¼ cups corn kernels
¼ cup chopped walnuts
¼ cup raisins
4 tablespoons (½ stick) butter, room temperature
3 tablespoons dry breadcrumbs
2 tablespoons unsalted shelled sunflower seeds
2 tablespoons grated onion
Salt and freshly ground pepper
2 tablespoons shredded cheddar cheese

Cook peppers in large saucepan of boiling water 5 minutes. Rinse under cold water; drain thoroughly.

Preheat oven to 350°F. Lightly butter 8-inch square ovenproof glass baking dish. Combine carrot, corn, walnuts, raisins, 2 tablespoons butter, 1 tablespoon breadcrumbs, sunflower seeds, onion, salt and pepper in large bowl and mix well. Arrange peppers in prepared dish. Divide mixture among peppers. Top each with cheese and remaining breadcrumbs. Dot with remaining butter. Bake until heated through, about 30 minutes. Serve immediately.

Orzo- and Feta-stuffed Tomatoes

24 servings

24 medium tomatoes
Salt

6 cups cooked orzo (3 cups uncooked)
12 ounces feta cheese, crumbled
1½ cups chopped Mediterranean olives
1½ cups pine nuts, toasted
1½ cups chopped green onions
¾ cup chopped fresh parsley
¾ cup olive oil
1½ teaspoons dried rosemary, crumbled
3 garlic cloves, minced
Fresh lemon juice
Freshly ground pepper

Cut ¼ inch of top off tomatoes. Scoop out pulp (reserve for another use). Sprinkle insides of tomatoes with salt. Turn over and drain 30 minutes.

Pat tomatoes dry. Mix orzo, cheese, olives, pine nuts, onions, parsley, olive oil, rosemary and garlic. Add lemon juice to taste. Season with pepper. Spoon mixture into tomatoes. Cover with plastic and chill until ready to serve. *(Stuffed tomatoes can be prepared 1 day ahead.)*

Stir-fried Red and Yellow Peppers

The vegetables for this colorful side dish can be cut up one day ahead and stored in the refrigerator.

12 servings

½ cup olive oil
3 large garlic cloves, crushed
2 pounds red bell peppers, cored and cut into 1-inch pieces
2 pounds yellow bell peppers, cored and cut into 1-inch pieces
1 2-ounce can flat anchovies, drained and minced
6 medium leeks (white part only), cut into 1-inch slices
20 ounces tomatoes, peeled, seeded and coarsely chopped
2 10-ounce packages frozen peas, thawed and drained
¼ cup (½ stick) butter
Salt and freshly ground pepper
Fresh parsley sprigs

Heat oil in wok or heavy large skillet over medium-high heat. Add garlic and stir until golden brown. Discard garlic using slotted spoon. Add peppers and anchovies to wok and stir-fry 2 minutes. Add leeks and stir until vegetables are crisp-tender, 8 to 10 minutes. Mix in tomatoes, peas and butter and stir until heated through. Transfer to platter using slotted spoon. Boil liquid until thick, about 5 minutes. Season with salt and pepper. Pour over vegetables. Top with parsley.

Brussels Sprouts and Chestnuts

8 servings

2 cups peeled fresh chestnuts*

2 cups brussels sprouts
1 cup Poultry Stock (see page 83)
1 cup whipping cream
2 tablespoons caraway seeds
1 tablespoon kümmel (caraway flavored liqueur) (optional)
¼ teaspoon freshly ground white pepper
Salt

Cut X in chestnuts. Simmer in water to cover 5 minutes. Remove chestnuts from water 4 at a time and peel.

Blanch brussels sprouts in boiling salted water until crisp-tender, about 8 minutes. Drain; rinse with cold water and drain. Combine chestnuts and stock in heavy large skillet. Simmer until chestnuts are tender, about 10 minutes. *(Can be prepared 1 day ahead. Cover brussels sprouts and chestnuts separately and refrigerate.)* Add cream and caraway seeds and simmer until liquid is reduced by half, about 5 minutes. Add brussels sprouts and stir until heated through. Add kümmel and pepper. Season with salt and serve.

*Canned peeled chestnuts can be substituted. Simmer in Poultry Stock to cover until tender, about 4 minutes.

Julienne of Carrots and Chayote with Olives

Peel the chayote squash first only if the skin is very tough and prickly.

8 servings

2 medium carrots, peeled

2 tablespoons (¼ stick) butter
1½ pounds chayote squash, cut into 3x⅛-inch julienne
1 teaspoon minced garlic
16 Nicoise olives, halved lengthwise and pitted
Salt and freshly ground pepper

Blanch carrots in boiling water until beginning to soften. Drain. Soak in ice water until cold. Drain well. Cut into 3x⅛-inch julienne strips.

Melt butter in heavy large skillet over medium heat. Add carrots, chayote and garlic and cook until vegetables are crisp-tender, stirring frequently, about 10 minutes. Mix in olives, salt and pepper. Serve immediately.

Steamed Cauliflower with Allemande Sauce and Vanilla

An interesting side dish that hints of nouvelle cuisine but is actually based on an age-old flavoring technique of using vanilla in savory dishes. Leave the head of cauliflower whole for a more spectacular presentation.

6 servings

3 tablespoons butter
3 tablespoons all purpose flour
2 cups chicken stock
2 egg yolks
½ cup whipping cream
2 tablespoons minced fresh parsley
2½ teaspoons vanilla
1 teaspoon fresh lemon juice
Salt and freshly ground pepper

1 2-pound head cauliflower, base trimmed

Melt butter in heavy medium saucepan over low heat. Add flour and stir 3 minutes. Whisk in stock. Increase heat and boil until thickened, stirring constantly, about 1 minute. Whisk yolks and cream in medium bowl. Slowly whisk in stock mixture. Return to saucepan and boil 1 minute, stirring constantly. Mix in parsley, vanilla, lemon juice, salt and pepper. *(Can be prepared 3 hours ahead. Press plastic wrap on surface. Reheat in top of double boiler over simmering water before using.)*

Meanwhile, steam cauliflower until crisp-tender, about 30 minutes. Arrange on heated platter. Cover cauliflower with some of sauce. Serve immediately, passing remaining sauce separately.

Chard, Zucchini, Onion and Turnip Torte in Whole Wheat Crust

6 servings

Crust

- **2¼ cups cake flour**
- **1¼ cups whole wheat flour**
- **1½ teaspoons salt**
- **¼ cup vegetable oil**
- **13 tablespoons cold water**

- **18 tablespoons (2¼ sticks) well-chilled unsalted butter**

Filling

- **4 tablespoons (½ stick) unsalted butter**
- **¾ pound turnips, peeled and thinly sliced**
- **Salt and freshly ground pepper**
- **4 garlic cloves, coarsely chopped**
- **1½ pounds Swiss chard, trimmed and sliced**
- **1 pound zucchini, thinly sliced**
- **1 large onion, thinly sliced**

- **3 tablespoons all purpose flour**
- **3 tablespoons minced fresh thyme**
- **1 egg, beaten to blend with ½ teaspoon water and pinch of salt (glaze)**

For crust: Combine flours and salt in bowl. Add oil and stir with fork to incorporate. Add water and stir with fork until soft dough forms; dough should be moist but not sticky. Cover and refrigerate dough 1 hour.

Set butter on lightly floured surface. Lightly flour top of butter. Pound with rolling pin until pliable but not too soft. Roll dough out on lightly floured surface to 18x8-inch rectangle. Spread butter over top ⅔ of dough, leaving ¼-inch border. Beginning with unbuttered third, fold dough over into 3 equal sections as for business letter, brushing off excess flour. Give dough quarter turn so it opens like a book. Roll again into 18x8-inch rectangle. Fold in thirds. (This is two turns.) Wrap dough tightly; refrigerate 1 hour. Give dough four more turns. Wrap and refrigerate until ready to use. *(Can be prepared 1 day ahead.)*

For filling: Melt 1 tablespoon butter in heavy large skillet over medium-high heat. Stir in turnips. Cover and cook until crisp-tender, stirring occasionally, about 5 minutes. Season with salt and pepper. Remove from skillet. Melt another tablespoon butter in same skillet over medium-high heat. Add garlic and stir to coat with butter. Add chard and cook until just wilted, stirring frequently, about 8 minutes. Season with salt and pepper. Remove from skillet. Melt another tablespoon butter in same skillet over medium-high heat. Add zucchini and cook until crisp-tender, stirring frequently, about 3 minutes. Season with salt and pepper. Remove from skillet. Melt remaining 1 tablespoon butter in same skillet over medium-high heat. Add onion and stir 3 minutes. Season with salt and freshly ground pepper.

To assemble: Preheat oven to 400°F. Roll ⅔ of dough out on lightly floured surface to thickness of about ⅛ inch. Fit dough into 9½-inch springform pan, allowing ⅛-inch overhang. Cover with ⅓ of chard. Sprinkle with 1 tablespoon flour and 1 tablespoon thyme. Season with salt and pepper. Continue layering with turnips, ⅓ of chard, 1 tablespoon flour, 1 tablespoon thyme, zucchini, onion, 1 tablespoon flour, 1 tablespoon thyme and remaining ⅓ of chard, seasoning with salt and pepper between each layer. Brush edge of dough with glaze. Roll out remaining ⅓ of dough to thickness of 1/16 inch. Drape dough over torte, pressing edges to seal. Trim and score edges. Roll scraps out on lightly floured surface. Cut out decorative shapes.

Brush torte with glaze. Arrange decorations atop torte. Brush with glaze. Using sharp knife, make 5 slits in center of torte to allow steam to escape. Bake 30 minutes. Cover loosely with foil and continue baking until golden brown, about 45 minutes. Let stand 30 minutes before serving.

Aunt Nicolassa's Corn Cazuela

A casserole named for the earthenware dish in which it is traditionally cooked. This one is lined with husks.

8 to 10 servings

12 ears corn, with husks

1 cup (2 sticks) butter, room temperature
¾ cup fine yellow cornmeal
¼ cup sugar
3 ounces cream cheese, room temperature

1 teaspoon salt
⅓ cup whipping cream
½ pound Monterey Jack cheese, grated
3 fresh Anaheim chilies, roasted, peeled, seeded and cut into 1-inch squares or strips

Remove husks from corn. Soak wide outer husks in boiling water until softened, about 15 minutes. Drain well. Line 9x13-inch baking dish with husks, overlapping if necessary and allowing excess to hang over sides.

Preheat oven to 375°F. Cut corn from cobs. Set aside 1 cup. Puree remainder in batches in processor. Beat butter in large mixer bowl until fluffy. Beat in cornmeal, sugar, cream cheese and salt. Stir in reserved corn and corn puree. Blend in cream. Pour half of corn mixture into prepared dish, smoothing top; do not spread to edges of husks. Cover with cheese and chilies. Pour in remaining mixture. Fold husks over to partially cover mixture. Cover with foil. Bake 1 hour. Uncover and let stand 20 minutes before serving; cazuela will firm as it cools.

Corn Terrine with Tomato and Red Bell Pepper Sauce

16 servings

14 ears young white or yellow corn, husked
4 tablespoons (½ stick) butter

2 large red bell peppers, seeded and coarsely chopped
2 medium leeks (white part only), coarsely chopped

6 tablespoons (¾ stick) butter
¼ cup all purpose flour
1½ cups half and half, scalded
2½ teaspoons salt or to taste
Freshly ground pepper
1 cup grated Gruyère cheese
6 eggs, beaten to blend

½ cup dry breadcrumbs
Tomato and Red Bell Pepper Sauce*
Fresh basil leaves

Cook corn in batches in large pot of boiling water 1 minute. Remove with tongs and plunge into bowl of ice water. Cut kernels off cobs. Using back of knife, scrape ears to remove remaining corn. Place 4 cups corn in heavy large skillet (reserve remainder for another use). Add 2 tablespoons butter. Cook over medium-low heat until corn is tender, stirring frequently, 3 to 5 minutes. Transfer to medium bowl.

Melt 1 tablespoon butter in clean skillet over medium-low heat. Add chopped bell peppers and cook until tender, stirring occasionally, about 10 minutes. Add to corn. Melt 1 tablespoon butter in same skillet over medium-low heat. Add leeks and cook until tender, stirring occasionally, about 6 minutes. Add to corn. Cool.

Melt 6 tablespoons butter in heavy medium saucepan and over medium-low heat. Add flour and stir 4 minutes. Cool 2 minutes. Whisk in hot half and half. Return to medium heat and simmer until thick, stirring constantly, about 5 minutes. Cool slightly. Add to corn with salt and pepper. *(Can be prepared 6 hours ahead. Cover tightly).* Mix in Gruyère and eggs.

Preheat oven to 325°F. Butter 9x5x3-inch loaf pan; coat generously with breadcrumbs. Spoon in corn mixture. Set loaf pan in roasting pan. Pour enough boiling water into roasting pan to come ⅔ up sides of loaf pan. Bake until terrine is firm to touch, about 1¾ hours. Cool 20 minutes. Invert terrine onto platter. Surround with sauce. Garnish with basil leaves.

***Tomato and Red Bell Pepper Sauce**

Also delicious over pasta.

Makes about 2⅔ cups

2 tablespoons (¼ stick) butter
4 large red bell peppers, seeded and cut into 1-inch pieces
2¾ pounds tomatoes, peeled, seeded and chopped
Salt and freshly ground pepper

Melt 1 tablespoon butter in heavy large skillet over medium-low heat. Add peppers and cook until tender, stirring occasionally, about 10 minutes. Transfer mixture to processor and puree until smooth. Return to skillet. Mix in tomatoes and remaining 1 tablespoon butter. Cook over medium heat until liquid evaporates and mixture mounds in spoon, stirring frequently, about 20 minutes. Season with salt and pepper. *(Can be prepared 1 day ahead and refrigerated. Reheat over low heat, stirring constantly.)*

Maui Onion Deep Dish

This is delicious with meat or chicken.

12 servings

1 cup plus 2 tablespoons rice (preferably Italian Arborio)

½ cup (1 stick) butter
3⅓ pounds Maui or yellow onions, coarsely chopped
1 cup plus 2 tablespoons shredded Swiss cheese
1 cup whipping cream
2 tablespoons minced fresh parsley
Salt and freshly ground white pepper
Paprika

Generously butter shallow 13x9-inch nonaluminum baking dish. Rinse rice thoroughly. Cook in large pot of boiling salted water 5 minutes. Drain well.

Melt butter in heavy large saucepan over medium-low heat. Add onions and cook until golden brown, stirring frequently, about 30 minutes. Mix in cheese and cream, then rice, parsley, salt and pepper. Turn mixture into prepared dish. Sprinkle with paprika. *(Can be prepared 1 day ahead. Cover baking dish and refrigerate. Bring to room temperature before continuing.)*

Preheat oven to 325°F. Bake onions until golden brown, about 1 hour.

Sauté of Peas, Shiitake Mushrooms and Prosciutto in Lettuce Cups

Serve as a light starter or a side dish. The filled lettuce cups can be picked up and eaten out of hand.

2 servings; can be doubled or tripled

3 large dried shiitake mushrooms
Boiling water

1 tablespoon butter
1 cup frozen baby peas
¼ cup slivered prosciutto or smoked ham (1½ ounces)
1 tablespoon minced fresh mint or 1 teaspoon dried, crumbled
1 teaspoon snipped fresh chives or minced green onion
½ teaspoon fresh lemon juice
Salt
4 large outer Boston lettuce leaves

Cover mushrooms with boiling water. Let soak until softened, about 20 minutes. Drain mushrooms; squeeze out water. Discard hard stems. Slice mushrooms thinly, then halve crosswise.

Melt butter in heavy medium skillet over medium heat. Add mushrooms and peas and stir 1 minute. Add prosciutto, mint and chives and stir until peas are heated through, about 2 minutes. Mix in lemon juice. Season with salt. Spoon mixture into lettuce leaves and serve immediately.

Rosemary Rösti

This is an easy version of the Swiss potato pancake.

2 to 4 servings

1¼ pounds baking potatoes, peeled and shredded
2 tablespoons (¼ stick) butter
2 tablespoons olive oil
2 teaspoons chopped fresh rosemary
Salt and freshly ground pepper
Fresh rosemary sprig

Pat potatoes dry with paper towels. Melt butter with oil in heavy 12-inch skillet over medium heat. Add potatoes to skillet and press to form cake. Sprinkle with chopped rosemary, salt and pepper. Cook until crisp, about 6 minutes per side. Garnish with rosemary sprig. Serve hot.

Risotto-stuffed Potatoes

6 servings

6 medium baking potatoes

3 cups Risotto Rapido*
½ cup freshly grated Parmesan cheese
3 egg yolks
½ teaspoon freshly ground pepper
All purpose flour
3 egg whites, beaten to blend
Fine dry breadcrumbs
Vegetable oil

Boil potatoes until tender, about 25 minutes. Peel, then halve lengthwise. Using small sharp knife, cut out and discard interior of each potato half, leaving ½-inch shell.

Mix risotto, Parmesan, yolks and pepper. Mound filling into six potato halves. Top with remaining potato halves, pressing to fit. Dredge in flour, shaking off excess. Dip in whites, allowing excess to drip back into bowl. Roll in breadcrumbs. Heat oil in deep fryer to 375°F. Fry potatoes in batches (do not crowd) until golden brown, 3 to 5 minutes. Remove using slotted spoon and drain on paper towels. *(Can be prepared several weeks in advance and frozen. Reheat 10 minutes in 350°F oven.)*

*Risotto Rapido

Makes about 4 cups

¼ cup (½ stick) butter
½ small onion, minced

5 cups very rich chicken stock (preferably homemade)
2 cups Arborio rice
Salt and freshly ground pepper

Melt butter in heavy large saucepan over low heat. Add onion and cook until softened, stirring occasionally, about 7 minutes; do not brown.

Meanwhile, bring stock to boil. Stir rice into onion. Stir in 2 cups stock. Cover and simmer until all liquid is absorbed, stirring occasionally. Stir in 2 more cups stock. Cover and simmer until liquid is absorbed, stirring occasionally. Add ½ cup stock and cook until absorbed, stirring occasionally. Add remaining ½ cup stock and cook until absorbed, stirring occasionally. Taste risotto. If rice is tender but just firm to bite, increase heat and boil, stirring constantly, until creamy. If too crunchy, stir in water in small amounts until grain is properly cooked. Season with salt and pepper. Let cool to room temperature before using.

Baked Spaghetti Squash with Two Cheeses

4 main-course or 8 side-dish servings

1 medium spaghetti squash (3 pounds)

1 cup fresh parsley leaves
2 medium garlic cloves

3 ounces mozzarella cheese, cut into 1-inch pieces
3 ounces soft goat cheese
¾ teaspoon salt
Freshly ground pepper

Bring large pot of salted water to boil. Add squash and cook until just tender, 20 to 25 minutes.* Drain well; cool. Halve lengthwise. Discard seeds and loose strings. Loosen spaghetti-like strands with fork and scrape out. Transfer to large bowl.

Position rack in center of oven and preheat to 350°F. Generously butter shallow 6-cup baking dish.

Place parsley in work bowl. With machine running, drop garlic through feed tube and process with steel knife until minced. Remove from work bowl.

Process both cheeses until smooth, stopping as necessary to scrape down sides of processor work bowl.

Stir parsley mixture, salt and pepper into squash. Transfer to prepared dish. Spoon cheese evenly over top. *(Can be prepared 2 days ahead, covered and refrigerated. Bring to room temperature and drain any liquid before baking.)* Bake until heated through, about 20 minutes.

Preheat broiler. Broil until cheese is lightly browned, 1 to 2 minutes, watching carefully. Serve immediately.

*Squash can also be cooked in microwave. Pierce with fork. Cook on High until just tender, about 15 minutes.

Zucchini and Yellow Squash Horseshoes

6 servings

3 medium zucchini
2 medium crookneck squash

3 tablespoons olive oil
1 large garlic clove, minced

1 large tomato, peeled, seeded and coarsely chopped
1 teaspoon dried oregano (preferably Mexican), crumbled
Salt and freshly ground pepper

Cut zucchini and squash into ¼-inch rounds. Cut out small triangular wedge from each round. Using melon baller, scoop out center from each zucchini and squash round, leaving shell (or use paring knife).

Heat oil in heavy large skillet over medium heat. Add garlic and stir 20 seconds. Add zucchini and squash and toss until almost tender, about 5 minutes. Add tomato and oregano and simmer 2 minutes. Season with salt and pepper. Serve immediately.

Sauté of Jerusalem Artichokes, Zucchini and Sweet Red Peppers

A pretty accompaniment to simple grilled meats.

6 servings

1¼ pounds small zucchini, trimmed and cut diagonally into ¼-inch-thick slices
1 pound Jerusalem artichokes, peeled and cut into ¼-inch-thick rounds

2 tablespoons (¼ stick) unsalted butter

2 tablespoons olive oil
2 medium red bell peppers, cut into 1-inch pieces
1 teaspoon dried thyme, crumbled
Salt

Cook zucchini in boiling salted water until just crisp-tender, about 2 minutes. Transfer to colander using slotted spoon. Add Jerusalem artichokes to water and boil until just tender, about 2 minutes. Drain in another colander. Pat vegetables dry.

Melt butter with oil in heavy large skillet over medium-high heat. Add bell peppers and cook until almost crisp-tender, stirring frequently, about 3 minutes. Add Jerusalem artichokes and stir 2 minutes. Add zucchini and stir until heated through, about 2 minutes. Season with thyme and salt. Serve vegetables in shallow bowl.

Pasta

Gourmet's Bucatini

If bucatini is unavailable, substitute spaghetti for this simple yet flavorful dish.

4 servings

- **2 Japanese eggplants**
- **3 tablespoons olive oil**
- **2 tablespoons (¼ stick) butter**
- **2 ounces pancetta* or bacon, thinly sliced**
- **2 large tomatoes, peeled, seeded and coarsely chopped**
- **1 small dried hot red chili**
- **¾ to 1 pound dried bucatini (hollow spaghetti-like pasta)**

Cut off peel and about ⅛ inch of pulp from eggplants. Reserve remaining pulp for another use. Cut peel into thin strips. Heat oil in heavy large skillet over medium heat. Add eggplant and cook until softened, stirring occasionally, about 5 minutes. Remove from skillet and pat dry. Melt butter in same skillet over medium heat. Add pancetta and fry 1 minute. Add eggplant, tomato and chili and cook until tomato liquid is absorbed, stirring occasionally, about 5 minutes.

Cook pasta in large pot of boiling water until just tender but still firm to bite. Drain well. Add pasta to skillet and stir to heat through.

*Dry-cured unsmoked bacon, available at Italian markets and specialty foods stores.

Pasta Shells with Sun-dried Tomatoes, Mushrooms and Goat Cheese

2 to 4 servings

- **¼ cup parsley leaves**
- **1 medium garlic clove**
- **12 large mushrooms, 2 opposite sides cut flat**
- **3 tablespoons olive oil (preferably extra-virgin)**
- **9 large sun-dried tomatoes* (1½ ounces total), cut into ⅛-inch-thick julienne**
- **½ teaspoon salt**
- **1 cup chicken stock**
- **8 large green onions, including green tops, cut into feed-tube lengths**
- **Freshly ground pepper**
- **6 ounces (about 3 cups) freshly cooked pasta shells**
- **1 tablespoon olive oil (preferably extra-virgin)**
- **4 ounces soft goat cheese (such as Montrachet), crumbled**

Place parsley in work bowl. With machine running, drop garlic through feed tube and mince using steel knife. Remove mixture from work bowl; set aside. Carefully remove steel knife and insert medium slicer.

Stand mushrooms on flat sides in feed tube and slice using light pressure. Heat 3 tablespoons oil in heavy 10-inch skillet over medium-high heat. Add mushrooms, tomatoes and salt. Cook until vegetables are soft, stirring occasionally, 4 to 6 minutes. Add stock and boil 2 minutes. Remove sauce from heat.

Stand green onions in feed tube and slice using light pressure. Add to sauce in skillet. Mix in pepper. Adjust seasoning. *(Can be prepared 2 days ahead, covered and refrigerated. Rewarm over low heat.)*

Toss pasta shells with 1 tablespoon oil and reserved parsley mixture in large bowl. Gently mix in cheese. Add sauce and toss well. Serve immediately.

*If using sun-dried tomatoes packed in oil, drain well and pat dry with paper towels.

Spicy Rice Noodles

4 to 6 servings

½ pound thin dry rice noodles*

3 tablespoons olive oil
3 dried hot red chilies, halved
2 tablespoons minced garlic
1 teaspoon minced fresh ginger
¼ pound red bell peppers, cored, seeded and cut julienne
2 tablespoons julienne of sun-dried tomatoes
½ pound zucchini, cut julienne
Salt and freshly ground pepper
1 cup basil leaves

Soak noodles in warm water until soft, about 30 minutes. Drain well.

Heat oil in heavy large skillet over medium heat. Add chilies, garlic and ginger and stir 3 minutes. Add bell peppers and sun-dried tomatoes and stir 2 minutes. Add noodles and zucchini and stir 5 minutes. Season with salt and pepper. Add basil leaves and stir until wilted. Serve immediately.

*Also called mai fun or rice sticks. Available at oriental markets.

Peppered Lemon Saffron Pasta with Onions and Dill

6 servings

¾ cup fresh lemon juice
2 tablespoons grated lemon peel
¼ teaspoon saffron threads, crushed

4 cups (or more) bread flour
4 eggs
4 tablespoons olive oil
3 tablespoons butter
36 pearl onions, blanched until tender, peeled
1 tablespoon minced fresh dill

Boil juice, peel and saffron until reduced by half. Cool completely.

Arrange 4 cups bread flour in mound on work surface or in large bowl. Make well in center. Add juice reduction, eggs and 1 tablespoon oil to well and blend with fork. Gradually draw flour from inner edge of well into center until all flour is incorporated. Knead dough on lightly floured surface until smooth, kneading in more flour if sticky. Wrap in plastic and let stand 2 hours.

Cut dough into 5 pieces. Flatten 1 piece of dough (keep remainder covered), then fold in thirds. Turn pasta machine to widest setting and run dough through several times until smooth and velvety, folding before each run and dusting with flour if sticky. Adjust machine to next narrower setting. Run dough through machine without folding. Repeat narrowing rollers after each run until pasta is 1/16 inch thick, dusting with flour if necessary. Hang dough sheet on drying rack or place on kitchen towels. Repeat with remaining dough. Set aside until sheets look leathery and edges begin to curl, 10 to 30 minutes, depending on dampness of dough. *Must be cut at this point or dough will be too brittle.*

Run sheets through fettuccine blades of pasta machine (or cut by hand into ¼-inch-wide strips). Arrange pasta on towel, overlapping as little as possible. Let dry until ready to cook. *(Can be prepared 1 week ahead. Let dry thoroughly. Wrap in plastic and refrigerate.)*

Melt butter with remaining 3 tablespoons oil in large skillet over medium heat. Add onions and heat through.

Meanwhile, cook pasta in large pot of boiling salted water until just tender but still firm to bite. Drain. Add to onions and toss. Garnish with dill.

Fettuccine and Mussels in Spicy Pecan Cilantro Butter

4 servings

- **32 mussels (2¼ pounds total), scrubbed and debearded**
- **1 teaspoon salt**
- **1 7-ounce red bell pepper**
- **1 cup pecans (4 ounces), toasted**
- **½ cup fresh cilantro leaves**
- **½ cup fresh parsley leaves**
- **1 large garlic clove**
- **1 jalapeño chili, stemmed**
- **½ cup (1 stick) well-chilled unsalted butter, cut into 8 pieces**
- **1 teaspoon fresh lime juice**
- **½ teaspoon salt**
- **6 ounces dried fettuccine, cooked al dente**

Combine mussels and 1 teaspoon salt in large saucepan. Add enough cold water to cover. Let soak 30 minutes. Drain. Rinse several times and drain. Rinse saucepan. Return mussels and liquid clinging to shells to saucepan. Cover and cook over high heat just until shells open, 5 to 7 minutes. Discard any mussels that do not open. Cool slightly. Remove mussels from shells; discard shells.

Char bell pepper over gas flame or in broiler until blackened on all sides. Transfer to paper bag and let stand 10 minutes to steam. Peel; rinse under cold water and pat dry. Cut lengthwise into 6 pieces, discarding core and seeds. Cut each bell pepper piece crosswise into ¼-inch-wide strips.

Chop pecans with steel knife in processor, using about 4 on/off turns, then process continuously until coarsely chopped, about 5 seconds. Remove from work bowl and set aside. Combine cilantro and parsley in work bowl. With machine running, drop garlic and chili through feed tube and mince. With machine running, drop butter pieces through feed tube and process until smooth, about 10 seconds, stopping as necessary to scrape down sides of work bowl. Add fresh lime juice and ½ teaspoon salt and blend 10 seconds.

Transfer butter mixture to heavy 12-inch skillet and melt over medium heat. Add fettuccine and mussels and toss to coat. Cook just until heated through, shaking skillet frequently to prevent sticking, about 6 minutes. Remove from heat. Mix in bell pepper and reserved nut. Adjust seasoning.

Linguine with Spinach, Cucumbers and Scallops

2 to 4 servings

4 large shallots
3 tablespoons unsalted butter
5 ounces frozen leaf spinach, thawed, drained and squeezed dry
1 teaspoon salt
1 English hothouse cucumber (1 pound), peeled, halved lengthwise, seeded and cut into feed-tube lengths
1 cup whipping cream
¼ teaspoon freshly grated nutmeg
¼ teaspoon dried red pepper flakes
8 ounces sea scallops, cut horizontally into thirds

6 ounces (about 3 cups) freshly cooked linguine
Minced or shredded Parmesan or Romano cheese (preferably imported)

With machine running, drop shallots through feed tube and mince with steel knife. Melt butter in heavy 12-inch skillet over medium heat. Add shallots and cook until beginning to soften, about 3 minutes. Add spinach and ½ teaspoon salt and cook until wilted, stirring frequently, about 2 minutes. Carefully remove steel knife and insert medium slicer.

Stand cucumber in feed tube and slice using medium pressure. Add to skillet and cook over medium heat until beginning to soften, about 2 minutes. Stir in cream, remaining ½ teaspoon salt, nutmeg and pepper flakes. Bring to boil. Reduce heat and simmer until sauce thickens, 5 to 6 minutes. Gently mix in scallops and cook until just opaque, about 30 seconds; do not overcook.

Toss linguine with scallop mixture in large bowl. Divide among plates. Serve hot, passing Parmesan separately.

Crabmeat Ravioli with Herb Oil

8 first-course or 4 main-course servings

2 tablespoons (¼ stick) unsalted butter
½ medium onion, finely chopped
1 pound lump crabmeat
½ cup ricotta cheese
1 egg yolk
¼ cup coarsely chopped walnuts
2 tablespoons freshly grated Parmesan cheese
Salt and freshly ground pepper

1 pound freshly made pasta dough

2 quarts chicken or fish stock
Herb Oil*

Melt butter in heavy large skillet over medium heat. Add onion and cook until translucent, stirring occasionally, about 8 minutes. Mix in crab and stir until heated through. Remove from heat. Mix in ricotta, yolk, walnuts and Parmesan. Season with salt and pepper. Cool filling completely.

Roll pasta out to thickness of 1/32 inch. Cut into 4-inch squares. Brush edges with cold water. Place heaping tablespoon of crabmeat filling in center of each square. Fold squares in half, forming rectangles. Press edges firmly to seal. *(Can be prepared 4 hours ahead. Arrange on baking sheet lined with floured kitchen towel. Cover with another kitchen towel and refrigerate.)*

Bring stock to boil in large pot. Season with salt. Gently drop in pasta. Reduce heat and simmer until pasta is just tender but still firm to bite, about 8 minutes. Drain pasta well. Heat Herb Oil in heavy large skillet until just warm. Add pasta and toss until coated.

***Herb Oil**

Makes about 1½ cups

2 cups packed watercress leaves
1 cup packed Italian parsley leaves
12 spinach leaves, stemmed
4 fresh sage leaves
2 tarragon sprigs, stemmed
⅔ cup extra-virgin olive oil
3 shallots, minced
2 garlic cloves, minced

Blanch watercress, parsley, spinach, sage and tarragon in large saucepan of boiling water until limp, about 1 minute. Drain, reserving liquid. Rinse herbs under cold water; drain well (do not squeeze dry). Puree herbs to smooth paste in blender, adding 1 tablespoon cooking liquid if necessary. Heat oil until just warm in heavy large skillet. Add shallots and garlic and stir 1 minute. Add herb paste and stir until just heated through. *(Can be prepared 1 day ahead and refrigerated.)*

Beans, Grains and Savory Pastries

Baked Black Beans

Plan ahead for this dish, as it takes ten hours to bake. It can cook overnight, however, or be prepared up to three days in advance.

12 servings

2 pounds dried black beans* or pinto beans, rinsed and sorted
12 cups water
2 onions, chopped
2 garlic cloves, minced
1½ teaspoons cumin seed
1 teaspoon salt or to taste
1 teaspoon freshly ground pepper
Chopped fresh cilantro or parsley

Preheat oven to 275°F. Combine all ingredients except cilantro in heavy 5-quart casserole. Cover and bake until water is absorbed and beans are tender, stirring occasionally, about 10 hours. Garnish with cilantro.

*Available at Latin American markets.

Saffron Rice with Chorizo

4 to 6 servings

¼ teaspoon saffron threads, crushed
1 tablespoon warm water
2 tablespoons (¼ stick) butter
1 small onion, finely chopped
¼ cup diced Spanish chorizo or Portuguese linguica sausage
1¼ cups long-grain rice
2 cups cold water
Salt and freshly ground pepper

¼ cup shelled fresh peas (4 ounces with pods), blanched 3 minutes or ¼ cup frozen peas, thawed
1 tablespoon olive oil

Dissolve saffron in 1 tablespoon warm water. Melt butter in heavy medium skillet over medium heat. Add onion and cook until beginning to soften, stirring occasionally, about 3 minutes. Add chorizo and stir 3 minutes. Add rice and stir to coat with butter. Mix in saffron, 2 cups water, salt and pepper. Bring to boil. Reduce heat to low, cover and cook until liquid is absorbed, about 13 minutes.

Mix peas into rice. Remove from heat, cover with kitchen towel and then lid. Let stand 20 minutes. Mix in oil.

Wild Rice with Shiitake Mushrooms

The earthy taste of the mushrooms is especially delicious with wild rice.

6 servings

- **3 cups water**
- **1 cup wild rice**
- **½ teaspoon salt**
- **5 tablespoons butter**
- **½ pound fresh shiitake mushrooms, stems trimmed**
- **Salt and freshly ground pepper**

Bring water, rice and ½ teaspoon salt to boil in heavy medium saucepan. Reduce heat to low, cover and cook 45 minutes. Drain well. Transfer rice to medium-size baking dish. Mix in 2 tablespoons butter. Set aside.

Preheat oven to 250°F. Melt remaining 3 tablespoons butter in heavy large skillet over high heat. Add mushrooms and stir until tender, about 4 minutes. Mix into rice. Season with salt and pepper. Cover and bake 20 minutes to blend flavors. Serve hot.

Couscous Salad Wrapped in Lettuce Leaves

16 servings

- **4 cups rich chicken stock**
- **4 cups medium-grain quick-cooking couscous**
- **¼ cup olive oil**
- **1 pound Kalamata olives, pitted and chopped**
- **4 carrots, peeled, coarsely grated**
- **2 cups minced fresh parsley**
- **1 cup olive oil**
- **12 green onions, chopped (including some of green tops)**
- **½ cup fresh lemon juice**
- **2 tablespoons oriental sesame oil**
- **Salt and freshly ground pepper**
- **Lettuce leaves**

Bring stock to boil in heavy large saucepan. Remove from heat. Stir in couscous and ¼ cup olive oil. Cover and let stand 5 minutes.

Transfer couscous to large bowl. Add remaining ingredients except lettuce. Toss well. Taste and adjust seasoning. Refrigerate until ready to serve.

Arrange lettuce on platter. Mound couscous on lettuce. Serve, enclosing salad in lettuce leaves as for tacos.

Cracked Wheat and Winter Squash Pilaf

2 servings; can be doubled or tripled

- **1½ tablespoons butter**
- **½ medium onion, chopped**
- **1 cup ⅜-inch-thick pieces peeled butternut squash**
- **½ cup bulgur wheat**
- **2 whole cloves**
- **1 2-inch rosemary sprig**
- **1 2-inch cinnamon stick**
- **1 bay leaf**
- **1 cup chicken broth**
- **Salt and freshly ground pepper**

Melt butter in heavy small saucepan over medium heat. Add onion and squash and cook until onion begins to soften, stirring frequently, about 5 minutes. Add bulgur, cloves, rosemary, cinnamon and bay leaf and stir until bulgur is golden brown, about 3 minutes. Stir in broth, salt and pepper. Cover and bring to boil. Reduce heat to low and cook 15 minutes. Discard cloves, rosemary, cinnamon and bay leaf. Fluff pilaf with fork. Serve hot.

Pumpkin and Wild Mushroom Stuffing

Makes about 8 cups

6 cups ½- to ¾-inch cubes Pumpkin Wheat Bread (see page 22)

1 cup peeled and diced parsley root (about 8 medium)
1 cup (2 sticks) unsalted butter
2 cups diced red onion
2 cups sliced fresh wild mushrooms (such as chanterelles, shiitake and/or porcini)
2 tablespoons minced fresh rosemary
2 tablespoons minced fresh tarragon
2 tablespoons snipped fresh chives
2 tablespoons minced fresh parsley
2 teaspoons salt
1 teaspoon freshly ground pepper
6 tablespoons (about) Poultry Stock*

Spread bread cubes on baking sheet. Let stand overnight to dry.

Butter 2-quart baking dish. Blanch parsley root in boiling water until just tender, about 2 minutes. Drain. Melt butter in heavy large skillet over medium heat. Add onion and cook until tender, stirring occasionally, about 8 minutes. Add mushrooms and cook until golden brown, stirring occasionally, about 6 minutes. Mix in parsley root, herbs, salt and pepper. Transfer to large bowl. Mix in bread cubes. Add enough stock to moisten. Transfer to prepared dish. Cover with foil, shiny side down. *(Can be prepared 1 day ahead and refrigerated.)*

Preheat oven to 375°F. Bake stuffing, covered, until hot, about 40 minutes.

*Poultry Stock

Makes about 10 cups

16 cups (or more) water
4 pounds poultry bones (combination of turkey necks and chicken bones)
Giblets from turkey
2 large onions, diced
2 large carrots, diced
2 bunches parsley stems
2 bay leaves
2 teaspoons whole black peppercorns

Combine 16 cups water with bones and giblets in large saucepan. Bring to simmer, skimming surface occasionally. Add remaining ingredients and simmer 5 hours, adding more water if necessary to keep ingredients covered. Strain. *(Can be prepared ahead. Refrigerate up to 3 days or freeze 1 month.)*

Cornmeal, Green Onion and Ginger Waffles

Terrific with Honey-Glazed Squabs (see page 44) or any other roasted poultry.

Makes 8 to 10 waffles

1 cup water
½ cup cornmeal
1 teaspoon salt

¾ cup milk
½ cup all purpose unbleached flour
½ cup (1 stick) unsalted butter, melted
3 tablespoons minced green onion
2 teaspoons minced fresh ginger
2 teaspoons oriental sesame oil
1 teaspoon baking powder
1 egg yolk
2 egg whites, room temperature

Bring water to boil in heavy small saucepan. Stir in cornmeal and salt and boil until thick, about 5 minutes. Cool mixture completely.

Preheat waffle iron. Blend milk, flour, butter, onion, ginger, oil, baking powder and yolk in processor to paste. Mix in cornmeal. Transfer to large bowl. Beat whites until stiff but not dry. Gently fold into cornmeal mixture. Spoon into hot waffle iron in batches. Cook until golden brown.

Tarts of Tomato and Zucchini with Goat Cheese and Pesto

4 servings

4 5x5-inch squares prepared puff pastry
2 tablespoons goat cheese (preferably imported)
2 tablespoons prepared pesto
1 small zucchini, cut into 12 slices
1 medium tomato, cut into 12 wedges
Freshly grated Parmesan cheese
Olive oil

Preheat oven to 400°F. Fold in ¼ inch of pastry around edge of each square to make raised border. Blend goat cheese and pesto. Spread 1 tablespoon in each pastry square. Arrange zucchini and tomato atop goat cheese mixture. Sprinkle with Parmesan and drizzle with olive oil. Bake until zucchini is tender and pastry is golden brown, about 30 minutes. Serve immediately.

6 Sauces and Condiments

You didn't find many heavy or complicated sauces coming out of the kitchen in 1986. But sauces, particularly spicy ones, are gaining new importance, becoming more refined and highlighting everything from simple veal chops to elegant vegetable timbales.

Here we offer a variety of versatile sauces and condiments, such as Garlic Butter Sauce (page 87), which is especially good with asparagus, spinach or cauliflower timbales. For a change, serve the Marsala-accented Cranberry Puree (page 88) with the holiday turkey this Thanksgiving. And make plenty of our classic Plum and Apple Butter (page 88) to spread on morning toast.

Apple-Horseradish Sauce

Serve this zesty sauce with boiled beef and other meat or game dishes.

Makes about 1½ cups

3 large Granny Smith apples, peeled, cored and thinly sliced
3 tablespoons water
2 tablespoons fresh lemon juice
2 tablespoons sugar
2 to 3 tablespoons well-drained prepared horseradish
1 teaspoon unsalted butter

Combine apples, water, lemon juice and sugar in heavy large saucepan. Cover and simmer 30 minutes, stirring occasionally. Uncover, reduce heat to low and cook until most of liquid is evaporated, about 15 minutes. Mix in horseradish and butter. Cool. *(Can be prepared 1 day ahead and refrigerated.)* Serve at room temperature.

Dill Cream Sauce

This sauce is particularly nice with asparagus, broccoli, carrot or winter squash timbales.

Makes about 1 cup

¼ cup dry white wine
2 dill sprigs
2 medium shallots, minced
1 cup unsalted chicken stock
1¼ cups whipping cream
Salt and freshly ground pepper
2 tablespoons snipped fresh dill

Combine wine, dill sprigs and shallots in heavy medium saucepan. Bring to boil. Add stock and return to boil. Reduce heat to medium-high and cook until liquid is reduced to 2 tablespoons, stirring frequently. Stir in cream. Season with salt and pepper. Bring to boil, stirring frequently. Reduce heat to medium and cook until sauce is thick enough to coat spoon, stirring frequently, about 7 minutes. Strain sauce. *(Can be prepared 1 day ahead, covered and refrigerated. To reheat, whisk over low heat until hot.)* Stir in dill. Adjust seasoning. Serve hot.

Quick Cumin Hollandaise Sauce

Serve this flavorful sauce with broccoli, cauliflower or spinach timbales.

Makes about 1 cup

3 egg yolks, room temperature
3 teaspoons strained fresh lemon juice
1 teaspoon ground cumin
Salt
¾ cup (1½ sticks) unsalted butter
1 tablespoon hot water
Cayenne pepper

Blend yolks, 2 teaspoons lemon juice, cumin and salt in processor or blender until light in color. Melt butter in heavy small saucepan over medium-high heat until butter is sizzling hot. With machine running, add 2 to 3 tablespoons hot butter to yolk mixture through feed tube, drop by drop. Add remaining butter in thin stream. Add hot water and mix briefly. Blend in remaining 1 teaspoon lemon juice and cayenne. Adjust seasoning. Serve immediately or keep warm 15 minutes in hot water bath or several hours in vacuum bottle. *If hollandaise sauce becomes too thick, thin with warm water, whisking in 1 teaspoon at a time.*

Garlic Butter Sauce

Especially good with asparagus, broccoli, cauliflower or spinach timbales.

Makes about 1 cup

⅓ cup dry white wine
2 tablespoons white wine vinegar
2 large garlic cloves
2 medium shallots, minced
2 tablespoons whipping cream
Salt and freshly ground white pepper
1 cup (2 sticks) well-chilled unsalted butter, cut into 16 pieces

Cook wine, vinegar, garlic and shallots in heavy small saucepan over medium heat until reduced to 2 tablespoons. Reduce heat to low. Add cream and simmer until mixture is reduced to 3 tablespoons, whisking frequently. *(Can be prepared 3 hours ahead and set aside at room temperature. Return mixture to simmer before continuing.)* Season with salt and pepper. Add 2 pieces of butter and whisk until almost melted. Add remaining butter 2 pieces at a time, whisking well after each addition. *(If at any time sauce becomes too hot and drops of melted butter appear on surface, immediately remove from heat, add 2 pieces chilled butter and whisk until warm. Return to low heat and whisk in remaining butter.)* Remove from heat immediately after last butter addition. Strain sauce. Adjust seasoning. Serve immediately or keep warm 15 minutes in hot water bath or 3 hours in vacuum bottle.

Basic Aïoli

This classic sauce can be prepared three days ahead, covered and refrigerated.

Makes about 1½ cups

6 medium garlic cloves, halved
2 egg yolks, room temperature
1½ cups extra-virgin olive oil, room temperature
2 tablespoons fresh lemon juice
Pinch of salt
Freshly ground pepper
3 teaspoons (about) lukewarm water

Food processor method: With machine running, drop garlic through feed tube and mince. Add yolks, 1 tablespoon oil, 1 tablespoon lemon juice, salt and pepper and blend, stopping to scrape down bottom and sides of work bowl. With machine running, slowly pour remaining oil through feed tube in slow, steady stream. Gradually add remaining lemon juice. Add enough lukewarm water 1 teaspoon at a time to thin to desired consistency. Adjust seasoning. Set sauce aside at room temperature 15 minutes before serving.

Mixer method: Chop garlic to puree. Blend garlic, yolks, 1 tablespoon lemon juice, salt and pepper in small bowl of electric mixer. Gradually beat in oil 1 drop at a time until sauce has thickened slightly. With mixer running, add remaining oil in slow steady stream. Gradually add remaining 1 tablespoon lemon juice. Add enough lukewarm water 1 teaspoon at a time to thin to desired consistency. Adjust seasoning. Set sauce aside at room temperature 15 minutes before serving.

Whisk method: Chop garlic to puree. Whisk garlic, yolks, 1 tablespoon juice, salt and pepper in heavy medium bowl to blend. Set bowl atop towel. Gradually whisk in oil 1 drop at a time until sauce has thickened slightly. Slowly whisk in 8 tablespoons oil in slow steady stream. Whisk in 1 teaspoon lemon juice. Slowly whisk in remaining oil in slow steady stream. Gradually add remaining 2 teaspoons lemon juice. Whisk in enough lukewarm water 1 teaspoon at a time to thin to desired consistency. Adjust seasoning. Set sauce aside at room temperature 15 minutes before serving.

Variations

Cilantro: Add 3 to 4 tablespoons chopped cilantro to finished sauce.

Basil or parsley: Add 5 tablespoons chopped fresh herb to finished sauce.

Jalapeño: Seed and mince 1 jalapeño chili. Add chili to garlic mixture before blending in olive oil.

Spinach: Boil 1 bunch stemmed spinach 1 minute. Drain; rinse under cold water and drain again. Squeeze spinach dry. Puree in processor or blender. Mix into finished aïoli sauce.

Roasted red pepper: Broil 3 medium red bell peppers about 2 inches from heat until skins are charred and blistered, turning often, about 15 minutes. Transfer to plastic bag; let stand 10 minutes. Peel peppers. Halve and core. Rinse if necessary; pat dry. Puree peppers in processor or blender. Blend puree into aïoli in three batches.

Cranberry Puree

8 servings

- **2 pounds cranberries**
- **4 cups sugar**
- **¾ cup Marsala**
- **½ cup Grand Marnier**
- **¼ cup bitters**

Cook cranberries and sugar in heavy medium saucepan over medium heat until cranberries are very soft, stirring occasionally, about 30 minutes. Puree mixture in blender with half of Marsala. Strain into medium bowl, pressing to extract as much fruit as possible. Whisk in remaining Marsala, Grand Marnier and bitters. Cover and refrigerate overnight. *(Can be prepared 5 days ahead.)* Serve well chilled.

Plum and Apple Butter

A wonderful use of late summer fruit.

Makes 3 pints

- **2 pounds slightly underripe red plums, quartered (do not peel)**
- **2 pounds Jonathan or McIntosh apples, quartered (do not peel)**
- **2 cups unsweetened, unfiltered apple juice**
- **2 cups sugar**
- **2 teaspoons cinnamon**
- **4½ teaspoons vanilla**

Combine plums, apples and apple juice in heavy nonaluminum saucepan. Bring to boil over medium heat. Reduce heat, cover partially and simmer 25 minutes, stirring occasionally. Uncover and cook until apples are very tender, stirring occasionally, 20 to 30 minutes. Cool slightly.

Force fruit mixture through food mill fitted with medium blade, discarding peel and seeds. Return puree to pan. Stir in sugar and cinnamon. Bring to boil over medium heat, stirring constantly. Reduce heat and simmer briskly until butter is thick and glossy, stirring frequently, about 40 minutes. Remove from heat and stir in vanilla. Spoon hot butter into hot jars.* Cool, cover and refrigerate. *(Can be stored in refrigerator up to 3 weeks.)*

*Can also be canned, processed in water bath 15 minutes and kept for 1 year.

Left to right: Romaine Lettuce Leaves Stuffed with Warm Rice and Vegetable Salad; Chard, Zucchini, Onion and Turnip Torte in Whole Wheat Crust; Calvados Ice Cream with Apple Calvados Compote

Irwin Horowitz

Left to right: Spicy Rice Noodles; Honey-glazed Squabs offered on Cornmeal, Green Onion and Ginger Waffles; Jade Prawns

Clockwise from top: Grapefruit and Pomegranate Tart; Grilled Comice Pears with Persimmon-White Chocolate Sauce; Chartreuse and Mint Chocolate Truffles; Pumpkin Ice Cream with Caramel Pecan Sauce

Irwin Horowitz

Corn Terrine with Tomato and Red Bell Pepper Sauce

Paul Elson

Rudi Legname

Clockwise from top: Chicken Chiricahua with Zucchini and Yellow Squash Horseshoes; Calamari and Greens with Lemon Vinaigrette; Kahlua-Milk Chocolate Cheesecake

Paul Elson

Chocolate Tortillas with Raspberries, Cream and Hot Fudge Sauce

Peach Dumplings

Brian Leatart

Victor Scocozza

Left to right: Frozen Chocolate Nougat Cream; Honey Cluster Pyramid; Raisin Nut Tartletts

7 ❦ Desserts

Despite a firmly established national passion for fitness and healthy eating, it seems the equally firm national devotion to desserts—the richer the better—shows no sign of fading.

Chocolate is still one of America's most beloved foods, as you can see in such confections as Reverse Chocolate Chip Ice Cream (page 95), White Chocolate and Macadamia Nut Parfait (page 97), Kahlúa-Milk Chocolate Cheesecake (page 103), and Chartreuse and Mint Chocolate Truffles (page 114).

The return of homey, old-fashioned desserts was an important aspect of 1986, and you'll see delicious new twists on many classics, such as baked apples (page 90) stuffed with pecans, brown sugar and applejack; tender Peach Dumplings (page 90) served atop a delicate orange-flavored custard sauce; and a crunchy Blueberry Buckle (page 92) topped with a cinnamon-bourbon sauce.

Of course, you'll still find the elegant, showstopping desserts for which *Bon Appétit* is famous, such as the Acropolis (page 99), an inspired construction of praline mousse and meringue; sensational Apricot Orange Pavé, topped with buttercream and chopped roasted pistachios (page 104); and luscious, mousse-filled Chocolate Butterscotch Torte (page 111), crowned with whipped cream and chocolate and butterscotch leaves.

One final food trend worthy of note, evident in recipes throughout this book but especially in this chapter of desserts, is a spirit of fun and invention. Where else would we find such delights as trompe l'oeil White Chocolate Ravioli (page 112), served with a rich hazelnut sauce, or Chocolate Tortillas with Raspberries, Cream and Hot Fudge Sauce (page 113)? These dishes are as much a delight to the eye as the palate, a playful celebration of the totally serious art of creating good food.

Fruit Desserts, Custards and Puddings

Baked Stuffed Apples with Brown Sugar and Applejack

Bake two extra apples and serve in the morning with yogurt for breakfast.

2 servings; can be doubled or tripled

2 tablespoons diced dried pears
2 tablespoons chopped toasted pecans
1 tablespoon firmly packed light brown sugar
¼ teaspoon grated lemon peel
Pinch of ground mace
2 large Golden Delicious or Rome Beauty apples

1 tablespoon butter, cut into small pieces
2 tablespoons firmly packed light brown sugar
½ cup applejack or apple cider

Whipping cream

Preheat oven to 375°F. Combine first 5 ingredients in small bowl. Core each apple without cutting through base; enlarge opening slightly. Peel top half of each apple. Press pear mixture into centers. Place apples in baking dish just large enough to accommodate. Dot with butter. Sprinkle with remaining 2 tablespoons brown sugar. Pour applejack over. Bake until apples are tender, basting every 15 minutes with pan juices, about 50 minutes.

Transfer apples to plates. Pour cooking juices into small saucepan and boil until reduced to thick syrup, about 2 minutes. Spoon over apples. Serve hot or warm, pouring cream over top.

Peach Dumplings

6 servings

Spiced Syrup
1½ cups sugar
1½ cups water
¼ teaspoon cinnamon
¼ teaspoon freshly grated nutmeg
3 tablespoons unsalted butter

Dumplings
6 medium peaches (unpeeled), cut into ⅜-inch-thick slices
⅓ cup sugar
Pinch of cinnamon

2 cups all purpose flour
2 teaspoons baking powder
¼ teaspoon salt
⅔ cup well-chilled unsalted butter
½ cup milk

6 tablespoons (¾ stick) unsalted butter
Sugar
Orange Custard Sauce*

For syrup: Cook first 4 ingredients in heavy medium saucepan over low heat, swirling pan occasionally, until sugar dissolves. Increase heat and boil until reduced to 1½ cups. Remove from heat and mix in butter.

For dumplings: Preheat oven to 375°F. Combine peaches, ⅓ cup sugar and cinnamon in large bowl. Mix flour, baking powder and salt in large bowl. Cut in ⅔ cup butter until coarse meal forms. Add milk to bowl and mix with fork until dough just holds together.

Gently roll dough out on lightly floured surface to 18x12-inch rectangle. Cut into six 6-inch squares. Mound ⅔ cup peach mixture in center of each pastry square. Fold corners of each pastry toward center, forming square package; pinch to seal. Arrange in 11x7-inch baking pan, spacing about 1 inch apart. Pour syrup around sides of dumplings. Dot each with 1 tablespoon butter. Sprinkle lightly with sugar. Bake until dumplings are golden brown, about 35 minutes. Cool slightly. Spoon sauce onto plates. Top with dumplings and serve warm.

***Orange Custard Sauce**

Makes about 2 cups

- **4 egg yolks, room temperature**
- **½ cup sugar**
- **1 cup whipping cream**
- **⅓ cup milk**
- **¼ cup fresh orange juice**
- **1 tablespoon grated orange peel**

Whisk yolks and sugar in medium bowl to blend. Scald cream with milk in heavy medium saucepan. Gradually whisk into yolks. Mix in orange juice and orange peel. Transfer to top of double boiler set over simmering water. Whisk until custard is well thickened and leaves path on back of spoon when finger is drawn across, about 15 minutes. Cool. Refrigerate until well chilled. *(Can be prepared 1 day ahead.)*

Grilled Comice Pears with Persimmon-White Chocolate Sauce

8 servings

- **¾ cup persimmon puree (from about 3 large peeled ripe persimmons)**
- **6 tablespoons fresh lemon juice**
- **¼ cup sugar**
- **5 egg yolks**
- **1 cup half and half**
- **5 ounces imported white chocolate, finely chopped**
- **¼ cup whipping cream**
- **4 large Comice pears, peeled, halved and cored**
- **1 lemon**
- **¼ cup shelled unsalted pistachios, skinned and chopped**

Combine persimmon puree, lemon juice and sugar in heavy medium saucepan. Simmer 5 minutes. Remove from heat. Whisk in yolks and half and half. Stir over medium-low heat until mixture thickens and leaves path on back of spoon when finger is drawn across, about 10 minutes; *do not boil.* Remove from heat. Add chocolate and stir until melted. Stir in whipping cream. Refrigerate until well chilled. *(Can be prepared 1 day ahead.)*

Preheat broiler. Cut pears lengthwise into ¼-inch-thick slices, without cutting through narrow ends. Squeeze lemon juice over. Arrange pears on baking sheet. *(Can be assembled 2 hours ahead. Cover tightly and refrigerate.)* Broil until heated through, about 3 minutes. Spoon sauce onto plates. Fan pears across sauce. Sprinkle with nuts.

Lemon Sorbet with Vodka-marinated Plums

2 servings; can be doubled or tripled

- **4 ripe sweet plums, pitted and sliced**
- **¼ cup vodka**
- **2 tablespoons (or more) sugar**
- **Lemon sorbet**

Combine plums, vodka and 2 tablespoons sugar in medium bowl. Taste and add more sugar if desired. Marinate at room temperature 1 hour.

Scoop sorbet into glasses. Top with plums and marinade and serve.

Blueberry Buckle with Cinnamon-Bourbon Sauce

6 to 8 servings

2 pints fresh blueberries
Sugar

1 cup (2 sticks) unsalted butter, room temperature
⅓ cup sugar
1 egg, beaten to blend
2 cups all purpose flour
2 teaspoons baking soda
1 cup buttermilk
1 cup all purpose flour
½ cup sugar
½ cup firmly packed dark brown sugar
½ cup chopped toasted pecans
½ cup (1 stick) unsalted butter, cut into small pieces
½ teaspoon freshly grated nutmeg
¼ teaspoon ground ginger

Sauce
½ cup (1 stick) unsalted butter
⅔ cup sugar
2 eggs
½ teaspoon cinnamon
1 tablespoon very hot water
½ cup whipping cream
½ cup bourbon

Combine berries with sugar to taste.

Preheat oven to 350°F. Butter and flour 8-inch square baking dish. Using electric mixer, cream 1 cup butter and ⅓ cup sugar until light and fluffy. Beat in egg. Sift together 2 cups flour and baking soda. Stir dry ingredients and buttermilk alternately into creamed mixture. Spread batter in prepared dish. Cover with berries. Mix next 7 ingredients until crumbly. Sprinkle over berries. Bake until top is browned and cake is firm, about 1 hour.

For sauce: Melt butter in double boiler over gently simmering water. Beat sugar, eggs and cinnamon in small bowl to blend. Stir mixture into butter. Add hot water and stir until mixture coats back of spoon, about 7 minutes. Remove from over water. Let cool to room temperature. Stir cream and bourbon into sauce.

To serve, cut cake into squares. Place squares on plates. Spoon sauce over.

Sweet Potato Flan

This dessert can also be cooked in a round cake pan.

6 to 8 servings

2 pounds dark orange sweet potatoes (yams)

2 cups sugar
2 cups water

2 cups whipping cream
6 eggs, room temperature
1⅓ cups firmly packed golden brown sugar
3 tablespoons dark rum
3 tablespoons brandy
1 tablespoon grated fresh ginger
2 teaspoons vanilla
1 teaspoon salt
½ teaspoon cinnamon
¼ teaspoon ground allspice
¼ teaspoon ground cloves

Preheat oven to 325°F. Bake sweet potatoes until very soft, about 1½ hours. Peel sweet potatoes. Puree in processor until smooth. Press puree through sieve to remove any lumps.

Heat 2 cups sugar and 1 cup water in heavy medium saucepan over low heat, swirling pan occasionally, until sugar dissolves. Increase heat and bring to boil, brushing down sides of pan with pastry brush dipped in cold water. Reduce heat to medium and boil until syrup caramelizes and turns deep golden brown, about 25 minutes. Immediately pour syrup into dry 2- to 3-quart glass loaf pan. Tip pan to coat bottom and sides evenly. Return excess caramel to saucepan. Mix 1 cup water into saucepan. Bring caramel to boil, stirring until smooth syrup forms. Pour sauce into bowl.

Preheat oven to 325°F. Combine 2 cups sweet potato puree and all remaining ingredients in large bowl. Mix until just blended; do not overmix. Spoon into caramelized pan. Place loaf pan in baking pan. Add enough boiling water to come ⅔ way up sides of loaf pan. Bake until center of custard is firm when pan is jiggled, removing pan immediately if custard begins to puff, 1½ to 2 hours depending on size of pan. Refrigerate at least 6 hours. *(Can be prepared 2 days ahead.)* Run knife around edge of pan. Invert Flan onto platter. Cut into slices to serve. Pass caramel sauce separately.

Bread Pudding Soufflé with Whiskey Sauce

8 servings

Soufflé

6 eggs, separated, room temperature
½ cup sugar
2½ cups Bread Pudding*
½ cup powdered sugar

Whiskey Sauce

2¼ cups water
1 cup sugar
1 tablespoon butter
Pinch of cinnamon
½ teaspoon cornstarch
1 tablespoon bourbon

For soufflé: Preheat oven to 375°F. Butter 2-quart soufflé dish; sprinkle with sugar. Whisk yolks and ½ cup sugar in double boiler over gently simmering water until thick and pale. Stir mixture into pudding. Using electric mixer, beat whites to soft peaks. Gradually add powdered sugar and beat until stiff but not dry. Gently fold whites into pudding mixture. Spoon into prepared dish. Bake until pudding is puffed and golden, 35 to 40 minutes.

Meanwhile, prepare sauce: Cook 2 cups water, sugar, butter and cinnamon in heavy small saucepan until sugar dissolves, swirling pan occasionally. Bring to boil. Dissolve cornstarch in remaining water. Add to pan and cook until sauce is reduced to 1 cup, stirring frequently, about 30 minutes. Remove from heat; blend in bourbon.

Serve soufflé immediately with sauce.

*Bread Pudding

8 servings

5 eggs
2 cups whipping cream
1 cup sugar
½ cup (1 stick) butter, melted
⅓ cup raisins
1 tablespoon vanilla
Pinch of cinnamon
12 1-inch-thick slices French bread

Preheat oven to 350°F. Lightly grease 9-inch square baking dish. Blend all ingredients except bread in large bowl. Pour mixture into prepared dish. Arrange bread in single layer in egg mixture. Let soak 5 minutes. Turn bread over. Let soak 10 minutes. Push bread down into custard. Set dish into roasting pan. Pour in enough simmering water to come within ½ inch of top of dish. Cover and bake until pudding is set but not firm, about 50 minutes. Uncover and bake until top is brown, about 10 minutes.

Mocha Armagnac Zabaglione

This dessert is also delicious served chilled.

2 servings; can be doubled or tripled

4 egg yolks, room temperature
3 tablespoons sugar
6 tablespoons Armagnac, Cognac or brandy
2 tablespoons cold brewed coffee
4 teaspoons grated bittersweet (not unsweetened) or semisweet chocolate

Using balloon whisk or electric mixer, beat yolks and sugar in large metal bowl until pale yellow. Set bowl over pan of gently simmering water. Gradually beat in Armagnac and coffee. Continue beating until mixture mounds softly, about 10 minutes. Divide between glass goblets. Top with chocolate and serve immediately.

Frozen Desserts

Mango and Boysenberry Sorbet Swirl

Makes about 1 quart of each

Mango Sorbet

1 cup sugar
1 cup water
3 cups mango pulp (from about 4 pounds mangoes)
1 cup fresh orange juice
6 tablespoons fresh lime juice

Boysenberry Sorbet

2 pints fresh or frozen, thawed unsweetened boysenberries
2 cups water
1 cup sugar
6 tablespoons fresh lemon juice
½ package liquid fruit pectin

For mango sorbet: Cook sugar and water in heavy small saucepan over low heat until sugar dissolves, swirling pan occasionally. Bring to boil. Let cool. Pour into blender or processor. Add remaining ingredients and puree. Strain to remove fibers. Refrigerate at least 30 minutes, or overnight.

Transfer mixture to ice cream maker and process according to manufacturer's instructions. Spoon into container. Freeze until ready to serve. *(Sorbet can be prepared 1 day ahead.)*

For boysenberry sorbet: Puree boysenberries with remaining ingredients in blender or processor (in batches if necessary). Refrigerate at least 30 minutes.

Transfer mixture to ice cream maker and process according to manufacturer's instructions. Spoon into container. Freeze until ready to serve. *(Sorbet can be prepared 1 day ahead.)*

Pack mango sorbet into half of standard ice cream scoop. Pack boysenberry sorbet into other half. Using knife, swirl sorbets. Release into dish. Serve immediately.

Apple, Walnut and Cognac Ice Cream

Makes 1½ quarts

2 eggs
1 cup sugar
2 Golden Delicious apples, peeled, cored and diced
2 cups whipping cream
⅜ cup chopped walnuts
⅓ cup Cognac, flambéed
Pinch of salt
1 cup milk

Whisk eggs in large bowl until frothy. Add sugar and whisk until thickened. Stir in apples, cream, walnuts, Cognac and salt. Pour in milk. Transfer to ice cream maker. Freeze according to manufacturer's instructions. Serve immediately.

Calvados Ice Cream with Apple Calvados Compote

6 servings

Ice Cream

1 tablespoon sugar
¼ cup Calvados

2 cups milk
1½ cups whipping cream
6 egg yolks
⅔ cup sugar

¼ teaspoon almond extract

Compote

1 tablespoon unsalted butter
2 pounds tart apples, peeled, cored and cut into 1-inch pieces
½ cup sugar
¼ cup Calvados
½ teaspoon vanilla

Additional Calvados (optional)

For ice cream: Stir 1 tablespoon sugar into Calvados. Let stand overnight.

Scald milk and cream in heavy large saucepan. Whisk yolks and ⅔ cup sugar in bowl until thick and pale. Whisk ⅓ of milk mixture into egg mixture. Whisk back into saucepan set over low heat and stir with wooden spoon until thick enough to coat back of spoon, about 15 minutes. Cool.

Stir Calvados and almond extract into custard. Refrigerate until well chilled.

Transfer Calvados custard mixture to ice cream maker and freeze according to manufacturer's instructions.

For compote: Melt butter in heavy medium skillet over medium-high heat. Add apples and sugar and cook until apples caramelize slightly, stirring frequently, about 15 minutes. Reduce heat to medium-low. Add ¼ cup Calvados and vanilla and cook until almost all liquid is absorbed.

To serve, top ice cream with compote. Drizzle with additional Calvados.

Reverse Chocolate Chip Ice Cream

This dark chocolate ice cream studded with white chocolate chips makes a delightful twist on an old favorite.

Makes about 5 cups

2½ cups milk
1 vanilla bean, split*

6 egg yolks, room temperature
½ cup sugar
½ cup unsweetened cocoa powder, sifted

1 cup whipping cream

½ pound white chocolate chips or finely chopped white chocolate, well chilled

Bring milk to boil in heavy large saucepan. Remove from heat. Add vanilla bean and let steep 10 minutes. Scrape vanilla seeds into milk.

Beat yolks and sugar until pale yellow and slowly dissolving ribbon forms when beaters are lifted. Slowly beat in hot milk. Return mixture to saucepan. Stir over low heat until mixture thickens and finger leaves path when drawn across spoon. *Do not boil or mixture will curdle.* Whisk in cocoa powder, then cream. Refrigerate until mixture is well chilled.

Process custard in ice cream maker according to manufacturer's instructions until beginning to set. Mix in white chocolate chips and process until set. Freeze in covered container 2 hours to mellow flavors. If frozen solid, soften slightly in refrigerator before serving.

*If unavailable, 1½ teaspoons vanilla extract can be substituted. Scald milk, then add to yolk mixture. Add vanilla to custard with cocoa powder and cream.

Pumpkin Ice Cream with Caramel Pecan Sauce

8 servings

Ice Cream

15 egg yolks
1 cup plus 2 tablespoons sugar
1 teaspoon vanilla
Pinch of salt
1 quart half and half
1 cup plus 2 tablespoons whipping cream
3½ cups canned solid pack pumpkin
½ cup pure maple syrup

Sauce

4 cups sugar
3 cups water
¼ cup fresh lemon juice
1 quart whipping cream

2 cups pecan halves

For ice cream: Combine yolks, sugar, vanilla and salt in heavy medium saucepan. Whisk in half and half and cream. Stir over medium-low heat until custard thickens and leaves path on back of spoon when finger is drawn across, about 30 minutes; *do not boil.* Remove from heat. Whisk in pumpkin and syrup. Strain into large bowl. Cover and refrigerate until chilled.

Process pumpkin mixture in ice cream maker according to manufacturer's instructions. Freeze in covered container at least 2 hours to harden.

For sauce: Cook sugar, water and lemon juice in heavy medium saucepan over low heat, swirling pan occasionally, until sugar dissolves. Increase heat and boil until rich caramel color, about 13 minutes. Remove from heat. Gradually whisk in cream (mixture will bubble up). Stir over medium-low heat until sauce thickens slightly, about 10 minutes. *(Can be prepared 4 days ahead and refrigerated. Rewarm in top of double boiler over simmering water.)* Mix in pecan halves.

To serve, scoop ice cream into bowls. Top with warm pecan sauce.

Frozen Chocolate Nougat Cream

8 servings

3 eggs, separated, room temperature
½ cup sugar
2¾ cups whipping cream
2 tablespoons dark rum
1 tablespoon vanilla
4 ounces bittersweet (not unsweetened) chocolate, finely chopped
3 ounces hard torrone,* crushed into rice-size pieces

1½ tablespoons powdered sugar
4 teaspoons unsweetened cocoa powder
Chocolate curls

Line 5x10-inch loaf pan with plastic wrap, allowing overhang. Whisk egg yolks and ½ cup sugar in bowl until thick and pale. Using electric mixer, beat 1¼ cups cream until soft peaks form. Using clean dry beaters, beat whites until stiff but not dry. Fold whipped cream, whites, rum and vanilla into yolk mixture. Combine chopped chocolate and torrone in small bowl. Sprinkle ⅓ of mixture into prepared pan. Top with ⅓ of cream, pressing firmly. Repeat 2 more times with remaining chocolate mixture and cream. Fold plastic wrap over top. Freeze at least 3 hours. *(Can be prepared up to 1 week ahead.)*

Unmold dessert onto platter. Let soften 30 minutes in refrigerator.

Sift together sugar and cocoa. Beat remaining 1½ cups cream until soft peaks form. Fold in cocoa mixture. Continue beating cream until stiff peaks form. Spread thin layer of whipped cream over dessert, covering completely. Spoon remaining cream into pastry bag fitted with large star tip. Pipe cream decoratively along edges and base of dessert. Garnish dessert with chocolate curls.

*Nougat candy, sold in both hard and soft forms, available at Italian markets, some supermarkets and specialty foods stores.

White Chocolate and Macadamia Nut Parfait

A luscious, simple-to-make frozen dessert.

6 to 8 servings

9 ounces imported white chocolate
6 egg yolks, room temperature
1 tablespoon sugar
1 tablespoon cold water
¼ cup crème de cacao
3 cups well-chilled whipping cream, beaten to soft peaks
¼ cup grated toasted unsalted macadamia nuts

Raspberry Sauce
1 pint raspberries
1 to 2 tablespoons powdered sugar

Fresh mint leaves

Melt chocolate in top of double boiler over hot (not simmering) water, stirring until smooth. Remove from over heat. Whisk yolks, sugar and cold water in large metal bowl set over saucepan of simmering water until pale yellow and slowly dissolving ribbon forms when whisk is lifted, about 5 minutes. Remove from over water. Whisk in chocolate and crème de cacao. Gently fold in whipped cream, then nuts. Cover and freeze overnight. *(Can be prepared 4 days ahead.)*

For sauce: Puree raspberries and 1 tablespoon sugar in processor until smooth. Strain through fine sieve to eliminate seeds. Taste sauce and add more powdered sugar if desired.

Let parfait soften slightly in refrigerator before serving. Coat plates with sauce. Arrange 3 small scoops of parfait in center of each. Garnish with fresh mint leaves.

❦ *Mousses, Charlottes and Meringue Desserts*

Lemon-Rhubarb Mousse

8 servings

Rhubarb Mousse
2 teaspoons unflavored gelatin
¼ cup water
1 cup Rhubarb Puree,* well chilled
½ cup whipping cream, beaten to stiff peaks

Lemon Mousse
2 teaspoons unflavored gelatin
¼ cup water
2 eggs, separated, room temperature
½ cup sugar
¼ cup fresh lemon juice
2 teaspoons finely grated lemon peel
½ cup whipping cream, beaten to stiff peaks

For rhubarb mousse: Sprinkle gelatin over water in small bowl. Set over pan of simmering water and stir until dissolved. Stir gelatin into Rhubarb Puree. Gently fold in whipped cream.

For lemon mousse: Sprinkle gelatin over water in small bowl. Set over pan of simmering water and stir until dissolved. Using electric mixer, beat yolks with ¼ cup sugar until thick and pale. Using clean, dry beaters, beat whites until soft peaks form. Gradually add remaining sugar and beat until stiff but not dry. Stir gelatin into yolk mixture. Blend in juice and peel. Fold in whites, then whipped cream.

To assemble: Alternate layers of rhubarb and lemon mousse in parfait glasses, wine glasses or glass serving bowl. Cover and refrigerate at least 3 hours. *(Can be prepared 2 days ahead.)*

***Rhubarb Puree**

Makes about 1 cup

- **¾ pound rhubarb, trimmed and cut into 1-inch pieces**
- **⅓ cup sugar**
- **¼ cup mashed strawberries or raspberries**

Combine rhubarb pieces and sugar in heavy medium saucepan. Cover mixture and let stand overnight.

Cook rhubarb over low heat to puree, stirring occasionally, about 30 minutes. Stir in strawberries. Cool completely. Cover puree and refrigerate until ready to use.

Charlotte Poire

8 servings

Biscuit
- **4 eggs, separated, room temperature**
- **⅛ teaspoon cream of tartar**
- **11 tablespoons sugar**
- **1 cup plus 1 tablespoon all purpose flour**

- **Powdered sugar**

Pears
- **6 cups water**
- **3 cups sugar**
- **3 tablespoons fresh lemon juice**
- **7 large pears, peeled, cored and halved**

Bavarois
- **1½ teaspoons unflavored gelatin**
- **1 tablespoon pear brandy (eau-de-vie)**
- **2 tablespoons whipping cream**
- **1 3-inch vanilla bean, split lengthwise**
- **6 egg yolks**
- **5 tablespoons sugar**
- **2 cups well-chilled whipping cream**

- **2 tablespoons pear brandy (eau-de-vie)**

- **¼ cup apricot preserves**
- **3 tablespoons water**
- **1 tablespoon red currant jelly**
- **2 teaspoons water**
- **3 ounces bittersweet (not unsweetened) or semisweet chocolate, melted**

For biscuit: Preheat oven to 375°F. Place dabs of butter in corners of 2 baking sheets. Draw 8-inch-diameter circle on parchment sheet. Arrange drawing side down on 1 baking sheet (butter will help hold in place). Draw 9x7-inch rectangle on another parchment sheet. Arrange drawing side down on another baking sheet. Beat whites and cream of tartar until soft peaks form. Gradually add 11 tablespoons sugar, beating until stiff but not dry. Beat in yolks 1 at a time, then beat 1 minute. Fold in flour.

Spoon batter into pastry bag fitted with ⅜-inch plain tip. Pipe batter in ½-inch-high spiral within circle on first baking sheet, covering completely. Pipe remaining batter in ½-inch-high crosswise strips within rectangle on second sheet, covering completely and making sure sides touch. Sprinkle top of batter with powdered sugar. Bake until light brown, about 25 minutes. Cool in pans.

For pears: Cook water, sugar and lemon juice in large saucepan over low heat, swirling pan occasionally, until sugar dissolves. Increase heat and boil 5 minutes. Add pears. Adjust heat so liquid barely shimmers and cook until pears are tender, about 20 minutes. Let pears cool in syrup.

For bavarois: Sprinkle gelatin over 1 tablespoon pear brandy in small cup. Let soften 5 minutes. Place cup in small pan of simmering water and stir until gelatin dissolves. Remove from heat. Drain 4 pear halves and puree in processor. Combine 1 cup pear puree and 2 tablespoons cream in heavy medium saucepan. Scrape in seeds from vanilla bean; add pod. Bring to boil. Beat yolks and 5 tablespoons sugar in medium bowl until thick and light in color. Strain pear mixture, pressing on pulp. Whisk into yolks. Return to pan and boil until consistency of very thick custard, whisking vigorously and constantly, about 4 minutes. Mix in gelatin. Strain custard into medium bowl. Cover and refrigerate until cool but not set, whisking occasionally. Beat 2 cups cream to soft peaks. Gently fold ¼ of cream into custard to lighten; fold in remaining cream.

To assemble: Remove 2 pear halves from liquid and pat dry. Cut into ¼-inch dice. Place 8-inch cake on 9-inch cardboard round. Close edges of 9-inch springform pan around base. Trim pastry rectangle. Cut into 6¾x1½-inch strips. Combine ⅓ cup pear poaching liquid and 2 tablespoons pear brandy. Brush lightly over cake base and on flat sides of cake strips. Arrange strips around sides of pan, placing rounded sides against pan and fitting between pan sides and pastry base (reserve remainder for another use). Pour half of bavarois into pan and smooth surface. Top with diced pears, leaving ½-inch border. Add remaining bavarois, smoothing top. Cover and refrigerate at least 3 hours. *(Can be prepared 1 day ahead. Refrigerate remaining pears separately.)*

Drain remaining pear halves. Trim to 2½x2-inch petal shapes, using fluted biscuit cutter held at angle for rounded end. Trim undersides to flatten. Wrap warm damp kitchen towel around dessert; release pan sides. Smooth edges of bavarois with metal spatula if necessary. Melt apricot preserves with 3 tablespoons water in heavy small saucepan. Strain. Brush over top of dessert. Arrange pear halves on top, points toward center. Melt currant jelly with 2 teaspoons water. Brush over pears only. Chill 5 minutes to set glaze. Spoon chocolate into parchment cone with small opening. Pipe in decorative border around edge of dessert and around pears. *(Can be prepared 4 hours ahead and refrigerated. Let stand at room temperature 30 minutes before serving.)*

Acropolis

Meringue and praline mousse are showcased in this special dessert. If the oven is not wide enough to accommodate baking sheets on same shelf (so they are not stacked), switch pan positions halfway through baking time.

8 to 10 servings

Meringue Française
4 egg whites, room temperature
1 cup plus 2 tablespoons sugar

Praline Mousse
1 cup plus 2 tablespoons (2¼ sticks) unsalted butter, room temperature
⅔ cup Praline Paste*
4 eggs, separated, room temperature
¾ cup sugar
6 tablespoons water

1 tablespoon sugar
¼ teaspoon cream of tartar

Unsweetened cocoa powder

For meringue: Preheat oven to 200°F. Place dabs of butter in corners of 2 baking sheets. Draw two 8-inch-diameter circles on sheet of parchment. Arrange drawing side down on 1 baking sheet. Line second baking sheet with parchment. Beat whites in large bowl until soft peaks form. Gradually add sugar and beat until stiff and shiny. Spoon meringue into pastry bag fitted with ⅜-inch star tip. Pipe meringue in ¼-inch-thick spiral within each circle, covering completely. Pipt remaining meringue across width of second sheet in 3/8-inch-wide strips, spacing 1 inch apart. Bake until meringue is crisp and dry, about 2 hours. Cool completely. *(Can be prepared 2 days ahead. Wrap tightly and store in dry area.)*

For mousse: Beat butter, Praline Paste and yolks until smooth. Scrape down sides and bottom of bowl and beat 2 minutes. Cook ¾ cup sugar and 6 tablespoons water in medium saucepan over low heat, swirling pan occasionally, until sugar dissolves. Increase heat and boil until thermometer registers 240°F (soft-ball stage).

Meanwhile, beat whites, 1 tablespoon sugar and cream of tartar in large bowl with clean dry beater until stiff but not dry. Gradually pour in hot syrup and beat until whites are cool, about 10 minutes. Gently fold ¼ of whites into praline mixture to lighten, then gently fold in remaining whites.

To assemble: Trim meringue circles to 7½-inch diameter. Place 1 layer on 8-inch cardboard round. Spread thin layer of mousse over inside of sides of 8-inch-diameter springform pan. Close sides around meringue on cardboard. Transfer remaining mousse to pastry bag fitted with medium plain tip. Pipe some mousse between meringue and pan sides. Then pipe in 1-inch-thick layer over meringue. Smooth and even surface. Top with second meringue layer. Pipe some mousse between meringue and pan sides, then pipe in 1-inch-thick layer over meringue (refrigerate remaining mousse). Smooth and even top. Refrigerate until set, at least 3 hours. *(Can be prepared 1 day ahead.)*

Wrap warm damp kitchen towel around sides of dessert; release pan sides. Smooth edges. Cut meringue strips into 1-inch-long pieces. Place 2 pieces next to each other in center of dessert. Arrange 2 more pieces perpendicular to and touching first 2 pieces. Repeat with enough pieces to cover entire surface. *(Can be prepared 6 hours ahead and refrigerated.)* Sift cocoa lightly over top just before serving.

***Praline Paste**

For best results, use the nuts while they are still warm from toasting.

Makes about 1⅓ cups

½ cup sugar
⅔ cup toasted blanched almonds
⅔ cup toasted and husked hazelnuts
¾ cup powdered sugar

Grease baking sheet. Cook ½ cup sugar in heavy medium saucepan over high heat without stirring until sugar begins to melt around edges. Stir until sugar dissolves. Reduce heat to low and stir until sugar turns amber. Add warm almonds and hazelnuts and stir until coated with syrup. Immediately pour onto sheet. Cool completely.

Break praline into 1-inch pieces. Transfer to processor. Add powdered sugar and mix using on/off turns until coarse paste forms. *(Can be refrigerated up to 3 months. Stir before using.)*

Cakes, Cheesecakes and Pastries

Swedish Gingerbread

Dust this light gingerbread with powdered sugar before serving for a pretty presentation.

8 to 10 servings

Butter
Vanilla wafer crumbs
½ cup (1 stick) butter, room temperature
1 cup firmly packed light brown sugar
2 eggs, room temperature
¾ cup sour cream
1¼ cups unbleached all purpose flour
2 teaspoons cinnamon
1 teaspoon ground cloves
1 teaspoon ground ginger
1 teaspoon baking soda

Position rack in lower third of oven and preheat to 350°F. Butter 7-cup bundt pan or tube pan. Coat lightly with crumbs. Using electric mixer, cream ½ cup butter and sugar until light. Add eggs 1 at a time and beat until light and fluffy. Mix in sour cream. Sift flour, cinnamon, cloves, ginger and baking soda. Add to batter and mix just until smooth. Spread evenly in prepared pan. Bake cake until tester inserted in center comes out clean, about 40 minutes. Cool in pan 20 minutes. Invert onto rack and cool completely. *(Gingerbread can be prepared 1 day ahead. Wrap tightly.)*

Arizona Pecan Cake

10 to 12 servings

Pecan Sponge Cake

½ cup pecan pieces
¾ cup all purpose flour
8 egg yolks, room temperature
¼ cup sugar
6 egg whites, room temperature
⅓ cup sugar
¼ cup (½ stick) butter, melted

Syrup

¾ cup sugar
½ cup water
2 tablespoons Praline liqueur

Pecan Crust

1 cup pecan pieces
1 cup pastry flour
1 cup (2 sticks) butter, room temperature
½ cup firmly packed light brown sugar
1 egg, room temperature

Praline Ganache

1 cup whipping cream
12 ounces bittersweet (not unsweetened) or semisweet chocolate (preferably imported *couverture*), coarsely chopped
2 tablespoons Praline liqueur

Buttercream

1¾ cups (3½ sticks) unsalted butter, room temperature
¼ cup powdered sugar, sifted
1 tablespoon solid vegetable shortening
1 tablespoon Praline liqueur

½ cup egg whites
1 cup sugar

For cake: Preheat oven to 375°F. Grease 9-inch round cake pan; line with parchment. Finely grind pecans with flour in processor using on/off turns. Using electric mixer, beat yolks with ¼ cup sugar until slowly dissolving ribbon forms when beaters are lifted. Using clean dry beaters, beat whites with ⅓ cup sugar until soft peaks form. Fold half of whites into yolk mixture. Fold in pecans. Fold in remaining whites. Fold ¾ cup batter into butter. Fold back into batter. Pour into prepared pan. Bake until cake is springy to touch, about 25 minutes. Cool 10 minutes in pan. Invert cake onto rack and cool completely. Wrap tightly. Refrigerate at least 2 hours. *(Cake can be prepared 1 day ahead.)*

For syrup: Cook sugar and water in heavy small saucepan until sugar dissolves, swirling pan occasionally. Bring to boil. Cool. Stir in liqueur. *(Can be made 2 days ahead and refrigerated.)*

For crust: Finely grind pecans with flour in processor. Using electric mixer, beat butter with sugar until light and fluffy. Beat in egg. Gently fold in pecan mixture. Gather into ball. Wrap in plastic. Refrigerate until firm, at least 3 hours or overnight.

Preheat oven to 350°F. Butter baking sheets. Roll dough out on lightly floured surface to thickness of ⅛ inch. Cut out one 9-inch round. Using cactus- or leaf-shaped cutter, cut out cookies from remaining dough. Transfer to prepared sheets. Pierce round. Bake until just golden, 20 minutes for round and 10 minutes for cookies.

For ganache: Bring cream to boil in heavy medium saucepan. Remove from heat. Add chocolate and stir until melted and smooth. Blend in liqueur. Cool ganache to room temperature.

For buttercream: Using electric mixer, beat butter, powdered sugar, shortening and liqueur until light and fluffy.

Heat whites and sugar in double boiler over gently simmering water until sugar dissolves and candy thermometer registers 100°F. Remove from over water. Using clean dry beaters, beat until whites are stiff but not dry. Carefully blend whites into butter mixture.

To assemble: Split cake into 3 layers. Set pecan crust on platter. Using spatula, beat ganache until slightly thickened. Spread ¼ onto crust. Top with 1 cake layer. Brush with syrup. Cover with about ¾ cup buttercream. Top with second cake layer. Brush with syrup. Spread with ¼ of ganache. Top with third cake layer. Brush with syrup. Spread with ¼ of ganache. Frost top and sides of cake with remaining buttercream. Spoon remaining ¼ of ganache into pastry bag fitted with star tip. Pipe 12 rosettes around edge of cake. Top each with cookie. *(Can be prepared 1 day ahead and refrigerated. Serve at room temperature.)*

Rougemont Apple Cake

The firm, sweet-tart McIntosh is the ideal apple for this classic dessert, but a combination of one part Granny Smith to two parts Golden Delicious can also be used. Serve with unsweetened whipped cream or slices of sharp cheddar cheese.

10 to 12 servings

Pastry

2½ cups unbleached all purpose flour
½ cup pastry flour
1 cup plus 2 tablespoons well-chilled solid vegetable shortening, cut into small pieces
7 tablespoons ice water
1 teaspoon salt
1 teaspoon sugar

Filling

¾ cup raisins
12 medium apples, peeled, cored and sliced ¼ inch thick
½ cup (1 stick) unsalted butter, melted and cooled
1 cup sugar
1½ teaspoons cinnamon
2 tablespoons all purpose flour
4 eggs
1 teaspoon Calvabec apple brandy, Calvados or vanilla

For pastry: Combine flours in large bowl. Cut in shortening until mixture resembles coarse meal. Make well in center. Add water, salt and sugar to well and blend with fork. Gradually draw flour from inner edge of well into center until all flour is incorporated. Turn dough out onto lightly floured surface. Flatten into disc. Wrap in plastic. Refrigerate at least 1½ hours.

Butter 9x2½- to 9x3-inch springform pan. Cut off ⅔ of dough. Roll out on lightly floured surface to thickness of ¼ inch. Cut out 9-inch circle. Fit into bottom of prepared pan. Roll remaining dough out on lightly floured surface to thickness of ¼ inch. Cut out 9-inch strip 2½ to 3 inches wide. Fit onto sides of pan, pressing to bottom dough to seal. Refrigerate.

For filling: Preheat oven to 350°F. Pour boiling water over raisins. Let stand 2 to 3 minutes. Drain. Toss apples with raisins. Turn mixture into prepared pan. Arrange top layer of apples in concentric circles. Bake until apples are browned, 50 to 60 minutes.

Whisk remaining ingredients in order given. Pour over apples. Bake until puffy and slightly set, about 20 minutes. Cool completely. Cover and refrigerate until set, at least 4 hours or overnight. Serve at room temperature.

Calvabec and Apple Cheesecake

12 servings

Crust
- ¾ cup graham cracker crumbs
- ½ cup finely chopped toasted walnuts
- ¼ cup (½ stick) butter, melted
- 2 tablespoons firmly packed light brown sugar
- ½ teaspoon cinnamon

Filling
- 4 8-ounce packages cream cheese, room temperature
- ¾ cup firmly packed light brown sugar
- 2 tablespoons all purpose flour
- 4 eggs, room temperature
- 2 egg yolks, room temperature
- 1¾ cups sour cream, room temperature
- 3 tablespoons Calvabec apple brandy or Calvados
- ½ teaspoon vanilla
- 1 tablespoon sugar

Topping
- ¼ cup (½ stick) unsalted butter
- 1 cup firmly packed light brown sugar
- ¼ cup half and half
- ¼ cup Calvabec apple brandy or Calvados
- 3 cups peeled and thinly sliced firm sweet apples (such as McIntosh or Golden Delicious; about ¾ pound)

For crust: Using fork, toss all ingredients in 9-inch springform pan. Press mixture into bottom of pan.

For filling: Preheat oven to 425°F. Using electric mixer, gently beat cream cheese and brown sugar until smooth. Blend in flour. Beat in eggs and yolks 1 at a time. Mix in ½ cup sour cream, brandy and ¼ teaspoon vanilla. Pour into crust. Bake 15 minutes. Reduce temperature to 225°F and bake until filling is just set, about 30 minutes. Increase temperature to 350°F.

Mix remaining sour cream, remaining vanilla and sugar. Spread over hot cake. Bake 5 minutes. Refrigerate cake immediately and chill overnight.

For topping: Melt butter in heavy medium saucepan over low heat. Stir in brown sugar, half and half and brandy and cook until syrup is thickened and candy thermometer registers 200°F. Stir in apples and cook until soft but not mushy, 5 to 8 minutes. Cool completely. Spread atop cheesecake.

Kahlúa-Milk Chocolate Cheesecake

8 to 10 servings

Crust
- ½ cup graham cracker crumbs
- 2 tablespoons firmly packed light brown sugar
- ¼ cup melted butter
- 1 teaspoon vanilla

Filling
- 12 ounces cream cheese, room temperature
- ½ cup sugar
- 3 eggs, room temperature
- 7 tablespoons whipping cream
- 2 tablespoons Kahlúa liqueur

- 3 ounces milk chocolate, coarsely chopped

Whipped cream
Shaved chocolate
Chocolate coffee bean candy

For crust: Preheat oven to 300°F. Combine crumbs and brown sugar in bowl. Stir in butter and vanilla. Press mixture into bottom of 8x1½-inch round cake pan. Bake crust for 10 minutes.

For filling: Using electric mixer, blend cream cheese and sugar until smooth, stopping to scrape down sides of bowl. Beat in eggs 1 at a time. Gently mix in 3 tablespoons cream and 2 tablespoons liqueur. Pour into prepared crust.

Melt chocolate with remaining 4 tablespoons cream in double boiler set over gently simmering water; stir until smooth. Drizzle spiral pattern atop filling. Stir with spoon to achieve marbling effect; do not overstir. Set on rimmed baking sheet. Transfer to oven. Pour water onto sheet to come halfway up sides of sheet. Bake cake until firm in center, adding more water to sheet if necessary, about 55 minutes. Cool completely. Refrigerate overnight.

To unmold, immerse bottom of pan in hot water for 2 minutes. Invert cake onto cardboard or platter, tapping bottom of pan if necessary. Invert cake from cardboard onto serving platter. Spoon whipped cream into pastry bag fitted with star tip. Pipe cream onto sides. Pipe one rosette in center of cake. Press shaved chocolate into sides. Top rosette with coffee bean candy.

Apricot Orange Pavé

6 to 8 servings

Sponge Cake

4 egg yolks
⅔ cup sugar
2 tablespoons fresh orange juice
2 tablespoons grated orange peel
½ cup sifted all purpose flour
½ teaspoon baking powder
5 egg whites, room temperature
Pinch of cream of tartar

Poached Apricots

2 cups water
2 cups sugar
3 tablespoons coarsely chopped peeled ginger
2 2-inch orange peel strips
9 apricots, blanched and peeled

Buttercream

4 egg yolks
1¼ cups (2½ sticks) unsalted butter, cut into tablespoons, room temperature
3 tablespoons orange liqueur

½ cup apricot preserves, melted and strained
¾ cup chopped roasted pistachios

For cake: Preheat oven to 375°F. Grease and flour 16x11x1-inch baking sheet, shaking off excess. Using electric mixer, beat yolks and sugar until slowly dissolving ribbon forms when beaters are lifted. Stir in orange juice and peel. Sift together flour and baking powder. Stir into yolk mixture. Using clean dry beaters, beat whites with cream of tartar until stiff but not dry. Fold ¼ of whites into batter to loosen. Gently fold in remaining whites. Spread batter on prepared pan. Bake until golden brown and springy, about 15 minutes. Cool in pan on rack.

For apricots: Cook water and sugar in heavy medium saucepan over low heat until sugar dissolves, swirling pan occasionally. Add ginger and orange peel. Increase heat and boil 5 minutes. Add apricots and cook until tender but still firm (time will vary according to ripeness of fruit.) Let poached apricots cool completely in syrup.

Drain apricots, reserving syrup. Strain. Set aside ½ cup for buttercream. Pour remaining syrup over apricots.

For buttercream: Boil reserved ½ cup apricot syrup until candy thermometer registers 238°F (soft-ball stage). Place yolks in large bowl. Using electric mixer, beat syrup into yolks a few drops at a time to start, then in slow steady stream. Continue beating until light, fluffy and cool, about 5 minutes. Beat in butter 1 tablespoon at a time. Beat in liqueur in slow steady stream.

To assemble: Cut cake crosswise into 3 pieces. Cut piece of cardboard same size as cake piece. Set 1 cake piece on cardboard. Brush cake with some of remaining syrup. Spread with thin layer of preserves. Let stand until firm. Spread with thin layer of buttercream. Top with second cake piece. Brush with some of apricot syrup. Spread with thin layer of buttercream. Top with third cake piece. Frost top and sides of cake with buttercream. Coat sides with pistachios. Spoon remaining buttercream into pastry bag fitted with star tip. Pipe rosettes along edge of cake. Refrigerate until firm.

Just before serving, drain apricots. Arrange rounded side up in 3 rows on top of cake. Serve at room temperature.

Fresh Blueberry Yogurt Tart

Any type of fresh berry would work well in this light and sophisticated tart.

8 servings

Crust

¾ cup (1¼ sticks) unsalted butter
6 tablespoons sugar
3 hard-cooked egg yolks, mashed
1½ cups all purpose flour
1 teaspoon finely grated lemon peel

Filling

1 cup ricotta cheese (10 ounces)
10 tablespoons plain yogurt (5 ounces)
⅔ cup sugar
3 eggs, room temperature
2 teaspoons all purpose flour
1 tablespoon fresh lemon juice

½ cup apricot jam
2 cups blueberries or other fresh berries
Powdered sugar
Shredded lemon peel (optional)

For crust: Cream butter, sugar and yolks in large bowl. Mix in flour and peel. Turn dough out onto lightly floured surface. Knead gently to blend ingredients. Wrap dough in waxed paper and refrigerate 1 hour.

Preheat oven to 375°F. Lightly grease 9-inch tart pan with removable bottom. Roll dough out between sheets of lightly floured waxed paper to thickness of ⅛ inch. Fit into pan; trim edges. Pierce dough. Line shell with parchment paper or foil; fill with dried beans or pie weights. Bake until pastry is set and edges are brown, about 15 minutes. Remove beans and foil.

For filling: Preheat oven to 350°F. Mix all ingredients in order given. Spoon into crust. Bake until filling is set and just golden brown, 40 to 45 minutes. Cool completely. Chill thoroughly.

To garnish: Melt jam in heavy small saucepan over low heat. Strain jam. Brush lightly over filling. Top with blueberries. Brush lightly with jam. Dust lightly with powdered sugar. Garnish with peel if desired.

Grapefruit and Pomegranate Tart

Pomegranate juice makes a beautiful topping for this elegant dessert.

8 to 12 servings

Crust

2 cups all purpose flour
6 tablespoons sugar
Pinch of salt
¾ cup (1½ sticks) well-chilled unsalted butter
1 egg

Filling

⅔ cup sugar
½ cup whipping cream
½ cup fresh grapefruit juice
5½ tablespoons fresh lime juice
4 eggs, room temperature
2 egg yolks, room temperature

¼ cup pomegranate juice*
1 egg yolk, room temperature

For pastry: Combine flour, sugar and salt in medium bowl. Cut in butter until mixture resembles fine meal. Add egg and mix just until dough binds together. Gather dough into ball; flatten to disc. Wrap with plastic and refrigerate at least 2 hours. Roll pastry out on lightly floured surface to thickness of ⅛ inch. Transfer to 10-inch tart pan with removable sides. Trim and finish edges. *(Crust can be prepared 3 days ahead. Cover and refrigerate.)*

Preheat oven to 375°F. Line pastry with foil, shiny side down. Fill with pie weights or dried beans. Bake until crust is set, about 20 minutes. Remove weights and foil and continue baking until brown, piercing with fork if puffy, 15 minutes.

Meanwhile, prepare filling: Combine sugar, cream and citrus juices in medium bowl, mixing until sugar dissolves. Beat eggs and 2 yolks until foamy. Add to citrus mixture. Strain through fine sieve. Whisk to blend.

Pour filling into crust. Bake until almost set, about 20 minutes. Mix pomegranate juice and 1 yolk. Drizzle some over top of tart in free-form pattern. Bake until topping is set, about 4 minutes. Cool on rack before serving.

*Pomegranate juice is available at natural foods stores and many supermarkets.

Pumpkin and Pecan Pie

10 servings

2 cups canned solid pack pumpkin
1½ cups whipping cream
¾ cup firmly packed light brown sugar
3 eggs, separated
1½ teaspoons cinnamon
1 teaspoon ground ginger
½ teaspoon salt
½ teaspoon freshly grated nutmeg
¼ teaspoon ground cloves
¼ teaspoon ground allspice
1 baked 10-inch pie crust

1 cup pecan halves
6 tablespoons apricot jam, heated and strained (glaze)
Whipped cream or maple ice cream

Position rack in center of oven and preheat to 300°F. Blend pumpkin, cream, brown sugar, yolks, spices and salt in large bowl. Beat whites until stiff but not dry. Gently fold into pumpkin mixture. Pour filling into pie crust. Set in baking dish. Add enough water to dish to come halfway up sides of shell. Bake until center of pie is almost set, about 75 minutes.

Move rack to lowest position. Transfer pie to rack. Arrange pecan halves around outer edge of pie; do not press into filling. Continue baking until center of pie is set, about 15 minutes. Cool completely. Coat with glaze. Top with whipped cream or maple ice cream.

Raisin Nut Tartlets

Delectable little treats filled with dried fruit, walnuts and grated chocolate.

Makes 24

Marsala Pastry
2 cups all purpose flour
¼ cup sugar
Pinch of salt
9 tablespoons well-chilled butter, cubed
3 tablespoons sweet Marsala
2 teaspoons grated lemon peel
1 egg, beaten to blend

Fruit Filling
¼ cup sweet Marsala
½ cup raisins
⅓ cup finely chopped dried figs (about 2 ounces)
⅓ cup finely chopped walnuts (about 1½ ounces)
3 tablespoons sugar
1½ ounces bittersweet (not unsweetened) chocolate, grated
¼ teaspoon cinnamon
Pinch of salt

Powdered sugar

For pastry: Sift flour, sugar and salt into large bowl. Cut in butter until mixture resembles coarse meal. Make well in center. Add Marsala, peel and egg to well and mix together to blend. Gradually draw flour from inner edge of well into center until all flour is incorporated. Gather into ball. Wrap dough in plastic. Chill at least 30 minutes. *(Can be prepared 2 days ahead.)*

Butter twenty-four 2-inch tartlet pans. Roll dough out on lightly floured surface to thickness of 1/16 inch. Using floured cutter or glass, cut out 3-inch rounds. Fit rounds into prepared pans; trim edges. Refrigerate shells.

For filling: Heat Marsala in heavy small saucepan. Remove from heat. Add raisins and let stand until plumped, about 30 minutes. Stir in remaining ingredients except sugar. *(Can be prepared 1 week ahead and refrigerated.)*

Preheat oven to 400°F. Spoon 1 tablespoon filling into each shell. Bake until pastry is lightly browned, 15 to 20 minutes. Allow to cool completely on rack. Remove tartlets from pans. Sprinkle with powdered sugar. *(Tartlets can be prepared 1 day ahead. Store at room temperature.)*

Plum Gallettes

Serve these beautiful fruit tarts the same day they are baked. You can also use the recipe to make one large gallette, baking it in a flat 15-inch pan.

16 servings

Dough

1 tablespoon dry yeast
¼ cup warm water (105°F to 115°F)

6 tablespoons sugar
1 tablespoon grated orange peel
1½ teaspoons grated lemon peel
3½ cups (or more) bread flour
¼ cup nonfat dry milk powder
¼ cup (½ stick) unsalted butter, melted and cooled
1 egg
1 teaspoon vanilla
10 tablespoons (or more) warm water (105°F to 115°F)

Filling

1 cup toasted pecans
¾ cup sugar
20 firm plums, quartered and pitted
3 tablespoons butter, cut into small pieces

1 cup plum preserves
1 tablespoon brandy
Grand Marnier Cream*

For dough: Sprinkle yeast over ¼ cup warm water in small bowl; stir to dissolve. Let stand 5 minutes.

Grease large bowl. Blend sugar and peels in processor 15 seconds. Add 3½ cups flour, milk powder, butter, egg, vanilla and yeast mixture. With machine running, pour 10 tablespoons water through feed tube and process until ball forms. If dough sticks to bowl, add more flour through feed tube 1 tablespoon at a time, incorporating each addition before adding next. If dough is dry, add more water through feed tube 1 teaspoon at a time, incorporating each addition before adding next. Process until dough is smooth and elastic, about 10 seconds. Transfer dough to prepared bowl, turning to coat entire surface. Cover bowl with plastic. Let rise in warm draft-free area until doubled in volume, about 1½ hours.

For filling: Grease two 10-inch pizza pans. Chop pecans medium finely with sugar in processor, using on/off turns. Cut dough in half. Press one piece out on lightly floured surface to 11- to 12-inch-diameter round with edges slightly thicker than center. Transfer to prepared pan. Repeat with second piece of dough. Divide nut mixture between pans. Arrange plums atop nuts, cut side down. Sprinkle with butter. Let dough rise in warm draft-free area until almost doubled in volume, 35 minutes.

Preheat oven to 375°F. Bake gallettes until crusts are golden brown, about 20 minutes. Transfer to racks.

Melt preserves in heavy small saucepan. Mix in brandy. Strain into small bowl. Brush over plums and crust. Serve gallettes warm or at room temperature with cream.

***Grand Marnier Cream**

Makes about 2½ cups

1 cup well-chilled whipping cream
¼ cup powdered sugar
2 teaspoons Grand Marnier
1½ teaspoons vanilla
2 tablespoons sour cream

Beat cream until soft peaks form. Beat in sugar, Grand Marnier and vanilla. Stir in sour cream. Serve over warm pastry.

Cookies

Vanilla Crescents

This classic Christmas cookie literally melts in your mouth. The vanilla sugar can be purchased in specialty foods shops. Or you can easily make your own: Simply empty a pound of powdered sugar into a canister, tuck in two vanilla beans and let the mixture season for at least a week.

Makes about 5 dozen

2⅔ cups sifted all purpose flour
1⅔ cups very finely ground, lightly toasted unblanched almonds or hazelnuts
½ cup sugar
1 cup (2 sticks) well-chilled unsalted butter, cut into small pieces
2 egg yolks
1½ teaspoons vanilla
1 cup vanilla sugar

Combine flour, almonds and ½ cup sugar in large bowl. Cut in butter until mixture resembles coarse meal. Knead in yolks and vanilla. Wrap dough in plastic. Refrigerate until firm enough to shape, 3 to 4 hours.

Preheat oven to 325°F. Lightly grease baking sheets. Form walnut-size pieces of dough into 3½x½-inch ropes, tapering ends. Bend into crescents and place on prepared sheets, spacing 1½ inches apart. Bake until cookies are firm to touch and beginning to color, 18 to 20 minutes. Cool on sheets 3 minutes. Transfer to rack and cool to room temperature. Roll cookies in vanilla sugar. Store in airtight container.

Gina's Island Shortbread Jewels

Coconut and macadamia nuts add a new dimension to these cookie favorites.

Makes about 36

1 cup (2 sticks) unsalted butter, room temperature
¼ cup sugar
1 teaspoon vanilla
2 cups sifted all purpose flour
¼ teaspoon salt
2 cups flaked unsweetened coconut
½ cup toasted chopped unsalted macadamia nuts
Powdered sugar
¾ cup (about) fruit jelly (such as guava, raspberry and/or black currant)

Preheat oven to 300°F. Grease baking sheets. Using electric mixer, cream butter and ¼ cup sugar until fluffy. Mix in vanilla. Sift flour with salt. Gradually mix into butter. Mix in coconut and macadamias. Shape dough into walnut-size balls. Arrange on prepared sheets, spacing 2 inches apart. Make depression in center of each cookie, using fingertip or handle of wooden spoon. Bake until cookies are beginning to color, 20 to 25 minutes. Sift powdered sugar onto sheet of waxed paper. Place hot cookies on waxed paper. Dust with additional powdered sugar. Place dollop of jelly in center of each. Cool on rack.

Pumpkin-Chocolate Chip Cookies

Makes about 6 dozen

Butter
½ cup (1 stick) butter, room temperature
1½ cups sugar
1 cup canned solid pack pumpkin
1 egg, beaten to blend
1 teaspoon vanilla
2½ cups all purpose flour
1 teaspoon baking soda
1 teaspoon baking powder
1 teaspoon cinnamon
1 teaspoon freshly grated nutmeg
½ teaspoon salt
1 6-ounce package semisweet chocolate chips

Preheat oven to 350°F. Lightly butter baking sheets. Cream ½ cup butter with sugar in large bowl until fluffy. Blend in pumpkin, egg and vanilla. Sift flour, baking soda, baking powder, cinnamon, nutmeg and salt into medium bowl. Add to butter mixture, blending well. Stir in chocolate chips. Drop batter by heaping teaspoons onto prepared sheets. Bake until lightly browned, about 15 minutes. Cool cookies on wire rack. Store in airtight container.

Caramel Candy Bar Cookies

Makes about 6 dozen

1½ cups pecans (6 ounces), lightly toasted

Cookie Crust
1 cup (2 sticks) unsalted butter, cut into 8 pieces, room temperature
¾ cup firmly packed light brown sugar (6 ounces)
1 egg yolk
1 tablespoon vanilla
¼ tablespoon salt
1¾ cups all purpose flour (8¾ ounces)

Caramel
1¾ cups sugar (12¾ ounces)
½ cup water
⅛ teaspoon cream of tartar
½ cup whipping cream
¾ cup (1½ sticks) unsalted butter, cut into 6 pieces

Position rack in center of oven and then preheat to 325°F. Butter 10½x15½-inch jelly roll pan.

Coarsely chop pecans in processor using about 4 on/off turns, then process continuously until evenly chopped, 3 to 4 seconds. Remove from work bowl.

For cookie crust: Blend butter, sugar, yolk, vanilla and salt in processor until completely smooth, about 1 minute, stopping as necessary to scrape down bowl. Add flour and blend just until incorporated using 3 to 4 on/off turns; do not overprocess.

Spread dough evenly in pan. Bake until light brown and edges are crisp, about 30 minutes. Cool completely.

For caramel: Cook sugar, water and cream of tartar in heavy 3-quart saucepan (do not use black pan) over low heat, swirling pan occasionally, until sugar dissolves. Cover, increase heat to high and boil 3 minutes. Uncover and boil until syrup begins to color, 4 to 5 minutes. Continue cooking until syrup turns golden amber, swirling pan occasionally; do not stir. Immediately remove from heat. Pour cream over (mixture will bubble); do not stir. When bubbling subsides, scatter butter pieces over; let melt. Stir with wooden spoon to incorporate thoroughly. Transfer to bowl. Cool completely; do not refrigerate.

Spread cooled caramel over crust. Sprinkle reserved pecans over top. Cover and refrigerate at least 1 hour. *(Can be prepared 1 day ahead or wrapped tightly and frozen 3 months. Thaw cookies in refrigerator.)* Cut into 1½-inch squares. Serve well chilled.

Sarah Bernhardts

Almond macaroons meet bittersweet ganache in these easy-to-make treats. The glaze is excellent for cakes and pastries that are served cold; it remains dark and shiny even after chilling.

Makes about 2 dozen

Almond Macaroons

⅔ cup whole blanched almonds
¾ cup sugar
3 tablespoons egg whites
½ teaspoon almond extract

Chocolate Ganache

4 cups whipping cream
16 ounces bittersweet (not unsweetened) or semisweet chocolate, finely chopped

Chocolate Glaze

8 ounces bittersweet (not unsweetened) or semisweet chocolate, finely chopped
12 tablespoons (1½ sticks) unsalted butter
1 tablespoon light corn syrup
5 teaspoons water
2 tablespoons minced unsalted pistachios

For macaroons: Line baking sheet with parchment. Finely grind almonds with sugar in processor. Add whites and almond extract and process to paste. Transfer to pastry bag fitted with ⅝-inch-thick plain tip. Pipe onto parchment in 1½-inch-diameter ¼-inch-high rounds, spacing 2 inches apart. Let stand for 30 minutes.

Preheat oven to 300°F. Bake macaroons until beginning to color, about 20 minutes. Immediately remove from paper; cool on rack. *(Can be prepared 5 days ahead. Wrap tightly and chill.)*

For ganache: Bring cream to simmer in heavy large saucepan. Remove from heat. Add chocolate and stir until partially melted. Let stand 15 minutes. Stir until smooth. Cover surface of chocolate with waxed paper to prevent crust from forming. Refrigerate until well chilled, at least 4 hours. *(Can be prepared 3 days ahead.)*

Beat ganache until color lightens and mixture is fluffy. Transfer to pastry bag fitted with ⅝-inch plain tip. Pipe 2-inch mound of ganache atop each macaroon. Refrigerate until well chilled, at least 30 minutes.

For glaze: Heat chocolate, butter and syrup in small bowl set over saucepan of barely simmering water, stirring until almost melted. Turn off heat. Stir mixture until completely smooth. Mix in water. Strain glaze and cool.

Hold cookie carefully and dip ganache into glaze. Set cookie on platter. Sprinkle with pistachios. Repeat with remaining cookies. Chill until ready to serve. *(Can be prepared 8 hours ahead.)*

Honey Cluster Pyramid

This traditional Neapolitan Christmas sweet is often the centerpiece of the holiday table. At the end of the meal, diners break off pieces of the fruit- and honey-coated struffoli *cookies that make up the pyramid.*

8 servings

2¼ cups sifted all purpose flour
3 tablespoons grated orange peel
1 tablespoon grated lemon peel
¼ teaspoon salt
3 tablespoons butter, room temperature
3 eggs, room temperature, beaten
½ teaspoon vanilla

Vegetable oil (for deep frying)

¾ cup honey
1 tablespoon sugar
1 cup mixed candied fruit

Additional candied fruit (optional)

Combine flour, 1 tablespoon orange peel, lemon peel and salt on work surface. Cut in butter. Make well in center. Add eggs and vanilla to well. Gradually draw flour mixture from inner edge of well into center until completely incorporated. Knead dough until smooth, adding more flour if necessary to prevent sticking, about 5 minutes. Cover dough loosely. Let stand 1 hour at room temperature.

Break off large walnut-size pieces of dough. Using palms, roll each piece out on work surface to 14- to 15-inch pencil-thin strip. Cut each strip into ¼-inch pieces.

Heat oil in deep fryer to 375°F. Lower pieces of dough into oil (in batches; do not crowd) and fry until golden brown, 45 seconds to 1 minute. Remove and drain on paper towels.

Butter large plate. Heat honey and sugar in heavy large saucepan over medium heat until clear, about 5 minutes. Add remaining orange peel, struffoli and candied fruit. Place on prepared plate. Let cool slightly, 5 to 7 minutes.

Moisten hands with cold water. Shape struffoli mixture into pyramid. Decorate with additional candied fruit if desired. *(Can be prepared 1 day ahead. Cover and store at room temperature.)*

Special Chocolate Desserts

Chocolate Butterscotch Torte

16 servings

Crust

- 1 8½-ounce box chocolate wafer cookies, coarsely chopped
- 3 ounces bittersweet or extra bittersweet (not unsweetened) chocolate, coarsely chopped
- ¼ cup butterscotch chips
- ¾ cup walnuts, lightly toasted and chopped
- ½ cup (1 stick) unsalted butter, melted and cooled

Filling

- 6 ounces unsweetened chocolate, chopped
- ⅓ cup butterscotch chips
- 2½ cups firmly packed dark brown sugar
- 1 8-ounce package cream cheese, room temperature
- 1 teaspoon vanilla
- 6 egg yolks
- ½ cup (1 stick) unsalted butter, cut into 8 pieces
- 3 egg whites, room temperature
- 1 tablespoon powdered sugar
- ⅛ teaspoon cream of tartar
- 2 cups whipping cream, whipped
- ¾ cup walnuts, lightly toasted and chopped

Leaves

- 3 ounces bittersweet or extra bittersweet (not unsweetened) chocolate, chopped
- ½ cup butterscotch chips
- ½ teaspoon butter
- 16 camellia leaves
- 1 cup well-chilled whipping cream
- 1 tablespoon powdered sugar, sifted
- 1 teaspoon vanilla

For crust: Mix cookies, chocolate and butterscotch chips in processor 20 seconds. Transfer to large bowl. Stir in chopped walnuts and melted butter, tossing until well blended. Press mixture into bottom and up sides of 9½-inch springform pan. Refrigerate crust while preparing filling.

For filling: Melt 3 ounces chocolate in double boiler over simmering water. Stir in butterscotch chips until well blended. Add remaining 3 ounces chocolate, mixing until smooth. Remove from over water.

Combine sugar, cream cheese and vanilla in large bowl over simmering water. Using electric mixer, beat until creamy, about 5 minutes. Beat in yolks 1 at a time. Continue beating until sugar dissolves and mixture is slightly thickened and forms slowly dissolving ribbon when beaters are lifted, about 10 minutes. Remove bowl from over water. Blend in butter 1 piece at a time. Stir in chocolate mixture. Cool to room temperature, stirring often, about 30 minutes.

Using clean dry beaters, beat whites with powdered sugar and cream of tartar until stiff but not dry. Fold whipped cream and whites into chocolate alternately in 3 additions. Gently fold in walnuts. Spoon into crust. Smooth top with spatula. Refrigerate at least 6 hours or overnight.

For leaves: Melt chocolate in double boiler or small bowl over simmering water. Melt butterscotch chips in another bowl over simmering water. Stir ¼ teaspoon butter into chocolate. Cool to room temperature. Stir remaining ¼ teaspoon butter into butterscotch. Cool to room temperature.

Spread chocolate over veined side of 8 leaves, being careful not to drip on edges. Arrange on plate, chocolate side up. Freeze until just firm, about 10 minutes. Starting at stem end, gently peel leaf away from chocolate, freezing briefly if too soft to work. Repeat with butterscotch and remaining leaves. *(Can be prepared 1 week ahead. Wrap and refrigerate.)*

Let torte stand at room temperature 20 minutes before serving. Meanwhile, whip cream with powdered sugar and vanilla to stiff peaks. Spoon some of whipped cream into pastry bag fitted with large star tip. Arrange leaves in center of torte, alternating colors. Pipe whipped cream around edge. Pass remaining cream separately.

White Chocolate Ravioli

A fanciful trompe l'oeil creation, served atop a rich hazelnut sauce.

8 servings

Chocolate Mousse Filling

- **8 ounces imported extra bittersweet or semisweet chocolate, coarsely chopped**
- **¼ cup (½ stick) unsalted butter**
- **2 eggs, separated, room temperature**
- **Pinch of salt**
- **Pinch of cream of tartar**
- **4 tablespoons sugar**
- **¾ cup well-chilled whipping cream**
- **1 teaspoon vanilla**

Ravioli

- **7 3-ounce bars imported white chocolate (preferably Tobler), halved crosswise**
- **Hazelnut Sauce***
- **½ cup toasted and husked hazelnuts, coarsely chopped**
- **8 mint sprigs**

For mousse: Melt chocolate and butter in top of double boiler over barely simmering water. Stir until smooth. Transfer to medium bowl. Whisk in yolks. Beat whites, salt and cream of tartar in another bowl until soft peaks form. Add 2 tablespoons sugar and beat until stiff but not dry. Fold into chocolate. Beat cream with 2 tablespoons sugar and vanilla in another bowl until slightly thickened. Fold into chocolate. Pour mixture into metal bowl. Cover and chill overnight. *(Can be made 3 days ahead.)*

For ravioli: Chill ravioli mold in freezer. Preheat oven on lowest setting 5 minutes. Turn off oven. Place white chocolate on baking sheets. Place in turned-off oven and let stand until soft enough to yield when pressed with finger, about 5 minutes.

Roll 1 piece of chocolate out on sheet of parchment to flatten slightly. Lift chocolate off paper, using thin knife if necessary. Turn pasta machine to widest setting. Run chocolate through. Adjust pasta machine to next narrower setting. Run chocolate through machine again. Repeat, narrowing rollers after each run until chocolate is 1⁄16 inch thick. Quickly press chocolate into chilled ravioli mold. Fill each ravioli with 1 to 1½ tablespoons filling. Repeat rolling with second piece of chocolate, resoftening in oven as necessary. Place atop ravioli. Seal with rolling pin. Invert mold, pressing gently to release ravioli. Cut into separate pieces with ravioli cutter or knife if necessary. Place on chilled baking sheet and refrigerate. Repeat with remaining white chocolate and filling, chilling ravioli mold between batches. *(Can be prepared up to 3 days ahead. Cover White Chocolate Ravioli tightly.)*

Let chocolate ravioli stand at room temperature for 30 minutes.

Spoon ¼ cup sauce onto each plate. Arrange 4 ravioli on each. Sprinkle nuts over sauce. Garnish with mint.

***Hazelnut Sauce**

Makes about 2 cups

1¾ cups half and half, scalded
¾ cup hazelnuts, toasted and husked

5 egg yolks, room temperature
¼ cup sugar
¼ teaspoon vanilla
Pinch of salt
2 tablespoons Frangelico (hazelnut liqueur)

Mix hot half and half and hazelnuts in blender until nuts are coarsely chopped. Cool completely.

Combine yolks, sugar, vanilla and salt in medium bowl. Bring nut mixture to simmer in heavy medium saucepan. Strain, pressing to extract as much liquid as possible. Whisk cream into yolks. Return mixture to saucepan. Stir over medium heat until custard thickens and finger drawn across back of spoon leaves path, about 3 minutes; *do not boil.* Remove from heat and whisk to cool. Strain sauce into bowl. Mix in Frangelico. Refrigerate. *(Can be prepared 3 days ahead. Cover tightly.)*

Chocolate Tortillas with Raspberries, Cream and Hot Fudge Sauce

8 servings

1½ cups all purpose flour
½ cup unsweetened cocoa powder
½ cup sugar
2 teaspoons baking powder
Pinch of salt
6 tablespoons lard or solid vegetable shortening, room temperature
½ cup (about) warm water

2 cups whipping cream, beaten to peaks with 2 tablespoons powdered sugar
1 pint raspberries
Hot Fudge Sauce*

Sift flour, cocoa powder, sugar, baking powder and salt into large bowl. Cut in lard until mixture resembles coarse meal. Add water and stir until dough is evenly moistened. Turn dough out onto lightly floured surface and knead until smooth, about 30 seconds. Cover with towel and let stand 30 minutes.

Shape dough into 16 rounds. Arrange on baking sheet. Cover with plastic wrap and let stand 30 minutes.

Roll each round out on generously floured surface as thinly as possible, 7½ to 8 inches in diameter. Heat large cast-iron skillet until very hot. Add tortilla to skillet using wide spatula and cook 30 seconds on first side; turn and cook 10 seconds on other side. Wrap in plastic to prevent drying. Repeat with remaining tortillas.

Preheat oven to 400°F. Wrap 8 tortillas in aluminum foil (refrigerate or freeze remainder for another use) and reheat. Set tortillas on plates. Spread whipped cream over half of each. Arrange berries on cream. Fold tortillas over filling. Spoon Hot Fudge Sauce onto plate.

*Hot Fudge Sauce

Makes 1 cup

- **⅓ cup light corn syrup**
- **¼ cup water**
- **¾ cup sugar**
- **¼ cup unsweetened cocoa powder**
- **2 ounces unsweetened chocolate**
- **2 tablespoons (¼ stick) butter**
- **⅓ cup whipping cream**

Boil corn syrup in heavy small saucepan 2 minutes. Stir in water (be careful; mixture may spatter). Sift together sugar and cocoa powder. Stir into corn syrup mixture. Bring to gentle boil, stirring until sugar is dissolved. Add unsweetened chocolate and butter and let melt. Add cream and bring to boil. Serve hot. *(Can be prepared 1 day ahead. Cool, cover and chill. Reheat gently.)*

Chartreuse and Mint Chocolate Truffles

Enjoy these rich confections with freshly brewed coffee.

Makes about 40

- **7½ ounces bittersweet (not unsweetened) or semisweet chocolate, coarsely chopped**
- **½ cup whipping cream**
- **2 tablespoons (¼ stick) unsalted butter**
- **2 egg yolks**
- **¾ cup powdered sugar**
- **1½ tablespoons Chartreuse liqueur**
- **1½ tablespoons crème de menthe liqueur**

Unsweetened cocoa powder (preferably imported)

Melt chocolate with cream and butter in top of double boiler over barely simmering water, stirring until smooth. Heat mixture to 100°F. Transfer to large bowl. Whisk in yolks. Sift in sugar ¼ cup at a time, whisking until smooth. Add liqueurs and whisk until smooth and shiny. Transfer chocolate to 9-inch square baking pan. Cover and refrigerate overnight.

Place cocoa in small bowl. Using spoon, scoop up 2 teaspoons chocolate mixture. Shape into ball. Roll in cocoa to coat. Place on baking sheet. Repeat with remaining chocolate. Cover and refrigerate until ready to serve. *(Truffles can be prepared 3 days ahead.)*

Index

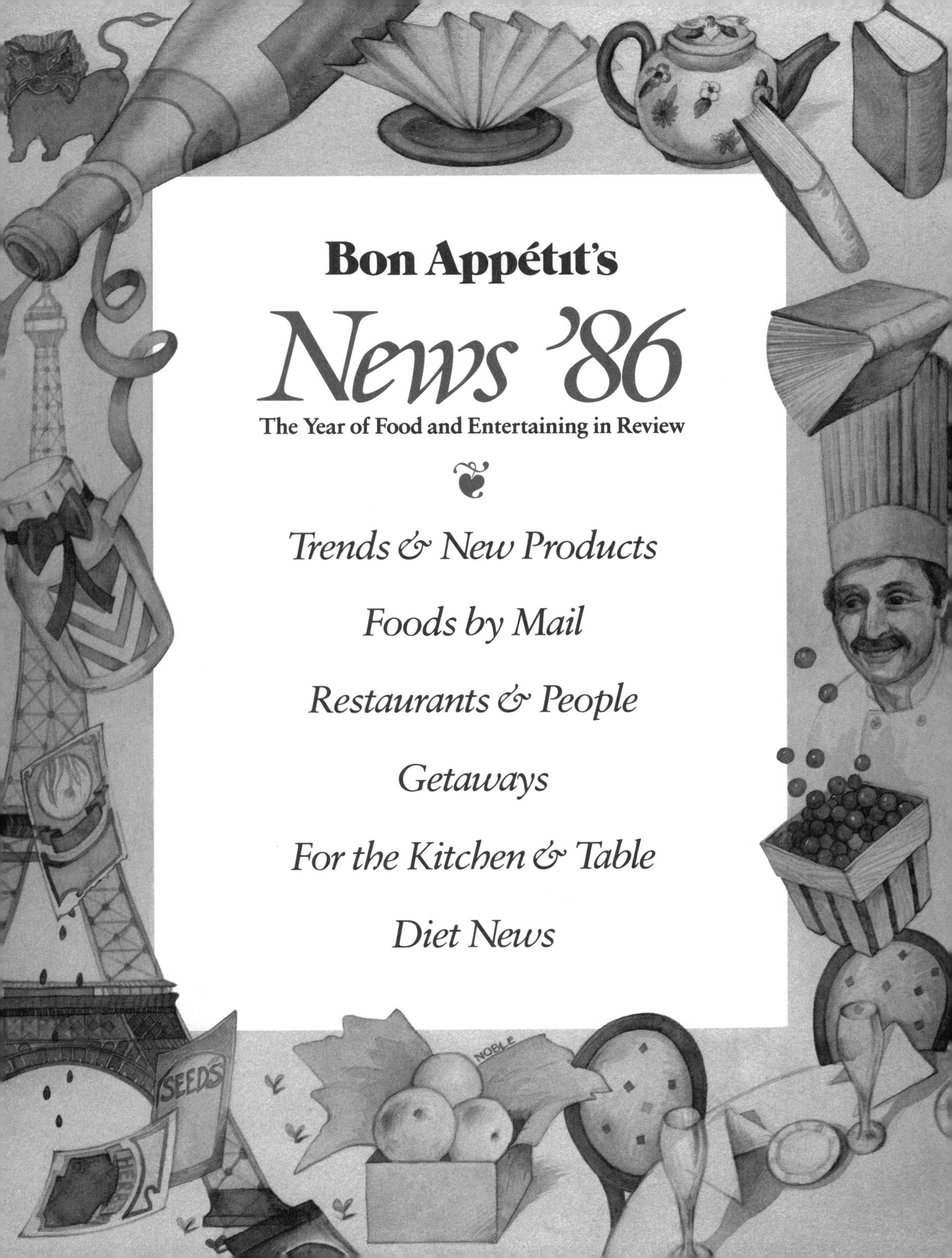

Bon Appétit's

News '86

The Year of Food and Entertaining in Review

Trends & New Products

Foods by Mail

Restaurants & People

Getaways

For the Kitchen & Table

Diet News

Trends & New Products

Cooking with flowers is now popular here, there and everywhere. Roses and marigolds, violets and day lilies, squash flowers and garlic blooms, nasturtiums and mums just begin the list. Paradise Farms in Summerland, California, is one such supplier of pretty posies that have blossomed their way as far east as Balducci's in New York City.

The new Gallup *Annual Report on Eating Out* states that seafood is the favorite, nudging out steak by about 8 percent. The same survey finds that food and restaurant aficionados who would rather eat all their meals out are predominantly single and under age 50. Then there is the Healthy Restaurant Salute from Sweet 'n Low, whose recent study indicates that Americans eat one meal out of three away from home. But the real question to consider is, does this include picnics and going to Grandma's house?

There is a great fish masquerade currently taking place, with hitherto unfamiliar fish standing in for other, more expensive ones. Take monkfish, a relative newcomer, also known to us as bellyfish, allmouth, anglerfish, fishing frog, lotte, baudroie or goosefish. Its meaty tail is white, firm and sweet. Served hot in bite-size chunks with melted butter, it tastes like lobster. Cold, it can be tossed with herbs and mayonnaise for a "lobster" salad. Another denizen of the deep that doubles for the real thing is mako shark, a good substitute for swordfish. And skate wings that are poached, shredded and treated to Newburg sauce will remind you of crabmeat.

New party ideas debuting around the country include "create your own chili" and "make your own curry." The former originated in Milwaukee restaurants, where setups similar to salad bars feature ingredients and toppings for building your own chili. For the curry affair, guests are offered chunks of seafood and lamb plus rice and an assortment of spices for blending your own curry powder into a bowl of basic sauce.

There is now a caviar on the scene to rival Russia's beluga and California's golden types. Mandarin caviar, a fresh-tasting one, with a rich, long-lasting flavor, has made its way from China to this country via the folks at California Sunshine Fine Foods. Look for it under the label of Tsar Nicoulai.

Vividly colored murals of fruits and vegetables cover the entire truck fleet of Northern Produce/Mushrooms, Inc., which whisks fine foods across the nation and purveys them to luxe hotels, cruise ships and, on occasion, to the White House or the Royal Yacht. The murals, airbrushed by California artist Thomas Suriya, have lifted dull delivery trucking to new heights with their graphics-for-the-road.

Twentieth-century Crystal Pears are so delicious, you would think they arrived straight from the Garden of Eden rather than the hilly orchards of Tottori, Japan. The crisp, sweet and juicy variety has the unique characteristic of looking just like a golden apple. But pears they are, and many people consider them to be the best of all. They are special from birth: First, the blossoms are pollinated by hand. Then, when the fruit begins to mature, it is wrapped in wax-treated bags while still on the tree, for extra protection from insects. Each pear is individually packed in a soft net cup to prevent bruising during shipping. One may weigh over a pound and cost as much as $3. You can find them in the very best produce markets and gourmet stores. Or write to Taky Kimura, Great Empire Trading Company, 908 Eighth Avenue, Seattle, WA 98104, for information on availability in your area.

Miniveggies are on the march now: finger-size zucchini and eggplant; radish-size golden minibeets; wee carrots, only as long as a teaspoon bowl; sweet, tender baby string beans akin to (but smaller than) French *haricots verts*. No need to pare, just blanch and eat—skins, tops and all. Beautiful for pickling whole, too.

Foods in tubes are the ultimate time-savers. Take, for example, catsup you can squeeze onto a hot dog, or icings with tips specially designed to decorate cakes. Now there is "mayo" in a tube, complete with a decorator tip for garnishing with flair. From Biffi di Milano, one of Italy's premier specialty foods manufacturers, this creamy, piquant mayonnaise is made with fresh eggs, light sunflower oil, wine vinegar, lemon juice and seasonings. Find it for about $2 in specialty foods shops; the 5.2-ounce tubes come packed in royal blue and gold boxes.

For those who prefer the savory to the fiery when it comes to condiments, Sable & Rosenfeld Foods, Ltd., has come up with a gift box that earned them the 1985 Specialty Foods Grand Award. The glossy black and red box contains 8-ounce jars of smooth Russian Style Mustard, The Tarragon Mayo and The Peaches 'N Peppers Relish. The gift pack, about $18, is available at fine food shops across the country.

Key lime pie is the queen of desserts throughout tropical Florida, a favorite of any piemaker worth his or her crust. But once out of the citrus belt, the cook is hard put to find the key limes with which to make it. At last, Grandma Ann's Florida Kitchen has come to the rescue by packaging the precious juice in eight-ounce bottles—enough to make two nine-inch pies. Each comes complete with a recipe for the tempting dessert. The juice is available in specialty foods shops and supermarkets across the country for about $1.99 a bottle. For information, write Grandma Ann's Florida Kitchen, P.O. Box 781, Altamonte Springs, FL 32714.

France has its Roquefort, Denmark its blue Castello and Italy its Gorgonzola. And England has that most royal of cheeses—blue Stilton. Dense, rich and evenly blue-veined, it is delicious with Port, crisp apple slices and crackers. This world-class product is now available in the U.S. under the banner of Tuxford & Tebbutt, which manufactures it in England's Stilton country. It is imported by Northfield Specialty Foods, and is available in fine food stores throughout the country. The cheese comes in rounds of 15½ pounds, and in half rounds of 6½ pounds, for $5 to $7 per pound. You will find it in ceramic half rounds and in Denby china jars as well.

Long a promoter of the art of Chinese cooking, Joyce Chen is also famous for her fine Chinese restaurants. Now she adds another dimension to her talents with a line of special sauces—the same as those used in her restaurants. The stir-fry sauces include Szechuan and zesty orange or lemon spice as well as Sweet & Tangy Duck Sauce and assorted soys. Look for them at specialty foods stores throughout the U.S.

Party givers this June will be pleased to hear about the release of Cuvée Spéciale Louise Pommery 1980, a Champagne from the French house of Pommery. This tête de cuvée, which translates as "top of the blend," is 50 percent Chardonnay and 50 percent Pinot Noir. The blend was created by Prince Alain de Polignac, whose great-grandfather is acclaimed for having made the first *brut* variety of Champagne.

Cuvée Louise is a delicate, well-balanced Champagne of pale gold with green glints. Its official introduction in France this April was heralded by a memorable meal prepared by food notables Paul Bocuse, Roger Vergé, Gérard Boyer and Gaston Lenôtre. It included rich consommé with black truffles; lamb chops in a delicate sauce accompanied by spinach-stuffed crepes and crusty potatoes; and *savarin* layered with Champagne mousse surrounded by passion fruit coulis and sorbet. The Champagne sells for about $50 in the U.S.

Two new oils have been introduced, just in time for summer salads. One is virgin cold-pressed peanut oil from Nuts D'Vine; the light oil contains no preservatives, additives or chemicals. What you do get is a fresh hint of peanuts. Order it in 16-ounce bottles for $3.95 plus $2.50 for shipping from Nuts D'Vine, Box 589, 185 Peanut Drive, Edenton, NC 27932.

And out in California, where avocado groves blanket the coastal mountains, there is another source for oil that is perfect for frying and baking, as well as for making dressings. Simply called Avocado Oil, it is cholesterol-free and has a buttery, nutlike taste that makes it nice with pasta and tortillas. For information on availability, write Avofood, 372 W. Blithedale, Mill Valley, CA 94941.

Chinese Walnuts are a fine finale to any meal with oriental flair. The Cookie Sheet bakes them every bit as good as homemade. The walnuts come in three flavors, Mandarin, candied and Szechuan. An 8-ounce tin is about $9.50 plus $3 for shipping and handling; a 16-ounce container is about $15.50 plus $3.50 for shipping. Contact The Cookie Sheet, Dept. B/A, P.O. Box 842, Bala Cynwyd, PA 19004. Allow two to four weeks for delivery.

Curd made from fruit, especially lemons, dates back to the seventeenth century and continues to this day to be popular as a lovely spread for hot biscuits or scones. It is also delicious as a base for tarts and cheesecakes and, lately, as a flavoring for ice creams. Now Crabtree & Evelyn offers two new ways with curd—passion fruit and orange. Each is made from a creamy mixture of butter, sugar and eggs plus the fruit and its peel. Both are packed in pretty hexagonal jars and cost about $4.00 apiece. For a catalog, send $3.50 to Crabtree & Evelyn, Ltd., P.O. Box 167, Woodstock, CT 06281.

Two great sweets for the breakfast table are the new cider products from Vermont, concocted and sold by Willis and Tina Wood. One is Cider Syrup, a concentrate of pure boiled cider and maple syrup from the local sugaring at their farm. Dark and rich, it is great on pancakes, waffles, French toast—even ice cream. The second delight is a highly concentrated Cider Jelly, which not only tantalizes on hot biscuits and toast, but also makes the ultimate "p.b. and j." sandwich. Four eight-ounce jars of the Cider Jelly are $7.50. A pint of the Cider Syrup is $6.00. For more information, contact Wood's Cider Mill, RFD 2, Box 477, Springfield, VT 05156.

Bruce Aidells, founder, owner and chef of a superb sausage company in Kensington, California, earned a reputation by creating some of the finest links in the country. His *andouille*, a Louisiana-style sausage, is most famous, but he is now getting kudos for his duck sausage and pork sausage with herbs, too. Hot on those links—in fact, very hot—are his Mexican-style chorizo and fresh creole-style Chaurice. These and more can be found in restaurants and top-drawer delis and food shops across the country. For information on availability, write Aidells Sausage Company, 618 Coventry Road, Kensington, CA 94707.

Speedy sparkle is what an alert company in Arlington, Virginia, offers as a toll-free gift service. Simply dial (800) BUBBLES and you may order a bottle of nicely wrapped Champagne delivered almost anywhere in the United States. The firm has even relayed the bubbly on ice with glasses. Customers can choose from more than two dozen kinds of imported Champagnes. For information, dial the 800 number or write Kathie Smith, 2347 S. Queen St., Arlington, VA 22202.

The Boston and Maine Fish Company has made it possible to stage an old-fashioned clambake anywhere. For $98.95, they will ship—overnight—everything needed for a group of four. That means four 1½-pound live lobsters, 4 pounds of fresh steaming clams, 2 pints New England clam chowder and four serving sets of bibs, crackers and picks and even a booklet of simple cooking instructions. The whole kit and caboodle makes a perfect midsummer gift. For further details, call (800) 6-BOSTON, or write Boston and Maine Fish Co., Quincy Market Building, Faneuil Hall Marketplace, Boston, MA 02109.

Those succulent Florida delicacies, stone crab claws, are at peak season from February until May 15. Smith Knaupp's Catch of the Day will send your order via overnight air express—any quantity, already cooked, and guaranteed to be super fresh on arrival. Simply crack them with a mallet, then serve the delectable claws with a good mayonnaise or a favorite seafood dip. Six of the largest ones (one pound) are about $17, as are eight of the medium claws (also one pound). The shipping charge is $29 for each order of any size. Contact the Smith Knaupp Co., 450 West McNab Road, Ft. Lauderdale, FL 33309; or call toll-free (800) 327-7723.

❦ *Foods by Mail*

An American classic, creamed dried or "chipped" beef on toast, is having a renaissance at brunches and luncheons. The dish, as good cooks have long known, depends ultimately on the quality of the dried beef. One great source is Youndt's Country Smokehouse, where the curing is the smokiest and the salt flavor just right. A pound is about $11 and comes complete with the original recipe for creamed dried beef. For a catalog, write Youndt's Country Smokehouse, 671 W. Church Rd., Ephrata, PA 17522.

It sounds as though it might be a strange animal, but in fact, *gubana* is a dialectic word—stemming from Slavonic roots—meaning to "curl up." And, indeed, curled within the snail-like convolutions of the Gubana Vogrig—a "wedding bread" from Italy's Friuli region—are enclosures of dried fruit, walnuts, hazelnuts, pine nuts, macaroons and raisins. Made without additives, this sweet loaf is leavened, and contains eggs, butter, sugar and oil. A good tea or brunch bread, it lasts several weeks after cutting and the Italians like to revive it when it finally dries out by drizzling the loaf with slivovitz. Available at Todaro Bros., 555 Second Avenue, New York, NY 10016, for about $12 per 2-pound loaf.

On the unsweet side is a gigantic 10-pound loaf called Holzofen, a sourdough rye bread made in Canada by the Dimpflmeier Bakery. Big, chewy, wholesome and healthy, it would be the perfect loaf to serve at a *charcuterie* party. Or it could be the star of a picnic, with pastrami and corned beef for make-your-own sandwiches. No artificial ingredients here, and the loaves are baked in stone-lined ovens. You can order one for $19.45 (including shipping) from Rondo Specialty Foods, Ltd., 307 Bering Avenue, Toronto, Ontario, Canada M8Z 3A5; telephone (800) 387-8702.

If your loved ones do not savor the flavors of caviar, then how about some chocolate caviar? Sprinkle these tiny crunchy beads over ice cream, mousse, cake, crêpes or crème fraîche-topped fruits. Dessert caviar is available by mail from Dearborn, 1 Christopher Street, New York, NY 10014; telephone (212) 691-9153. In a colorful 4-ounce box sealed in a moisture-resistant pouch, the faux roe is $9 plus $2 for shipping.

Panache Chocolatier in Kansas City is the source of some of the newest and best chocolate fantasies. In this smart pink and black shop in the Country Club Plaza, superb quality chocolate is available solo or as a topping on the likes of cookies, caramels, nuts and even popcorn. Yes, the marriage of two of America's favorites emerges as "Choco Poppo," a provocative mélange of sweet milk chocolate and crisp golden popcorn. Improbable as it sounds, the combination is a winner in its airtight 20-ounce plastic jar decorated with a black, white and gold label and a black satin bow tie around the neck. Contact the source for information about receiving this and other delights (Killer Brownies and Chunk Chocolate Cookies, for instance). Write directly to Panache International, Inc., 4709 Central, Kansas City, MO 64112; (816) 931-3191.

More and more and better and better—that is the way of American-produced cheeses. Combining European methods with American needs has resulted in a selection of new low-sodium, low-calorie and fresh milk (goat and cow) varieties. One low-salt, semisoft, mild-flavored cheese available in supermarket delis and cheese shops is called Lorraine. It is produced in Illinois by a company of the same name. Made from whole milk with only 35 mg of sodium per ounce, it is about $5 per pound. Other Lorraine cheeses include smoked, jalapeño pepper and chives and onions.

And, not so deep in the heart of Texas—in Dallas, to be exact—is the award-winning Mozzarella Company, now three years old and one of the few outfits in the country producing Italian-style fresh mozzarella. It is available directly from the factory along with salt-free ricotta (only 27 calories per ounce), *crème fraîche* and a thick and creamy Texas goat cheese. Another favorite is mascarpone, the high butterfat cream cheese reminiscent of clotted cream. For a list of available cheeses write the Mozzarella Company, 2944 Elm Street, Dallas, TX 75226, or call (214) 741-4072.

New from The Spice Hunter are nicely packaged dried herbs, specially mixed for flavoring grilled beef, poultry or seafood. The aromatic beef blend, for instance, combines marjoram, thyme, basil, rosemary, juniper and bay leaf. Just soak the herbs for about 20 minutes, scoop up a tablespoon at a time and sprinkle on the barbecue just before cooking. The savory smoke wisps slowly around the food. Available in two-ounce packages, Grilling Herbs are $2.50 each plus postage from The Spice Hunter, 850-C Capitolio Way, San Luis Obispo, CA 93401.

Restaurants & People

Terrace-five is the unheralded restaurant located in New York's Trump Tower. It can be found only if you know that the tower elevator to level five operates after the building closes at 6 P.M. The softly lit decor is a charming backdrop to the cooking of two young chefs, Laurie Segel and Rag Brandston. They offer such tempting spa-inspired dishes as seafood ragout with saffron, steamed vegetables with tamari ginger sauce and brown rice, and poached Norwegian salmon with basil sauce. Everything is prepared with natural, fresh ingredients (there is not even a freezer in sight), purchased each day. The twinkling lights of Trump Tower's trees give the restaurant a special glow in winter, and the set-back terrace is opened for summertime dining outdoors with a splendid view of Fifth Avenue. A pre-theater dinner for under $24.50 is served from 6 to 7 P.M. and an *à la carte* dinner menu is offered until 10 P.M. The wine list is an extraordinarily good one, and there are wines by the glass from a Cruvinet. Reservations are a must. (Terrace-five, 725 Fifth Ave., New York, NY 10022; telephone 212/371-5030.)

Increasingly these days we are finding that from great restaurants come even more great restaurants. Such is the case in Los Angeles. There, restaurateurs are meeting the challenges of expansion by opening new spots—sibling establishments, if you will—where they can continue to experiment with a variety of dishes and decor.

The Mandarin, a long-established sophisticated version of Cecilia Chiang's famous San Francisco Chinese restaurant, has recently given rise to The Mandarette, located across town. Son Philip Chiang reigns at this stark green and black new-age cafe, where the tradition of offering representative dishes from all the provinces continues.

Valentino, where Piero Selvaggio earned quite a reputation for innovative, authentic cuisine and established his prize-winning wine cellar, has led the way for Primi. Chefs have been rounded up from the great restaurants of northern Italy, and the menu they have developed features *primi piatti,* Italian for first courses, which include soups, salads, pastas, risottos and desserts.

Yuji Tsunoda's La Petite Chaya, which has been credited for inspiring the Franco-Japonaise craze, has a sister restaurant called Chaya Brasserie. This warehouselike space serves cosmopolitan food with noticeable attention to Japanese flavors, especially in the appetizer department.

Gérard and Virginie Ferry first created the lovely L'Orangerie, a sophisticated elite French restaurant in the heart of the city, where the service is formal, the flower arrangements are spectacular and the food is Gallic with a touch of nouvelle. Then they turned their attention to Pastel for a more casual atmosphere and a simpler style of cooking. An outdoor patio overlooks fashionable Rodeo Drive, making Pastel the perfect place for lunch or dinner.

Hisae is a name well known to Manhattan aficionados of cuisine with oriental influences. But Backstage, the newest venture, is unknown except to those who frequent the theater district. A sleek and gleaming hideaway tucked into 45th Street, its black-and-brass decor belies the lightness of the cooking. A "Light & Lean" lunch of buffalo mozzarella and opal basil salad, roasted whole fish with coriander and mild chili pesto and fresh fruit flan is their answer to a "businessman's luncheon," and it boasts the lowest calorie tab in town. Evenings, the regular menu features such delights as sautéed wild mushrooms, pasta dishes with delicate Asian touches, and a mountain of steamed mussels in a deliciously flavored broth. (Backstage, 318 West 45th Street, New York, NY 10036; 212/489-6100.)

No Los Angeles restaurant captures the spirit of a true Parisian bistro better than Le Chardonnay. Its *belle époque* decor sparkles from beveled mirrors that line the room, reflecting candlelight and crystal and the fireworks of the glass-enclosed mesquite grill. The menu is a little bit French and a little bit Californian. Dinner selections may include superb tortellini with escargot and garlic butter sauce, warm leek salad with Louisiana crayfish and sea scallops, grilled Hawaiian tuna with ginger-lime sauce, and medallions of venison sautéed with *sauce poivrade* and green apples. Whom to thank for perhaps the most romantic dining spot in town? Partners Robert Bigonnet and Claude Alrivy. The former is the charming host, the latter the skilled chef, and together they have transformed a Melrose Avenue storefront into every Francophile's dream. (Le Chardonnay, 8284 Melrose Ave., Los Angeles, CA 90046; 213/655-8880.)

In New York City's Flatiron District, the trendy Lola restaurant presents a stunning menu on Sunday, with a plus: At 2:30 P.M., gospel singers rock that attractive spot with their revival-style singing. It all seems magnificently appropriate with the brunch that includes such friendly down-home dishes as eggs Benedict and scrambled eggs with Andouille sausage. The newest program, called the Saints & Sinners BLD (Breakfast/Lunch/Dinner), features an all-day menu and tops off Sunday with a resounding evening of blues and jazz. Hosted by the vivacious and charming Yvonne "Lola" Bell (she is manager/owner/designer Eugene Fracchia's partner), this popular place offers Caribbean, Italian and regional American cuisines at lunch from Monday through Friday and for dinner Monday through Saturday. Hours are from noon to midnight. (Lola, 30 West 22nd Street, New York, NY 10010; telephone 212/675-6700.)

Not yet 30 years old, Raymond Haldeman runs one of the most stylish restaurants in Philadelphia. Masterminding both a thriving catering business and the establishment named for him, this enthusiastic chef serves forth various temptations. For starters, try escargots with hazelnuts in cream sauce swirled into fresh pasta. Another of his fine specialties is a sampler of hot and cold *bouchées*—crabmeat-stuffed snow peas, baked potato with sour cream and caviar, a cube of spinach quiche, mini spinach-mushroom pie, kebab of sesame chicken breast and frills of exotic greens. The entrée might be poached salmon with two caviars in Champagne sauce or crisp boneless duck in ginger sauce.

The service here is faultless. Part of his success, in a city now known for great restaurants, is attributed to the fact that Haldeman never takes a day off: He even lives on the premises. Reservations are a must. (Raymond Haldeman, 110 South Front Street, Philadelphia, PA 19106, telephone 215/925-9888.)

Petrossian is well known as one of the prettiest and most luxe dining spots in New York City, And if you thought the tab would match the surroundings, guess again. Their $29 after-theater supper is a bargain. You can enjoy the same lush art deco quarters in the landmark Alwyn Court at the corner of Seventh Avenue and 58th Street that made the restaurant famous and be pampered too: The menu, served every evening from 10:30 P.M., offers a glass of Veuve Clicquot Champagne with a choice of the Petrossian family's own sevruga caviar, pressed caviar with blinis, smoked wild salmon, Russian salmon roe with toast, or goose foie gras from the Périgord. Then choose from a "Dessert Chariot" filled with such treats as imported wild strawberries, pear tart, chocolate mousse and cassis cake. All this is served in the glitter of Lalique and mirrors, on a table set with Limoges china, Christofle silver and handmade linen. It is posh all the way. (Petrossian, 182 West 58th Street, New York, NY 10019; telephone 212/245-2214.)

On Chicago's elegant lakefront is a new restaurant whose architectural statement is as much a part of the dining experience as its food. Spiaggia (which means "beach" in Italian) is thoroughly contemporary, designed with the classical references that characterize post-modern architecture. A Palladian archway leads to a marble table with a still-life display of cheeses, wines, vegetables and glass "pillars" of antipasti. Subdued lighting picks up the colors of the walls, punctuated by Italian marble columns.

Patrons can enjoy an Italian sparkling brut rosé before sampling the crisp pizzas (no tomato sauce here). One tasty palette combines duck sausage and goat cheese; another, the classic *quattro formaggi,* blends mozzarella, provolone, Romano and Gorgonzola. Specials are featured daily, with the veal dishes among the most delicious. The wine list offers a wide variety of wonderful Italian bottles, with a separate reserve list of older vintages. The open kitchen is visible along one side of the restaurant but is designed to harmonize with the decor of the room as well as add some lively visual activity. At Spiaggia, attention to detail is as apparent in the fresh Northern Italian fare as it is in the comfortable setting. (Spiaggia, 980 N. Michigan Avenue, Chicago, IL 60611; 312/280-2750.)

In San Francisco, a city full of talented chefs, there is no brighter star than Joyce Goldstein, kitchen designer, writer, former chef at Cafe Chez Panisse in Berkeley and creator of San Francisco's first international cooking school. Now she has a successful restaurant of her own, appropriately called Square One.

As the name suggests, the menu here changes daily, taking advantage of the season's bounty and the chef's mood. While some dishes harken back to Joyce's several years at the helm of Chez Panisse's cafe, in general the fare is broader—more strikingly international. Hungarian cauliflower soup, wild mushroom and prosciutto lasagne, squash ravioli, lamb tajine with artichokes, and spicy sausage with lentils are examples of the colorful variety to be found on any given day's menu. While deciding what to order, savor the restaurant's crusty signature bread—homebaked, earthy Italian loaves. And at meal's end, there is another choice to make—dessert. Try honey mousse with raspberries, fig tart, or even a simply delectable cookie.

The decor is stylishly minimal, intended to show off the food, the crowd and the view into Sydney Walton Park. What color is lacking on the walls, however, is more than made up for in the well-designed cuisine. (Square One, 190 Pacific at Front Street; 415/788-1110.)

Dakota's restaurant is solidly ensconced well below the sidewalks, traffic and hurly-burly of city life in the Dallas Metroplex. Why "Dakota's"? Because it features Dakota granite—in the outdoor courtyard with its water wall, and in the restaurant itself, where bar, tabletops and floor are granite. The handsome dark mahogany wainscoted interior is punctuated with gleaming brass brads and rails and illuminated by gas lights—it all gives the dining room a clublike atmosphere. Guests can dine elegantly at tables, informally at the bar or in cozy, quiet niches. It is a showplace that dazzles, even in dazzling Dallas.

The food matches the glorious surroundings. The menu runs the gamut from down-home American to nouvelle cuisine with such specialties as prime steaks, baby back ribs, Cajun-spiced red snapper, pheasant and duck, all of which are grilled over aromatic woods. (Dakota's is located at 600 North Akard; 214/740-4001.)

Crisp salmon skins are the tasty crunch in the special salad at Katsu, the place to go for the best sushi in Los Angeles. That salad is made complete with bonito shavings, enoki mushrooms, greens and flecks of raw tuna, all enhanced by the julienne of toasted salmon skins—a terrific stand-in for bacon. And very easy to make, according to the chef. Simply place them in a toaster oven on a sheet of foil and bake until golden and crisp. Then cut them into fine julienne. Katsu is located at 1972 N. Hillhurst Avenue, Los Angeles, CA 90027; the telephone number is (213) 665-1891.

The Tap Room in New York is a new spot for hoisting a cool one. Beer lovers gather here in the New Amsterdam Amber Beer brewery to quaff the brew, watch it being brewed and eat such go-withs as Manhattan chili and beer bread. The drink, to be sure, is freshly drawn from taps into chilled mugs. The publike atmosphere is convivial and clubby.

Getaways

So you would like to improve your technique at the wok or perhaps master some of the more difficult French sauces? But you would also like to take a vacation—one that provides more stimulus than a week on a nice but awfully quiet beach. The solution is a cooking course held in a distant land by a contagiously enthusiastic teacher. Spend mornings at the stove and afternoons touring the sites for a holiday unlike any other.

Classic Chinese cuisine in the Orient is being offered for the seventh year by Nina Simonds, well-known author and teacher, and Stella Lee, a native of Taiwan. Together they provide culinary tours of Taiwan, Hong Kong and China. Highlights include a Peking duckling class by master chef Leung Kit, and study at the Wei-Chuan Cooking School in Taipei with three Chinese chefs who specialize in Eastern regional cooking, Szechwan, Hunan and Cantonese cuisines. For a brochure and additional details, write Nina Simonds, 400 Essex Street, Salem, MA 01970.

Going into his twelfth season of Hong Kong cooking courses is teacher, best-selling author and TV chef Ken Hom of Berkeley. His superb week-long series is offered twice a year, and students learn how to make everything from potsticker dumplings to Shanghai crab. This accomplished and zealous devotee of Chinese cooking literally infuses the novice with his glorious "Hom cooking." Write for details: Ken Hom in Hong Kong, 23B Orinda Way, Orinda, CA 94563; or telephone (415) 254-8433.

Anne Willan's success with Ecole de Cuisine La Varenne in Paris has led her to open a new school in Burgundy at Château du Fey. In addition to being an excellent series of classes, this program offers French country living at its best. Several one-week gastronomic courses are scheduled throughout the year. For details write La Varenne in Burgundy, P.O. Box 15313, Seattle, WA 98115; or telephone (202) 337-0073.

Down under (as the Americans, but not Aussies, say) is the Howqua Dale Gourmet Retreat, now in its ninth year. About 200 kilometers from the city of Melbourne, it has become known as a place of supreme serenity and sublime foods and wines. For the first time, co-owners Sarah Stegley and Marieke Brugman are offering a deluxe trio of tours. Called the Gourmet Tours of Australia, the three packages celebrate that country's newfound sophistication, bracketing three major cities and their fine restaurants. For details and prices, write World Travellers Inc., 19032 66th Avenue South, Suite C-107, Kent, WA 98032, or call (800) 426-3610.

Imagine living for a week at Badia a Coltibuono, a wine estate in Tuscany, staying at a great stone abbey built in the twelfth century by monks. Imagine having as your hostess the gracious Lorenza de' Medici, who shares the secrets of her hospitality, for which she is famous.

Imagine hands-on cooking lessons that concentrate on the food of that Italian countryside—authentic traditional recipes that Lorenza has adapted to today's way of life. Imagine, too, dinners in great private houses in the area, eating wholesome Tuscan food and participating in a way of life only rarely enjoyed by outsiders. Imagine all this if you can, and then learn that every year eleven groups of Americans make it a reality. Lorenza de'Medici opens Badia a Coltibuono for six-day stays in May, June, September and October. The total cost of $2,200 per person includes room at the abbey, all meals, cooking classes, excursions and transfers. For more information, write Badia a Coltibuono, 2561 Washington Street, San Francisco, CA 94115.

The picturesque Horse & Hound Inn in Franconia, New Hampshire, at the base of Cannon Mountain just north of Franconia Notch, is the ideal retreat for lovers of fall foliage. The living and dining rooms offer three cheery fireplaces to travelers. Chef Joe Peterson creates specials daily from chicken, duckling and veal, all with innovative twists. New England's freshest and best fish dot the menu. Telephone (603) 823-5501 for your reservations.

For elegance reminiscent of an era past, consider touring the Scottish Highlands via a slow-rolling train that travels along little-used railway lines winding through the mountains and glens of this dramatic countryside. The Royal Scotsman departs from Edinburgh's Waverly Station Tuesdays and Fridays for either of its two three-day trips or the more complete and doubly relaxing six-day sojourn. The stately mahogany-framed cabins provide wonderfully comfortable accommodations en route to tours of famous estates, castles and gardens, most of which are not open to the general public.

The good food aboard highlights the native dishes, such as black pudding for breakfast and just-caught seafood, including salmon, *langoustines* and turbot. Dessert might be homemade amaretto ice cream with fresh berries. All meals are served in the handsomely decorated saloon car, which was constructed in 1912. The train has eight railway carriages, yet the number of guests is restricted to just 28, giving passengers plenty of room for relaxation. Fares are fully inclusive and range from $1,790 to $3,770. For more information write Abercrombie & Kent International, Inc., 1420 Kensington Rd., Oak Brook, IL 60521, or call (800) 323-7308.

Come Father's Day, give that sportsman a really extravagant gift—a packaged three-day weekend at the unique Yes Bay Lodge in Alaska. All Dad needs to pack is his toothbrush; the inn provides everything else, including warm Alaskan hospitality and some of the finest fishing in the world. From June to the end of October, there are three species of trout and four of salmon running at various times, among them sea-run cutthroat trout, king salmon, rainbow and Dolly Varden trout. Family-style meals here include shrimp and crab and local fish, all fresh from the adjacent waters. Operated by the Hack family, Yes Bay Lodge is a secluded luxury inn nestled in a picturesque alpine setting, a 20-minute flight from Ketchikan Airport. (For details, write Yes Bay Lodge, Yes Bay, AK 99950.)

Travelers to Toronto will find sublime happiness in quarters at the landmark King Edward Hotel, located close to theater and concert halls, galleries and fine shops as well as the financial center. Built in 1903, its wonderfully spacious rooms, each with a sitting area, have all been modernized since the days of its namesake. The lobby, however, is still evocative of all the grandeur and elegance of the turn of the century, complete with tiers of balustrades, a vaulted glass ceiling and Corinthian marble columns. There is 24-hour room service and every old-world amenity you could wish. The grand dining room, Chiaro's, offers fine French specialties in a comfortably formal setting. General manager Ibrahim Fahmy keeps the whole thing humming quite smoothly. (The King Edward is located at 37 King Street East, Toronto, Ontario M5C 1E9; 416/863-9700.)

Santa Barbara has become one of the best weekend getaways in Southern California, and as its popularity grows, so does the number of charming bed and breakfast inns there. How to choose among them? You might try one with a delicious difference: bed, breakfast—and dinner.

At The Old Yacht Club Inn, hard by the blue Pacific and an easy bike ride (this is the weekend, after all) from the shops and trendy restaurants downtown, co-owner Nancy Donaldson tends the stove once a week at suppertime. It is a delightful bonus for lucky guests. Nancy is an accomplished cook, and her five-course meals—created from what is freshest and most appealing from the purveyors that day—rival the finest the city has to offer. There is also a small, well-chosen wine list featuring vintages of the nearby Santa Ynez Valley.

The inn actually consists of two buildings. One, which once served as the Santa Barbara Yacht Club, was built in 1912 and has been fully restored. There is an inviting parlor with fireplace adjacent to the dining area, and upstairs are four large and sunny guest rooms. The Hitchcock House just next door has four more renovated suites, each with its own sitting area and private bath.

Along with Nancy Donaldson, the other innkeeper-owners are Gay Swenson, Lucille Caruso and Sandy Hunt. They keep everything humming along smoothly, and can direct you to what to do in town, what to see and where to shop in nearby Montecito, as well as arrange a wine country tour. (The Old Yacht Club Inn, 431 Corona Del Mar, Santa Barbara, CA 93103; telephone 805/962-1277.)

It's time for East Coast tourists to head for the country—motoring to an inn in New England, upstate New York or Connecticut—searching out the first signs of spring. One of the most charming and one of the oldest (a mere two centuries) is the rambling, rustic and utterly peaceful Silvermine Tavern on the Silvermine River in Norwalk. It has been operated by the Whitman family since 1955. Here are but ten guest rooms, all delightfully decorated with honest-to-goodness American antiques. Since there are no TVs and no telephones, you are practically guaranteed solid rest and comfort.

A 200-seat dining room fills the main floor, and an outdoor dining area on a tree-shaded porch overlooks a tranquil millpond. Three fireplaces help take the chill off the nights in spring and winter. And then there is the old-fashioned menu of traditional New England favorites: roast duck, chicken potpie, broiled scrod, their famous honey buns, Indian pudding and fresh fruit pies. (Write the Silvermine Tavern, Norwalk, CT 06850; or call 203/847-4558.)

The expanded specialty foods emporium, evocative of Harrod's in London or Fauchon in Paris, is the wave of the future. But here now, and an award-winner in the field, is the West Point Market in Akron, Ohio. It is indeed *super* in every sense of the word, beginning with its nationally famous selection of exotic cheeses—over 350 varieties. The go-with, of course, is an extensive wine department with three wine stewards on hand to give expert advice. The vast array of foods comes not only from all over the United States, but also from foreign countries far afield. Owner Russ Vernon has just one credo to which he adheres in stocking this palace of delights—"go for the best." And he has done just that. (West Point Market, 1711 West Market Street, Akron, OH 44313.)

For the Kitchen & Table

Aeons ago the Chinese discovered the route to nutritious cooking via the steam pot. Vegetables are brighter in color, crisper and more flavorful. Fish and poultry are tender, moist and quickly done. And dried grains—rice, especially—plump up in the most toothsome way. Now designer Kira Fournier has taken a cue from the ancient Orient and crafted a white porcelain version of the steam pot—but with a twist. Hers collects all the natural juices as a broth, which bastes the contents of this casserole by way of a spout in the middle. Good looking, and with a cover that doubles as a trivet, it is a natural to go directly to the table as a serving piece. In three sizes, with a colorful cookbook, The Steampot is priced approximately as follows: one-quart size, for custards and quiches, $32; two-quart, $42; and four-quart, for large, one-pot dinners, $58. Available at specialty cookware stores or from Kira Designs, Inc., 1 Faneuil Hall Marketplace, Boston, MA 02109.

Taka Industries has debuted a handy, foolproof device for making sushi quickly and uniformly at home. A perfect do-ahead dish, sushi can be made the night before, packed in lacquer or straw boxes with chopsticks, napkins and dipping sauce, and taken to a picnic or an outdoor concert in the grand tradition of the Japanese. Sold by mail order only, it is $75 postpaid from Taka Industries, P.O. Box 1218, Oak Brook, IL 60521.

Sunday brunch takes a new turn when eggs are baked, perhaps with cheese or bacon bits. Foolproof baking is assured in heat-resistant handblown-glass bakers, each holding one to three eggs. They are sold in sets of two for $14, and are available at kitchen shops across the country. Available by mail from Trans Duck International, P.O. Box 534, Palo Cedro, CA 96073; or call (800) 223-DUCK.

Princess Di has a royal blue one; it is rumored that Paul McCartney's is red and John Updike's is green. And the Frank Lloyd Wright house in Falling Water, Pennsylvania, had one installed 40 years ago. The legendary British cookstove, The Aga, is classy to the *n*th, with an even classier tab—$6,000 for the four-oven model and $5,000 for the dual oven. Designed long ago by a Swedish Nobel Prize laureate, it has such desirable features as an odorless all-night cooking facility; heat "storage" (the ovens remain on all the time, much like your refrigerator); moisture retention, which eliminates the need for basting; and, best of all, low-cost fuel consumption. It is 58 inches wide and fits into the average kitchen cabinet depth. This handmade jewel works equally well in both ultramodern and colonial settings. And it will stand you in good stead for better than a lifetime. For more information write The Aga Sales Office, RFD 1, Box 477, Stowe, VT 05672.

The Grillery is easily the classiest grill in town. It is hand built of the finest stainless steel with the precision and durability of a fine automobile. This wood-burning setup with twin rotisseries and six-station locking system was James Beard's favorite. It allows the home chef to cook on an open flame, just as the professionals do. A special V-channel cooking surface carries juices away from the fire to a collecting pan where, with the addition of herbs, wine, a clove of garlic or dash of the "hot stuff," a delectable basting sauce is made. Designed to last a lifetime, just 250 such units are currently in circulation. The handsome barbecue measures 18x23x39 inches. The grilling surface is 18½x20 inches. The legs can easily be disconnected, so the top can slide into your fireplace and serve as an off-season grilling center, or as a magnificent addition to that ski cabin in the mountains. Available for about $525 plus $65 for a vinyl-lined canvas cover from Grillworks, Inc., 1211 Ferdon Road, Ann Arbor, MI 48104. The phone number is (313) 995-2164.

Stark white and black, half and half, is Emilio Bergamin's dinnerware design called "Intermezzo." Basic as the little black dress, the line will be at home in everything from an art deco dining room to a sleek oriental setting. Black on one side, white on the other, the plates also come in blue and brick red, yellow and blue and black and dark green. Coffee mugs and demitasse cups are available, too. The dinner plate is about $17, the salad plate $10.50 and service plate $46.50. Demitasse sets are $17, and mugs are $9.25 each. All items are from Taitu's spring 1986 collection and can be found in fine china departments throughout the country. Or for a listing of stores near you, write Taitu at 2156 Irving Blvd., Dallas, TX 75207.

The month of June brings to mind tea parties, bridal showers and other such intimate gatherings. And now, a company called Paper Windows has brought out a line of serving pieces and accessories perfect for those occasions. Their delicate teapots, creamers and sugar bowls, all designed by Linda de Sapio and Carol Lee Veitch, are hand-formed, hand-painted and hand-decorated. The pots come in white with flowers of pink, yellow or blue, and green leaves. And for sipping alone, there is the precious "Tea-for-One," a single-size pot complete with a butterfly top and crowned with a lone cup. There is also a pretty pot made especially for serving hot chocolate. The teapot ($50), hot chocolate pot ($50), cream and sugar set with spoon ($48), as well as the Tea-for-One ($40) can be ordered directly from Paper Windows, 9021 Dicks St., Los Angeles, CA 90069.

A Swedish Orrefors handblown crystal vase would be ideal for that first clutch of spring flowers from your garden or florist. These versatile vases are suitable for any setting, contemporary or old-fashioned. Designer Anne Nilsson's Crocus pattern features a fired, hand-painted lavender-colored blossom. It comes in four sizes, ranging in price from about $40 to $95. Available at Orrefors Crystal Gallery, 58 East 57th St., New York, NY 10022; (212) 753-3442.

Le Jacquard Francais, the manufacturer of fine French household linens, has been licensed by the Colonial Williamsburg Foundation to produce woven linens based on objects and designs found in the Abby Aldrich Rockefeller Folk Art Center in Williamsburg, Virginia. Two damask kitchen towels, one called Vines and the other Lion, are adapted from nineteenth-century coverlets. Vines features a white background with a blue or rose-brick grapevine border. Lion is available in the same colors and combines a daisy and star interior with a fruit tree and picket fence border; a lion stands in each corner. They cost $10 each plus $1.50 shipping per order. The towels are available through the Colonial Williamsburg Foundation Mail Order Department, P.O. Box CH, Williamsburg, VA 23187, and at fine department stores nationwide.

Hoya is the world's largest manufacturer of fine crystal. Their contemporary designs range from museum pieces to functional ones, which include fine stemware, vases, bowls, barware and clocks. With characteristic Japanese artistry, these dazzling *objets* blend the best of both worlds, joining ancient skills and modern technology. Using a combination of handblown and hand-formed glassmaking with specially designed technical innovations, each full lead crystal piece is individually finished to an extremely high degree of brilliance and reflection. Whether hand-cut saké glasses for $35 each, or artwork worth $30,000, anything from Hoya is destined to become a collector's item. Find it at the new Hoya Crystal Gallery, 450 Park Avenue at 57th Street, New York, NY 10022.

Whether you park your knife or your chopsticks on Villeroy & Boch's elegant little porcelain rests, you will be doing the proper thing and saving the napery at the same time. This quaint, withal practical, custom also makes for pretty table ornamentation. The rests are available in five charming patterns, Botanica, Petite Fleur, a marbleized design called Siena, classic blue and white Vieux Luxembourg and a pastoral Naïf. Look for them in fine china departments. They come in sets of two for about $20.

A trio of blue and white serving dishes in the shapes of squashes is a whimsical addition to the autumn table. The three range in size from a small pickle plate to a large platter. The gently modern design is part of a collection from Brooke Harvey, purveyor of oriental porcelain. The dishes are all handcrafted yet dishwasher safe. The tiny squash is 4x2½ inches and sells for about $10; the medium size, 8½x5½ inches, is about $15; and the large 12x8-inch one is about $60. The pieces are sold in fine china departments across the country. Or for the address of a shop near you, write to Brooke Harvey at 35 Malaga Cove, Palos Verdes Estates, CA 90274.

Something new always seems to be coming our way from the skilled glassblowers of Finland. Now it is a patio light. Called Balladi (ballad), the small 2½x2x¾-inch frosted and clear holder from iittala cups a votive candle to shine through its arched windowlike design. It can be hung in its red enameled sling or set on the table. Find it at fine glassware departments throughout the country for $16.50. The same company, by the way, has just introduced Alvar Aalto's famous green glass vase in the original design of 50 years ago. It is available for about $125 wherever fine glass is sold.

Diet News

Medical science has taken up the cause of wine as a food containing vitamins and minerals and natural grape sugars. Wine has long been recognized as an appetite stimulant and an aid to digestion. Now we learn that red wine in particular is instrumental in lowering the cholesterol in the blood. It is low in sodium, as well.

The oldest documented fish is a new one in this country. Often called St. Peter's fish, though we know it as tilapia, this 2,000-year-old species is presently being flown in fresh from Israel. It is sweet and tender-flaked, best served quickly broiled, grilled or pan-fried. A lean fish, with only 1½ to 3 percent fat, it is a boon to cholesterol watchers.

That best-selling salt-free seasoning Mrs. Dash adds a new dimension to its original blend with a Lemon & Herb flavor. It incorporates 14 natural herbs and spices, including basil, savory, rosemary and orange peel. And for those who like things really hot-hot, there is Mrs. Dash Extra Spicy. This company offers an interesting brochure for kicking the salt habit, called *Taming Your Taste for Salt*. It is available at no charge from Mrs. Dash, Department HA, 2525 Armitage Avenue, Melrose Park, IL 60610. You can also phone the Sodium Information Center hotline at (800) 622-DASH.

Sorrell Ridge Farms of Port Reading, New Jersey, has introduced a line of 14 flavorful sugar-free conserves such as cranberry and black raspberry. Each kind is sweetened only by fruit, and the calorie count comes in at 14 per teaspoon. The conserves are available in natural foods stores and specialty foods shops at about $2.50 for each 10-ounce jar.

A reminder: Given 24 hours' notice, most airlines can cater to low-calorie, low-sodium, diabetic and low-cholesterol needs. Vegetarian and kosher meals have long been available.

Buffalo is "in" for the epicure who counts calories and cholesterol. It offers more protein, vitamins and minerals than beef, far fewer calories and half the cholesterol. All this has its price, though: Buffalo costs 25 percent to 50 percent more than beef. Many restaurants across the country are serving it and specialty butchers purvey it. By mail, Wilderness Gourmet offers buffalo (also venison and wild boar) raised specifically as a food source without hormonal and chemical additives. For further details, write Wilderness Gourmet, Enzed Traders, Inc., P.O. Box 3257, Ann Arbor, MI 48106.

Cattlemen of America now have an answer to appeals for low-fat meats: Brae Beef, a meat of truly exceptional quality. The cattle are raised in Vermont, and on an organically nutritious diet. The meat is lean, tender and juicy. Steaks come in a variety of sizes and cuts. For ordering and additional information write Brae Beef, 100 Greyrock Place, Stamford, CT 06901, or phone (800) 323-4484.

Here a diet, there a diet, and which to choose should certainly be a matter between you and your physician, whether you need advice and counsel on a diet for hypertension, stress, diabetes, adding or losing weight, high cholesterol or for any other problems. But there are also several associations that provide information on these subjects. You can write the American Dietetic Association, the American Heart Association or the American Diabetes Association. (Check your phone directory for local addresses.)

Another helpful hotline is offered by the Hain Pure Food Company to answer questions about cholesterol and provide diet tips. The number is (800) HAIN-123 (or in New York, 800/223-4242). And a general information booklet with recipes to help lower cholesterol counts is yours for the writing: Hain Nutrition Information Bureau, Lewis & Neale, Inc., 928 Broadway, New York, NY 10010.

From Shamitoff Foods of Redwood City, California, comes a line of frozen natural fruit bars. Ranging in calories from 50 to 195 and in flavors of Peaches 'n Cream, Piña Colada, Dark Sweet Cherry, Pineapple, Raspberry, Lemon, Bananas 'n Cream, Strawberry, and Chocolate Coconut Cream, they are a great way to cool off those end-of-summer heat spells. Look for them in supermarkets throughout the country.

"Down with Salt" appears to be today's message from the American Heart Association, as well as that of doctors and nutritionists. And right on target are companies such as Armour, which are now making low-sodium bacon, ham, bologna, salami, hot dogs and cheeses. Varieties of cheese include Colby, Monterey Jack and cheddar, all at about 120 milligrams of sodium per ounce, rather than the usual 170 to 200 milligrams.

News is out that David's Cookies has joined the less-is-better-bandwagon. The company is producing the chocolate chip delectables, now with 30 percent less sugar, 15 percent less butter and, well, 15 percent less chocolate. The name? What else but David's Lite Cookies. About $6.50 per pound in David's Cookies shops in 26 states.

Galaxy Cheese Company's super healthy Formagg makes its way to us straight from New Castle, Pennsylvania. Available in 25 flavors, including mozzarella, Parmesan, Monterey Jack with jalapeño, regular and low-salt cheddar, it is the only cheese product with no cholesterol. Formagg has high-quality protein and more vitamins, calcium and other essential minerals than natural cheese and is lactose free, with 35 percent fewer calories and one-third the saturated fat of natural cheese. Try it for pizzas, tacos, enchiladas and pasta. It can be found now in supermarkets throughout the East and soon will be nationally distributed. Parmesan and Romano come in one-pound rolls and in grated form in a shaker container.

Snacking on seaweed has proven to be a successful route for weight loss. Nori is that paper-thin, dark, sea-flavored variety used as a wrapper for sushi. Laden with minerals and vitamins, it has 10 kinds of vitamin B (including B-1, 2 and 6) and vitamin C, as well as 23 essential minerals. And if all that were not enough, it is delicious, too, when shredded and sprinkled on soups and salads, on rice and in omelets. More ideas for using it, including recipes, are available from the California Business Corporation, Suite 1339, 234 S. Figueroa Street, Los Angeles, CA 90012. Cheese-stuffed nori, anybody? Just alternate layers of nori and sliced cheese and bake at 300°F until the cheese is soft, about five minutes.

If you are a dieter or a cook who measures by weight, if portion control is of concern to you, then make note of Ohaus Scale Corporation's new Lo Pro Lume-O-Gram. This neatly designed portable electronic scale computes small portions quickly and accurately with instant readouts in grams or ounces. Battery-powered (or by an optional AC adapter), its power-saver circuit automatically shuts off after a reading is taken. With 1,000-gram capacity (or 35 ounces), it works with a light tap on the front panel and displays the weight figures in large, bright LED numbers. At about $85, it is available nationwide. For a store near you write Ohaus Scale Corp., 29 Hanover Road, Florham Park, NJ 07932; or call (201) 377-9000.

This has been a banner year for diet and health books, with something for every taste. Here are a few of our favorites:

Diet-book writer Merle Schell (*The Chinese Salt-free Diet Cookbook*) has come out with a new book, *The Mexican Salt-free Diet Cookbook* (NAL Books, 1986, $16.95). With recipes for full-course meals, from appetizers to desserts, this book includes many popular Mexican dishes that the health-conscious previously had to forego.

Francine Prince's *The Dieter's Gourmet Cookbook* (Fireside Books, 1986, $8.95) offers low-calorie haute cuisine for perennial dieters.

Donald S. and Carol P. Robertson have written *The Snowbird Diet* (Warner Books, 1986, $8.95), aimed at frostbitten folk heading for the Sunbelt and revitalization. It has everything from shopping lists, menus, recipes, a maintenance plan, diary and exercise guide.

Credits and Acknowledgments

The following people contributed the recipes included in this book:

Jean Anderson
Nancy Verde Barr
Lena Cederham Birnbaum
Patricia Brooks
Ron Brown
Ginger Chang
Rebecca Chase
Commander's Palace, New Orleans, Louisiana
Jamie Davies
Anita and Paul DeDomenico
Judy and Washington Falk III
Helen Feingold
Susan Feniger
Carol Field
Flea St. Cafe, Menlo Park, California
The Four Seasons, New York, New York
George Germon
Bunny and Sidney Goldman
Marcy Goldman-Posluns
Joyce Goldstein
Ken Hom
Larry Jacobs
Ronda Jones
Jane Helsel Joseph
Karen Kaplan
Kristine Kidd
Johanne Killeen
Heidi Landers
Vivian Levine
Faye Levy
Little City Antipasti Bar, San Francisco, California
Mimmetta Lo Monte
Susan Herrmann Loomis
Abby Mandel
Kathleen Martin
Michael McLaughlin
Jacqueline H. McMahan
Alice Medrich
Catherine Merlo
Mary Sue Milliken
Jefferson and Jinx Morgan
Bruce Naftaly
Noemi, Venice, Italy
Cindy Pawlcyn
Stephan Pyles
Restaurant Jasper, Boston, Massachusetts
Elizabeth Riely
Betty Rosbottom
David Rosengarten
Julie Sahni
Richard Sax
Jimmy Schmidt
Edena Sheldon
Judy Shermann
The Silvermine Tavern, Norwalk, Connecticut
Nina Simonds
Denise and Jerry St. Pierre
Stephanie, Peoria, Illinois
Laurent Terrasson
Whiskers, Stowe, Vermont
Wild Winds Farm, Naples, New York
Wine Cask, Santa Barbara, California
The Winnetka Grill, Winnetka, Illinois
Alan Zeman

Special thanks to:
Editorial Staff:
Angeline Vogl
MaryJane Bescoby
Graphics Staff:
Bernard Rotondo
Gloriane Harris
Rights and Permissions:
Karen Legier
Indexer:
Rose Grant

The Knapp Press
is a wholly owned subsidiary of
Knapp Communications Corporation

Composition by PTH Typographers, Los Angeles, California

This book is set in Sabon, a face designed by Jan Teischold in 1967 and based on early fonts engraved by Garamond and Granjon.